I0482076

POSITIONING FMCG BRANDS

Findings from the Indian Market

Dr. SUBHO CHATTOPADHYAY
MBA, PhD.

Associate Professor
LBSIMT, Bareilly

CONTENTS   Page

ACKNOWLEDGEMENT

The book consists of a collection of research work conducted on the brand positioning strategies of MNCs dealing with FMCG brands in the Indian market. Some work conducted during my doctoral research has also been included in the book. I take this opportunity to pay tribute to my research guide Dr. Sanjay Mishra under whose guidance I conducted my doctoral research. I also express my heartfelt thanks and sincere gratitude to my teacher Prof. A.K. Sarkar for his valuable guidance and supervision during the course of my doctoral research. I am deeply indebted to both of my teachers for their expert guidance, unwavering support and compassionate approach.

Words fall short to express my gratitude to Prof. Rajendra P. Bharti, Director, Lal Bahadur Shastri Institute of Management & Technology, for his invaluable guidance and diligent mentorship. He has been a mentor in the true sense of the word and has encouraged and cajoled me to author a good book since the time I have been in touch with him.

One's success very often is the outcome of unsung sacrifices of his loved ones and the relentless support of a few, selflessly supporting from the obscurity of the wings. I attribute the successful completion of this book to a few such people in my life who have lent an unconditional support to me not only throughout the course of the research work but throughout my life. Had it not been for the encouragement, guidance, motivation and support of my parents, Dr. Shyamal Kumar Chattopadhyay and Mrs. Ranu Chattopadhyay, I would not have become what I am today. My life has been shaped by their love, care and sacrifice. I shall remain ever indebted to them. Today, it also gives me an immense pleasure to pay tribute to my Mother-in-law Mrs. Gauri Bhattacharjee. I thank her for her blessings and good wishes. My wife Mrs. Ruby Chattopadhyay has been a constant source of inspiration and encouragement. I thank her for her unswerving support and relentless motivation and treasured companionship. I see her as the 'wind beneath my wings'. My twin sisters Dolon (Mrs. Kuntala Chakrabarty) and Julia (Mrs. Sharmistha Banerjee) have been my strength since the day I remember. Their love, care, understanding and help are deeply valued and cherished. They have been by my side whenever I needed them. My sisters have made my life beautiful and my memories worth cherishing.

I would like to take this opportunity to express my thanks to my dear friends and my brothers in law Mr. Surajit Chakrabarty and Mr. Kaushik Banerjee for their constant moral support. They are the people who have stood by me through thick and thin. It also gives me a sense of elation to vocalise my gratitude and utter a word of thanks to my sisters in law Basabi Didi (Mrs. Basabi

Bhattacharjee) and Devi (Mrs. Chinmoyee Bhattacharjee) for their love, concern and moral support.

The task of collecting data for the researches used in this book could not have been completed without the help obtained from Mr. Sandeep Banerjee (Sandeepda), my students Mr. Sanjoy Mukherjee, Mr. Manmohan Singh and Mr. Shashilesh, my sister Mrs. Kuntala Chakrabarty, my brothers in Law Mr. Kaushik Banerjee and Mr. Kaushik Acharjee and my friends and colleagues Mrs. Harsimrat Sharma and Mr. Abhinav Nath.

My desire to acknowledge the most important people in my life would remain unfulfilled if I fail to mention the names of four wonderful little kids from whom I draw inspiration, happiness and strength. These little darlings are my nephew Ryan Banerjee, my nieces Indrani Chakrabarty and Abhilasha Majumdar and last but not the least, a little angel who keeps me energised and has made my life really sweet with his beautiful smile, amusing acts and innocent mischief. That little angel is my adorable son Saptarshi Chatterjee.

-Dr. Subho Chattopadhyay

****

PREFACE

In the midst of advertisement clutter in an over-communicated society getting a brand noticed is a gargantuan task. The foremost desire of every brand manager in such a market is to create a distinctive identity and a pre-emptive position for the brand in the consumer's mind space. Finding a position that is meaningful for the consumer and assures him of a distinctive benefit offered by no other competitor ensures survival and sustainability for the brand. So the key to successful positioning lies not in the product, not even in the marketer's mind but in the mind of the consumer (Ries & Trout, 1981). Ries & Trout, 1981, have further clarified that positioning starts with the product. But positioning is not what you do to the product. It is what you do to the mind of the prospect.

Like every nation, India also has a unique set of values, beliefs and customs which further vary from one region to another within the country itself. These values and beliefs have a strong influence on the perception and attitude of the people and their predisposition towards any object, product or brand. If a brand is able to reflect these values and conform to the beliefs of the people, it is likely to experience a favourable impact on its brand acceptability and brand preference. So the challenge of a company lies in identifying the need of the people, their values, beliefs, preferences, likings and disliking and in finding their expectations from a product or a brand so as to inculcate the desired values into the brand. A knowledge of customer preference and an understanding of the customer's perception and attitude helps in positioning the brand in a suitable manner and in establishing some favourable, strong and unique associations that may result in strong brand equity.

For a Multinational company, that finds itself in the midst of a culture and customs which are absolutely different from those of its home country, brand positioning may involve several critical decisions like whether or not to use a standardized strategy for all the markets, up to what extent to adapt to the local culture, what values to inculcate into the brand and what values to emphasise while positioning it, and whether to emphasise the country of origin of the brand or not.

PROBLEMS OF THE STUDY

The Indian market is characterized by a unique blend of traditional values and modern approaches, and the evaluation criterion used by the consumer to judge a product or place value on a brand consists of a varying mix of such contrasting parameters. In this marketing environment marked by such psychographic characteristics of an average consumer it is interesting to get an insight into the strategies that are being used or can be used by the MNCs dealing in Fast Moving Consumer Goods to position their brands in the Indian market.

Some specific questions that are likely to arise in this context are related to:

- The types of positioning strategies being used by MNCs dealing in fast moving consumer goods in the Indian market.

- Identification of the various factors that affect the brand positioning strategies of the MNCs.

- The types of message content elements likely to be used by the MNCs and relevant for them while promoting and positioning their FMCG brands in India.

- Whether the 'Country of Origin' of the brand has an impact on the brand positioning strategy used by the MNCs in the Indian market.

Several studies, related to the positioning of multinational FMCG brands in the Indian market, have been conducted by the author to find answers to such questions. These studies have been aimed at developing a broad understanding of the brand positioning strategies of multinational companies dealing in fast moving consumer goods in India and the factors affecting their positioning strategies. The present book is a compilation of a few of those studies.

Thus some of the objectives with which the present book has been compiled are:

1. To understand the nuances of brand positioning strategies being used by the MNCs in India.
2. To identify the factors which affect the brand positioning strategies of MNCs dealing in FMCG brands in the Indian market.
3. To evaluate the importance of social, cultural and economic factors in the brand positioning strategies of MNCs dealing with FMCG brands in India.
4. To identify the elements of message content used in brand positioning and the relative significance of those elements in brand positioning strategies of multinational companies selling FMCG brands in the Indian market.
5. To find out if the MNCs (dealing with FMCG) using Indian cultural element i.e., companies which use Local Consumer Culture Positioning (LCCP), have a competitive advantage as compared to those which don't (or those which use GCCP).

6. To trace the impact and significance of the 'country of origin' of the brand on the brand positioning strategies adopted by the MNCs selling FMCG brands in India.

The product categories for which the studies have been conducted are: Food & Beverage, Confectionary, Soaps & Detergents, Cosmetics and Home Care products and Over-the-Counter products (OTC).

The critical evaluation of brand positioning strategies by MNCs dealing with FMCG products in India, undertaken in this book would help in enhancing the understanding of the various factors which should be taken into account while positioning the brand in the Indian market. The studies presented in the book would help the researchers and the industry to ponder upon the impact of socio-cultural factors on brand image and brand positioning. The book would also help the researchers to gain an insight into the relative significance of the elements of the message content strategy used while positioning a brand and targeting it to different market segments. The findings of the studies included in the book would help the FMCG companies in giving an appropriate direction to their brand positioning strategies so as to enable the consumer in selecting the product and brands that would solve their needs more effectively thus satisfying them in a better way.

****

CHAPTER 1

BRAND POSITIONING -AN INTRODUCTION

BRAND: MEANING AND SIGNIFICANCE

In this era of global business expansion and product proliferation, consumers virtually have a limitless option and are faced with a countless number of ways to satisfy their needs and wants. The onus lies on the manufacturer/ seller not only to provide the best means of satisfaction (i.e., products that deliver the best satisfaction) to the consumers but also to persuade the customers to seek out the manufacturer's offerings and specifically ask for the same. In the world of 'me-too' products and a number of manufacturers, the process of such specific search and the promotion of such specific demand can only be generated when the products are endowed with a very clearly visible mark of identification that facilitate the recognition of the origin and differentiates the offering from those of the other companies. This mark of distinction can be provided in an easy way and most conveniently in the form of a distinctive name that would get associated with the company's offering, a logo and an identification sign. This part of the product that can be vocalized (the brand name) along with the accompanying mark, sign or logo (used for its identification and differentiation) gives rise to a brand.

The concept of brand and the phenomenon of branding have been in existence, though in a crude form since the beginning of human civilization. When man left his nomadic life, settled in villages and took to agriculture as a profession and as a means of livelihood, he honed the skill of rearing animals to aid the agricultural production and enhance his agricultural produce. Livestock thus became a prized possession and an apt indicator of wealth and affluence. The size of livestock went on to acquire a functional and symbolic significance. One of the challenges facing our earliest civilized ancestors was to keep a count of the animals under their possession, differentiating them from those of others and preventing their animals to mix with those of others. A simple solution that ensued was to make a mark on the bodies of the animals with a hot metal (SaifUllah & Owais, 2007). This differentiating mark was a brand in the crudest form and this is where the modern word 'brand' has derived its meaning from. 'Brand' as we know it today, has its origin in the Norse word '**Brandr**' which means 'to burn' (Verma, 2002). Much later, during the Roman Empire, the slaves of the Roman dynasty were also identified and differentiated using a similar branding process (Samson, 1992). The phenomenon of branding slaves, lawbreakers and criminals was also prevalent in the bygone era in Britain (William, 1899).

With the advent of the industrial era, the genesis of marketing as a discipline and the further evolution of this discipline, the concept of brand acquired a new dimension and the phenomenon of branding took on a new significance. The basic purpose however remained the same and that was to differentiate.

Brand became the most important tool in the arsenal of the marketer to distinguish his products from those of the competitors. The firms and the marketers started using a combination of name (to vocalize the company's offer), sign, symbol and insignia to distinctly identify the company's product, to help the consumer associate it with the company that offers the product and to distinguish it from the competitors' products. This combination came to be known as a brand in the marketing parlance (Kotler, 1996). According to the American Marketing Association, "A brand is a name, term, sign, symbol or design or a combination of them, intended to identify the goods and services of one seller or group of sellers and to differentiate them from those of competitors."

The strongest brands emerged to be those that not only differentiated but also conveyed in a lucid way the functional and tangible benefits offered by the product and simultaneously evoked an array of emotional feelings in the customers in addition to conveying some intangible benefits. These brands were thus responsible for creating a strong and sustainable bond between the product and the consumer.

In today's era of intense marketing competition, brand is not merely an identifier. It stands for the value associated with the product and enhances it. Brand is a symbol of assurance to the customer, an assurance of quality, assurance of delivery, assurance of safety and much more depending on the perception of the customer regarding the brand in question. Besides being an identifier and a symbol of assurance, a brand may be used by the consumer as a conspicuous or at times subtle means of expression of the self. As a matter of fact all brands evolve over a period of time and predominantly perform a different function at each stage of its evolution (Ghodeswar, 2008). The different stages of evolution of a brand along with the predominant function performed during these stages as pointed out by Ghodeswar, 2008 are:

Stage I: Expresses the identity of the producer (i.e., label)

Stage II: Establishes functional superiority (Perceived by customers as differentiation)

Stage III: Establishes the emotional touch.

Stage IV: Generates the power of self expression.

Stage V: Becomes a cult.

Thus A comprehensive look at brand may depict its ability to convey a functional benefit, a sensory experience and/or an emotional bonding of the customers with the product (Park et al, 1986). A brand is therefore:

- Is A Promise To Consumers

- Is How A Company/Product/Service Defines And Differentiates Itself

- Is Dynamic And Evolving

- Is Defined By Consumers Perceptions And

- Expectations

- Is a symbol of assurance

- Speaks Loudly About What A Product Stands For

The ability of a brand to convey a functional message or generate a sensory stimulus or create an emotional connect determines the level of brand awareness, brand acceptance and brand preference amongst the consumers which in turn is responsible for determining the brand equity of a given brand (Kotler, et al, 2007).

For a brand to generate a lucid functional meaning and a distinctive emotional connect, it should occupy a distinctive and valued position in the perceptual space of the consumer in such a way that it conforms to the expectations of the consumers not fulfilled by the other competing offerings in the market. This is Brand Positioning.

BRAND POSITIONING

In this era of cut throat competition the success of any Company depends up to a large extent on its ability to satisfy and delight the consumers in the target market. Survival in this age of globalisation can be ensured up to a certain extent only if the goods and services offered by the company conform to the requirements of the target consumer. Thus every Company, be it a global company or a local company, wants to establish itself in the mind of the consumer and eventually into the market in which the company is operating. This calls for an appropriate positioning of the brand in the perceptual space of the consumer as well as in the market.

Brand Positioning implies finding a valued place for the brand in the mind of the target consumer. The significance of Brand Positioning lies in the fact that it differentiates the company's offer from those of the competitors and establishes a brand image or brand association which if designed properly may go a long way in establishing a long term relationship with the customers. Brand Positioning doesn't simply mean finding or creating a suitable place in the mind of the target customer but doing so with a watchful eye on the competitor (Ries & Trout, 1981) and simultaneously making points of parity with the competitor and establishing relevant and sustainable points of difference so as to achieve the required competitive advantage (Keller, 2008 & Kotler et al, 2007). According to Kotler, 1996, "Positioning is the act of designing the company's offer and image so that it occupies a distinct and valued place in the target consumer's mind." Thus a brand Positioning exercise starts with understanding the target market segment, and is followed by understanding the competitor and establishing points of parity and points of difference.

Thus Brand positioning is all about identifying the optimal location in our customers' minds for our Brand vis-à-vis our competitors. Proper positioning makes it easier to facilitate understanding of our Brand.

In order to Position a Brand one must decide

- Who the Target Consumer is

- Who your main competitors are

- How the Brand is similar to your competitors

- How the Brand is different from your competitors

Positioning is always done with respect to the competing brands in the mind of the target consumer. The reference points employed for positioning a brand are the competing brands and their images in the consumer's mind or perceptual space. These two i.e. the target market and the nature of competition therein constitute the frame of reference for positioning (Keller, 2008). Once the competitive frame of reference has been established, the act of positioning commences with identifying the 'category membership endowing' Points of Parity and 'benefit promising' Points of Difference (Kotler et al, 2007).

Point of Difference (POD)

Points of Difference are strong, favorable and unique brand associations. These are associations which promise a unique benefit as compared to the other competing brands. Points of Difference may be any association based on either the physical attributes of the

Point of Parity (POP)

Points of Parity are the associations that are shared with other brands. Points of Parity may be of two types:

- Category POP: 'Category Points of Parity' are the brand associations essential to establish the claim to the membership of a particular category. These are the attributes that are required to include your product as a member of that category.

- Competitive POP: These are the associations that match the Point of Difference of the competitors, negate those Points of Differences and nullify the uniqueness promised by those Points of Differences.

Brand Positioning in a Foreign Market

Positioning a brand, in the foreign market, calls for a carefully planned and cautious approach. Besides deciding on points of Parity and Points of difference, the brand manager has to be sensitive to:

- Local Culture- Failure to understand the local culture may lead to blunder. A classical example is the failure of KFC in India during its initial launch in mid 90's. In keeping with its global practice Kentucky Fried Chicken was selling its wares fried in beef tallow, unaware of the religious sentiments of the majority Hindu population of the country that refrains from beef consumption due to the religious reverence to cow.

    Research indicates an emerging use of culture for developing brand identity and the emergence of the concept of cultural positioning whereby culture is used as an element of positioning and as a communication element to convey the brand identity. Wherever required, a brand may be positioned using elements of the local culture. Such type of positioning is called Local Consumer Culture Positioning (LCCP) (Steenkamp et al, 1999).

- Local Language- Difficulties faced by the brand name 'Nova' by Chevrolet in the Spanish market was on account of the meaning of 'Nova' in Spanish language. In Spanish language 'Nova' means 'It doesn't move'. In the foreign markets local meaning of brand names may enhance or destroy brand equity.

  It has been found that pronouncing or spelling a brand in a foreign language triggers cultural stereotypes and influences product perceptions and attitudes of the consumers towards the brand (Leclerc et al, 1994).

- Relevance of the product category in the market- a product category that is highly relevant and meaningful in one market may not be equally relevant in some other market. Such a situation may call for adaptation of the product offered by the company in different markets or repositioning of the product or the brand according to the nature of the market.

BRAND REPOSITIONING

Repositioning is the phenomenon of altering the brand identity so as to change the perception of the brand in the consumers' mind. It involves identifying and offering a value proposition different from the one currently offered by the brand.

A company may reposition its brand to make it more meaningful, relevant and appealing to the consumer and to give it a distinctive edge in the market. Repositioning makes sense when the present positioning doesn't give access to a substantial market or when the company contemplates expanding the scope of the brand and achieving a greater market penetration. Also when the present positioning of the brand becomes less effective and somewhat obsolete, repositioning may be attempted to make the brand contemporarily relevant. In such cases repositioning helps the brand to keep pace with the changing taste and preferences of the consumers.

A brand may need to change its positioning when it enters into a new market segment whose characteristics are substantially different from the characteristics of the market in which the brand presently operates.

POSITIONING FMCG BRANDS IN THE INDIAN MARKET

An Overview of the FMCG Sector in India

As the current study focuses on the brand positioning strategies adopted by multinational companies dealing in fast moving consumer goods in India, it warrants a discussion on the Indian FMCG sector. The size of the FMCG market in India as on 2011 was Rs. 1,463 billion which is expected to grow at 12 percent to 17 percent up to 2020 and would reach a market size of Rs. 4000 to 6,200 billion (Source: Dabur Annual Report 2010-2011). The affluent in India who comprise about 1 percent of the population and the upper middle class which comprise 2 percent of the population forms the main market for the premium products and brands. The middle class in India comprises 11 percent of the population and is expected to grow to 30 percent by the year 2020. This forms the main segment to be targeted for the mass market products. Another segment is the Bottom of the Pyramid segment. The consumers in this segment spend mainly on essentials. The demand for expensive lifestyle products is almost missing in this segment. The rural market which for many years was blatantly neglected by the corporate world, today contributes significantly to the growth of the FMCG sector.

A study conducted by AC Neilsen shows that in more than half of the FMCG categories, rural India's contribution to their growth exceeds the contribution of the urban market. This market is expected to become a $100 billion market by the year 2025 (Source: AC Nielsen, November, 2010).

An important factor that influences the growth of the Indian FMCG industry is the favourable demographic profile of the consumer. Fifty percent of the country's population is below 25 years and 65 percent of the population is below 35 years of age (Source: Dabur Annual Report 2011). This offers a tremendous potential for growth to the FMCG sector in India.

With the increase in the overall population of the country, an increase in the average income of the consumer, a general improvement in the lifestyle, increased urbanisation and an enhanced media exposure for the urban and rural population the growth potential of the Indian consumer goods industry has significantly increased over the years. The market now offers a scope for the introduction of a variety of products, proliferation of product variants and the growth and survival of numerous brands that may be targeted at various segments of the market.

Multinational Companies in the Indian FMCG Sector

FMCG companies in India have an immense potential of growth owing to the vast population of the country and the improved economic situation ushered in by the rapid growth and development of the economy in the last two decades. The Indian FMCG market is populated by a bevy of domestic and international companies. The market offers a level playing field for regional players, domestic companies operating at the national level, homegrown multinationals and the global giants of foreign origin. These companies offer a wide range of products that can be broadly categorised under the categories of personal care products, home care products, food products and over-the-counter products (OTC).

There are a total of 143 listed FMCG companies in the Indian market. The total number of multinational companies operating in the FMCG sector in India as on December 2011 is 50 (Source: www.fundoodata.com). These multinational companies offer products and brands in product categories like soaps, detergents, oral care, hair care, skin care, dairy products, chocolates, confectionaries, food and beverage, etc.

The foreign multinational companies operating in the FMCG space in India get a tough competition from the homegrown multinationals as well as from the domestic players with a national presence (Shashidhar, 2010). In many regional, suburban and rural pockets of the Indian market these multinationals have to compete with several local and regional brands with a strong local acceptance.

Drivers of Growth of the Indian FMCG Sector

The Indian FMCG sector is a rapidly growing sector that has exhibited a growth rate of 11 percent per annum over the last decade (Source: Marico Annual Report 2010-2011). It has an immense potential that lures the international giants, domestic companies as well as regional players into the fray. According to the Annual Report 2010-2011 of Marico, "Robust growth in India's Gross Domestic Product (GDP), growing urbanization, evolving consumer lifestyles and increased income in rural areas are some of the key drivers of growth" for this sector. According to the Annual Report 2020-2011 of Dabur, the factors that are responsible for the increased consumption in the urban and rural areas and those that are driving the growth of the Indian FMCG sector can be enumerated as:

- Demographic Characteristics of the Market: 50 percent of the Indian population is below 25 years and 65 percent of the population is below 35 years of age. The young consumer makes the market vibrant and dynamic.
- Economic Growth: Consistently robust economic growth results in an increased per capita income of the Indian consumer. The per capita income of the Indian consumer is expected to increase from $1,017 in 2009 to $3,231 in the year 2020 (Source: Dabur Annual Report 2011-2012) which translates into a bright future for the FMCG industry.

- Growth of Organised Retail Sector and Demand for Branded Products: Increasing patronage of the consumer for the organised sector and an increased preference for branded products provides a fillip to the FMCG sector.

- Increase in the Per Capita Income of the Indian Consumer.

- Changing Consumer Lifestyle: Tremendous improvement in the lifestyle of the consumer has triggered a change in the consumption pattern.

- Market Penetration of FMCG Industry: Improved penetration of the packaged consumer goods into the various strata of the market and an overwhelming enthusiasm amongst manufacturers and sellers for the rural market has kindled new hopes and avenues of growth for the Indian FMCG industry.

- Growing Size of the Indian Middle Class: The middle class which constituted 5 percent of the population in 2007 is expected to grow up to 40 percent of the population by 2025 (Ablett et al, 2007).

- Rapid Urbanisation and Increased Participation of Women in the Workforce.

- The Growth of Modern Trade Channels in India which Make Shopping Convenient and Enjoyable.

- Arousal of the Rural Market: There is an increased awareness about quality amongst the rural consumers, a rising demand for branded goods in the rural markets and an overall evolution of the purchase behavior and consumption pattern of the rural consumer.

Brand Positioning of FMCG Brands by Multinational Companies in the Indian Market

Many multinational companies find it difficult to compete against Indian companies that have learnt the art of manufacturing and marketing on a shoestring budget. These Indian companies having acquired the skill of operating on a frugal budget are rapidly emerging as effective players. Another reason for the difficulty faced by several western MNCs in the Indian market lie in their strategies based on a faulty assumption that the modern day Indian market is similar to what the western market was several decades ago. The fact, on the contrary, is that the emerging markets have leapfrogged several stages of development (Inkpen & Kannan, 2007).

Kumar and Gupta, 2003, found that for a multinational company of western origin, positioning its brands of FMCGs in the Asian market in general and in the Indian market in particular is a challenging task. Because of the culture based differences in consumer behavior, brands in the western market have a rugged identity that signify freedom, independence and individuality but South Asian brands in general have a smooth and soft identity that signify and emphasize the concern of the consumer for his family, friends, community and the society. So the dimensions and nuances of brand positioning for an MNC in India are different from those in the western markets (Kumar & Gupta, 2003). Multinationals need to chalk out different value propositions for consumers in the emerging markets like India. Their marketing programmes need to be specifically adapted to the needs of the emerging market consumers (Dawar & Chattopadhyay, 2000).

In order to effectively position a foreign brand of fast moving consumer goods in the Indian market, the company should use the marketing mix with which the host country consumer is familiar with. Secondly it should be positioned as complementary to the existing products. Using a positioning that would challenge the conventional consumption practices of the consumer and attack or demean the well accepted cultural habits and beliefs of the consumer would not stand the brand in good stead (Kumar & Gupta, 2003).

The three things essential to be considered while positioning a brand are

(a) The target customer
(b) The target competition and
(c) The company or the brand.

Verma, 2002 calls these as the 3Cs of brand positioning. These are also the factors that determine and influence the positioning of a brand.

(a) Customers (The First 'C'): The Indian consumer of FMCG are highly diverse in their income levels, education background, language, lifestyle, locational background (urban/rural), culture, customs, habits and beliefs (Kumar, 2007). The consumers of FMCG can broadly be categorised as urban and rural consumers. The purchase behaviours and motives of consumption may be different in consumers from varied backgrounds. Thus the products may have to be positioned differently for different types of consumers. Even in the urban market the consumers may be classified and targeted on the basis of their lifestyles or on the basis of their incomes. While premium brands are targeted at consumers from the upper income level, the mass market brands are targeted at the middle income consumers and the economy brands and sachets are targeted at the consumers at the lower income level.

(b) Competitors (The Second 'C'): Competing in the Indian FMCG space are International brands, brands from the stable of homegrown multinationals, national brands and brands sold by regional companies. While certain categories like chocolates, shampoos and toilet soaps are dominated by international brands from multinational companies, categories like hair oil, edible oil, branded flour, etc. are dominated by Indian brands operating at a national level and brands from the stable of Indian multinationals. In product categories like tea, spices, etc.

unbranded products or local and regional brands have an overbearing market share. While positioning a brand of FMCG in any market segment, such competition related factors invariably need to be taken into account.

(c) Company or Brand (The Third 'C'): What positioning and image a company envisages for its brands also depends on the broad strategy of the company, its vision, its history, its standing in the market and its market philosophy.

As far as the rural market is concerned it has been found that even strong brand awareness may not lead to a heavy consumption of the FMCG brand in rural India (Bishnoi & Bharti, 2008). To effectively position an FMCG brand in the rural market, the brand should be differentiated by virtue of its quality, value for money and proximity of its association with the consumer (Anand & Krishna, 2008).

****

REFERENCES

Ablett, Jonathan, Baijal, Aadarsh, Beinhocket, Eric, Bos, Anupam, Farell, Diana, Gersch, Ulrich, Greenberg, Ezra, & Gupta, Shishir, "The 'Bird of Gold': The Rise of India's Consumer", *Report Mckinsey Global Institute*, May 2007, pp. 9-18

AC Nielsen (2010), "India's Rural FMCG Market to Grow to $100 Billion by 2025", November 24

Alden, Dana L., Jan-Benedict EM Steenkamp, and Rajeev, Batra (1999), "Brand Positioning Through Advertising in Asia, North America and Europe: The role of global consumer culture", *Journal of Marketing*, Vol. 63 (January), pp. 75-87

Andrews, William (1899), *Bygone Punishments*, William Andrews & Co., London, pp. 44-45

Bishnoi, Vinod Kumar, & Bharti (2008), "Does Branding Matter: An Empirical Study of FMCG Products in Rural Haryana", *Pragyan: Journal of Management*, Vol. 6, No. 2 (Dec.), pp. 39-44

Dawar, Niraj, Chattopadhyay, Amitava (2000), "Rethinking Marketing Programs for Emerging Markets", *William Davidson Institute Working Paper*, No. 320, pp. 1-22

Ghodeswar, B.M. (2008), "Building brand identity in competitive markets", *Journal of Product & Brand Management*, Volume 17, Number 1, pp. 4 – 12.

Inkpen, Andrew, Ramaswamy, Kannan (2007), "End of Multinational: Emerging Markets Redraw the Picture", *Journal of Business Strategy*, Vol. 28, No. 5, pp. 4-12

Kapferer, Jean Noel (2004), *The New Strategic Brand Management: Creating and Sustaining Brand Equity Long Term*, 1st South Asian ed. (New Delhi: Kogan Page India Pvt. Ltd.), *pp.96-106*

Keller, Kevin Lane (2008), *Strategic Brand Management- Building, Measuring and Managing Brand Equity*, 3rd ed., Pearson, New Delhi, pp. 120-139

Khan, SaifUllah, & Mufti, Owais (2007), "The Hot History & Cold Future of Brands", *Journal of Managerial Sciences*, Vol. 1, No. 1, pp. 75-87

Kotler, Philip (1996), *Marketing Management Analysis, Planniing, Implementation, and Control*, 8th ed. New Delhi, PHI, pp. 444-445

Kotler, Philip, Keller, Kevin Lane, Koshy, Abraham, & Jha, Mithileshwar (2007), *Marketing Management-A South Asian Perspective*, 12th ed., Pearson Prentice Hall, New Delhi, pp. 254-257, 288-295

Kumar, S. Ramesh (2007), *Marketing and Branding: The Indian Scenario*, New Delhi: Pearson Education, 1st ed, pp. 443-445

Kumar, S. Ramesh, Gupta, Vipin (2003), "Repositioning Western Brands in the Asian Culture: Insights from the Indian Context", *Asia Pacific Journal of Economics & Business*, Vol. 7, No.1 (June), pp. 57-72

Leclerc, France, Schmitt, Bernd H., & Dube Laurette (1994),; "Foreign Branding and its Effect on Product Perceptions and Attitudes", *Journal of Marketing Research*, Vol. XXXI (May), pp: 263-270

Park, C.Whan, Jaworski, B.J., & Macinnis, D.J. (1986); "Strategic brand concept-image management", *Journal of Marketing*, Vol. 50, October, pp. 135-45.

Ries, Al, & Trout, Jack (1981), *Positioning: The Battle for Your Mind*, 20th ed., McGraw-Hill Professional, New York, USA, pp. 5-10

Sagar, Mahim, Singh, Deepali, Agrawal, D.P., & Gupta Achintya (2009), *Brand Management*, Anne Books Pvt. Ltd, pp.55-72

Samson, R. (1992), "Slavery, The Roman Legacy", *in Fifth Century Gaul: A Crisis of Identity?*, eds Drinkwater, John, Elton, Hugh, Cambridge University Press, 1st ed., New York, USA, pp.218-227

Shashidhar, Ajita (2010), "Good to Global", *Outlook Business*, July 24, pp. 42-46

Van den Putte, Bas (2002), "An Integrative Framework for Effective Communication", in Bartels, G & W. Nellissen (ed.s), *Marketing for Sustainability: Towards Transactional Policy Making*, (Amsterdam: IOS Press), pp. 83-95

Van den Putte, Bas (2009), "What Matters the Most in Advertising Campaigns? The Relative Effect of Media Expenditure and Message Content Strategy", *International Journal of Advertising*, Vol. 28, No. 3, pp. 669-690

Verma, Harsh V., *Brand Management: Text and Cases*, 2nd ed, New Delhi: Excel Books, 2002, pp. 135-138

Verma, Harsh, V. (2002), *Brand Management*, 1st ed. (New Delhi-Excel Books), pp. 44-46

Anand, Sandip, & Krishna, Rajneesh (2008), "Rural Brand Preference Determinants in India, Conference on 'Marketing to Rural Consumers- Understanding and Tapping the Rural Market Potential, 3-5 April, 2008

CHAPTER 2

BRAND POSITIONING STRATEGIES OF MNCS SELLING FMCG BRANDS IN INDIA

TYPES OF BRAND POSITIONING STRATEGIES

The point of reference of a brand positioning strategy is the market and the competitor. On the basis of these points of reference the different positioning strategies may be built upon the features of the product offered to the market, the benefits offered by the product and sought by the market, the purpose for which the product is used, the consumers/ users who constitute the market, the price and quality sought by the market and the competitors. Thus the broad categorization of the brand positioning strategies may be:

a) **Attribute positioning:** A brand positioning strategy in which the product is differentiated from its competitors and positioned in the perceptual space of the consumer on the basis of the product attributes and features incorporated into the product. Example, when BMW positions itself on the basis of its superior technology and the specialised features that are present in the car, it is using attribute positioning.

b) **Benefit positioning:** A brand positioning strategy in which the company positions its brand on the basis of the distinctive benefit that the product offers to its customers. Example, Maggi was positioned using the proposition of instant satisfaction to hunger and the benefit of a tasty meal within a very short time. Later on the brand of noodles was positioned by promising the benefit of health and taste.

c) **Use/ Application positioning:** Positioning the brand on the basis of the distinctive use of the product or by virtue of the number of different uses of the product. Example milkmaid positions itself by professing the number of uses it can be brought into. Krack cream is differentiated from the other creams in the market on the basis of its very specific use and has occupied a preemptive position of a cream meant to be used to cure cracked heels.

d) **User positioning:** User positioning means positioning the brand on the basis of the target consumer. The brand positions itself by promising to portray an image of the user that he aspires to have. The brand may position itself by establishing a conformance between the self image of the user and the image that the brand carries or portrays. Example when Bajaj

Pulsar used the punch line 'Definitely male" in its advertisement, it established a conformance between the characteristics of the bike and the self image of the target consumer. It also promised a macho image to its users and thus appealed to the young boys who aspired to have such an image.

e) **Quality/ Price positioning:** The brand is differentiated from its competitors on the basis of the quality that it offers and/or the price at which it is available. Quality and/or price are then used to craft a distinctive image of the brand in the minds of the customer.

f) **Product category positioning:** The brand positions itself by claiming to be in a product category that is different from its immediate competitors as well as different from that in which it is expected to be. Example Dove positions itself by claiming that it is not soap.

g) **Competitor positioning:** Positioning the brand by directly comparing it with its competitor. Example 'Rin' detergent powder tried to position itself by directly comparing itself with the detergent powder 'Tide'.

Besides these usual positioning strategies, of late the multi national companies coming to India have realized the potential of the rural markets and hence the need for a distinctive positioning strategy exclusively designed for the rural market as well as the bottom of pyramid market. Today rural India, with a population of 73 crores (i.e, 60% of Indian population) is an important market not only for the domestic companies but also for the multinational companies. The potential of the Indian rural market becomes evident from the fact that about 12 % of the global population lives in rural India.

BRAND POSITIONING STRATEGIES IN THE FMCG SECTOR IN INDIA

The FMCG Sector

The Indian FMCG market is characterized by a plethora of brands, spanning several categories of products and a fierce competition being fought over by a slew of domestic and multinational companies targeting a varied segment of the Indian consumer. One can have an inkling of the enormity of the FMCG market by taking a look at the market size that stands at around $ 25 billion as on 2010. "From a $9 billion industry in 2000, the Indian FMCG industry has catapulted to become a $25 billion industry in 10 years" (Source: Shashidhar, 2010). The industry has recorded a CARG of 14.5 percent over the past decade (Source: Outlook business, July 24, 2010). According to AC Nielsen, India is amongst the fastest growing FMCG markets in the world, with an annual growth of 16 percent in the non food sector. (Source: Business Standard, December 29, 2009). "There is also evidence that as Indians get richer, and more and more people sail past the poverty line, the demand for FMCG will grow. According to a recent McKinsey report, the number of households in the deprived segment is likely to drop from 101 million in 2005 to 74 million in 2015. That means 27 million households will have entered the market in 10 years to 2015- the size of many a mid-size country's population" (Iyer, 2009).

"A big part of this growth story has been written by Indian FMCGs, which have recorded CARG of 15-16 percent over the past decade, compared to the industry average of 14.5%" (Shashidhar, 2010). Many of these Indian FMCG companies (including Godrej, Marico, Dabur and Emami) are no more complacent with just the domestic market but are expanding aggressively in the global market as well. Much of this aggressiveness comes from the confidence garnered by these companies by having successfully competed with the MNCs and global giants such as HUL, P&G and GSK in the domestic turf. "In 2000 Hindustan Unilever commanded more than 60% of the market in most key FMCG categories such as soaps, detergents and shampoos. A decade later, HUL's sales in most categories are less than half of the rest of the listed Indian FMCG players" (Shashidhar, 2010). In such a situation the battle of brands in the Indian FMCG sector have tremendously intensified. The various categories under which the brand battle is fought in the Indian FMCG space are: Oral care, Toilet soap, Detergent, Hair care (Shampoo, Hair oil, Hair colour), Beverages (Carbonated Drinks, Non-carbonated Drinks, Fruit Juices, Tea, Coffee, etc.), Food Items (Noodles, Ketchup, Packaged Food, Packaged Cereals, Spices, Snacks, Edible Oil, etc.), Confectionary (Biscuits, Chocolates, Candies, Cakes, etc.), Cosmetics & Skin Care Products (Face Cream, Body Lotion, Shaving Cream, Shaving Gels, Razors, Lipstick, Nail Polish, Fairness Cream, etc.), Body Care Products, Cigarettes and Tobacco Products, Home care products, etc. The market size of some of these categories is as shown in the table 2.A:

Table 2.A: Market Size of Certain Categories of FMCGs in India

Category	Market Size	Source
Fabric Care	Rs. 13,000 Crores	Strategist July 11, 2011
Toilet Soap	Rs. 10,000 Crore	Strategist, August 2, 2010
Instant Noodles	Rs. 1,137 Crore	Strategist August 2, 2010

Skin Care (Growing at 20% per annum)	Rs. 5,000 Crore	Business Today, November 13, 2011
Branded Snacks (Growing at 15-20% per annum)	Rs. 3,200 Crore	Strategist, October 13, 2009
Biscuit(Growing at 5-7% per annum)	Rs. 10,000 Crore	Strategist, October 20, 2009
Chewing Gum	Rs. 800 Crore	Strategist, July 5, 2010
Decorative Paints	Rs. 10,000-11,000 Crore	Strategist June 7, 2010
Fruit Juice Packaged fruit juice	Rs. 7,000 Crore Rs. 2,500 Crore	Strategist August 9, 2010
Chocolate	Rs. 2000 Crore	Strategist June 30, 2009
Household Cleaning Care Utensil Cleaners **Surface Cleaners:** Toilet Cleaners Floor Cleaners Specialist Cleaners	Rs. 1,240 Crore Rs. 950 Crore Rs. 180 Crore Rs. 75 Crore Rs. 35 Crore	Strategist, September 15, 2009
Packaged Water	Rs. 254 Crore	Strategist, January 12, 2010
Branded Edible Oil	Rs. 10,000 Crore	Strategist, March 9, 2010

Fairness Cream (Annual Growth 13-15%)	Rs. 1,700 Crore	Strategist, June 28, 2010
Coffee	Rs. 2000 Crore	Business Today, April 6, 2008
Packaged Tea	Rs. 4396 Crore	Business Today, April 6, 2008

The major players in the Indian FMCG space are global giants like HUL, P&G, Nestle, Colgate Palmolive, Coca Cola and Pepsi, Multinational Companies like Cadbury, Heinz, Garnier and Perfetti and homegrown stalwarts like Dabur, Godrej, Marico, Emami and ITC. With a number of strong, well established and well entrenched players in a crowded market space and with so many brands within each category, the challenge for a brand lies in effectively differentiating itself from the other brands. Whereas the new brands need to consciously strive to identify a vacant position (perceptual space of the consumer) and occupy it, the older brands need to periodically evaluate their position and point of difference viz-a-viz the competing brands and in case of a diluting point of difference need to harp upon new points of difference, revamp the differentiation and reposition the brand to maintain the competitive advantage.

Besides effectively positioning the brands in the conventional urban markets almost all the FMCG players have been making a serious endeavour since the last few years to spruce up the growth rate and expand their market by penetrating into the rural markets and the semi urban pockets, which hitherto remained an unexplored market. The rural market came as a rescue to some of these companies during the recessionary phase of 2008-2010. Thus besides positioning the brands in the urban market an additional task at hand for these FMCG companies (both multinational and domestic) is to simultaneously position their brands in the rural markets. While price and packaging strategy plays an important role in this endeavour, promotional efforts also have to be tweaked intelligently and strategically to achieve this objective. Companies also work upon new product formulations or modify the existing product offerings to develop an appropriate value proposition that suits the rural market.

Positioning of Oral Care Brands

According to the Technopak Advisors, the oral care market in India was valued at Rs. 3976 Crore in the year 2008 and is expected to reach Rs. 4373 Crore by 2012. The market can be segmented into mouthwashes, toothpastes, toothpowders and toothbrushes. The greatest contribution to this market comes from the toothpastes, the market of which was estimated to be of Rs. 2,866 Crores and is expected to reach Rs. 3,226 Crore by 2012. This is followed by the toothbrush market that was valued at Rs. 539 Crore in the year 2008. The mouthwash market in the same year was valued at Rs. 74 Crore and is expected to reach Rs. 89 Crore by 2012. The toothpowder market, with its major sales coming from the rural segment, was valued at Rs. 497 Crore and is expected to reduce to Rs. 458 Crore by the year 2012. (Source: Business Standard, October 14, 2008).

In the toothpaste segment, Colgate stands as the undisputed market leader with a market share of more than 49 percent followed by HUL at 30 percent with its brands Pepsodent and Close-UP (Carvalho, 2008). The other significant players in the market are Dabur (with its brands Dabur Babool, Dabur Red and Dabur Meswak), Henkel India with its 'Neem Active' brand of toothpaste and Vicco Laboratories with its product Vicco Vajradanti.

The brand Colgate that is the undisputed market leader in toothpastes, is synonymous with oral care in the Indian market. The strong position of the brand becomes evident from the fact that Colgate emerged as India's most trusted brand in the Brand Equity Annual Survey 2011 conducted by AC Nielsen for the Economic Times. It is the only brand to be in the top three consistently for the last eleven years (Irani, 2011). The Colgate toothpaste brand line consists of several variants of the brand, each positioned distinctively from the other and each promising a different benefit and value proposition. Colgate dental cream is positioned as a product that prevents tooth decay and acts even on those points on a tooth where the toothbrush cannot reach. The brand/product tries to occupy a perceptual space in the consumer's mind by using benefit positioning (prevention of tooth decay) strategy. The brand and the promotional campaign harps on the functional elements of positioning. One of the advertisement copy shows the inside corner of a newly painted door. The corner which couldn't be painted becomes vulnerable to decay. The door is compared to a tooth that is brushed superficially. Another ad copy shows a dentist exhibiting and demonstrating the reason of tooth decay using a model of the teeth. The brand 'Colgate' fortifies itself by associating with dentists and the Indian Dental Association and by claiming to be endorsed by the dentists. The expert opinion card is played by the brand by mentioning in its ad copy "Dentist ka sujhaya number one brand" ("The number one brand as suggested by the dentist").

Another brand from the stable of Colgate is the 'Colgate Active Salt' that is positioned as a salt-laced toothpaste to fight germs and strengthen gums. When the brand was initially launched, the positioning for the brand started off as cultural positioning. The positioning and promotional endeavour focused on the fact that salt was used as an essential element of oral care by our forefathers and older generation Indians. The positioning later on changed to a combination of attribute positioning and benefit positioning (citing the benefit of an important ingredient of the toothpaste). The positioning for the brand harps upon the presence of salt in the toothpaste and the advertisement copies dwell upon the germicidal and gum strengthening benefits of salt, an important ingredient of the toothpaste. The Functional element of message content strategy is used for positioning this brand of toothpaste.

A relatively new product from the stable of Colgate is Colgate Total. The brand is positioned as one that offers complete protection from all tooth related ailments. It claims to provide protection from twelve tooth related ailments in particular including gingivitis, cavities and plaque. Like in the advertisement copies for other brands of Colgate toothpastes, this brand also makes use of expert opinion and shows recommendations from dentists to use the brand. The positioning strategy used is benefit positioning.

The second biggest player in the Indian toothpaste market is HUL having a market share of 30 percent. Pepsodent and Close-Up are the brands from HUL in the Indian market. Close-Up is specifically targeted to the young segment of the market. It is positioned as a product that endows the user with a confidence to get close by giving him a fresh breath and sparkling white teeth. Thus the positioning strategy is benefit positioning and the benefits promised are: social acceptability and the confidence to get close, confidence to smile, fresh breath and sparkling white teeth. The promised benefit also reflects in the jingle for the television commercial for the brand "Pass aao, pass aao, pass aao na" ("Come close, come close, please do come close"). Hedonistic element is used to communicate the benefit to the target audience and the consumer.

On the other hand Pepsodent Germickeck from the same company, though using benefit positioning promises a different benefit: that of fighting against and killing germs. The brand is differentiated from the other brands in the market by laying a claim on its ability to fight germs for a longer period of twelve hours. Thus it is positioned as a product that kills germs and fights germs for a longer duration. Shah Rukh Khan has been roped in as the brand ambassador for pepsodent.

Dabur is perceived as a company that manufactures Ayurvedic, herbal and natural products. The strength of the company and the brand lies in its legacy of providing natural products and products derived from the traditional knowledge of Ayurveda. Strictly in line with the perceived image of Dabur, it positions two of its toothpaste brands: Dabur Babool and Dabur Meswak. The product formulations and the brand names are rooted in Ayurveda and traditional Unani medicine respectively. Dabur Meswak in its positioning highlights the natural ingredients of the product (the extract of Meswak plant), the bactericidal and germicidal properties of which strengthen the teeth and give fresh breath and protect it from cavity, plaque and tartar. The positioning strategy consists of a mix of attribute positioning (the product made up of pure extracts of Meswak plant) and benefit positioning (Fresh breath, strong teeth, prevention of cavity, plaque and tartar). The advertisement uses celebrity appeal wherein Bipasha Basu, the brand ambassador for Dabur Meswak, advocates the use of the brand. The promotional campaign makes use of humour appeal in its advertisement copy.

Dabur Babool is positioned as a product that gives strong teeth and a lively day. The advertising campaign for the brand is characterized by a series of advertisement copies used over a period of time, each of which is very lively. The very first ad copy showed a young man becoming very active and filled with liveliness and energy after brushing his teeth with Babool. The jingle for the advertisement copy went as "Subah Babool ki to din tumhara" which means "If you start the morning with Babool, the day is yours". The advertisement copy effectively communicated the benefit positioning of "A lively day with Babool". A subsequent advertisement copy used humour appeal while showing a young white man solving the water problem of a village by breaking open a fountain of water by biting on an underground/concealed water pipe using his teeth and earning the title 'Fountain Guru'. The benefit positioning of 'Strong teeth' with Babool is conveyed in a humorous way. Another advertisement copy uses the film star Vivek Oberoi in it. This advertisement copy is also lively and full of energy and dwells on the benefit positioning (strong teeth and lively day) of the brand. Dabur Babool has used the hedonistic element throughout its advertising campaign to promote and position the brand.

Positioning of Toilet Soap Brands

The size of the toilet soap market in India is Rs. 10,000/- crore (Source: The Strategist, July 11, 2011). HUL leads the race with lifebuoy having 16.6% of the market share followed by Lux at 15.5%. Godrej NO.1 from Godrej Consumer Products Ltd. occupies the third rank with 6.45% of the market share. (Source: The Strategist, August 25, 2009). Other important brands in the market are Pears, Dove, Liril and Breeze from HUL, Santoor from Wipro, Nirma and Dettol from Reckitt & Benckiser.

Initially lifebuoy was position as a carbolic soap for the sportsman, for the rugged people leading a rough and tough life. The value proposition chosen to distinctively position the brand was health. The advertisement Jingle "Lifeboy Hai Jahan, Tandurusti Hai Wahan" remains deeply embedded in the memories of the television viewers till this date. Later the brand was further extended into the beauty soap category and was positioned as a toilet soap for the entire family. The health proposition was however retained by the brand in all its extensions from the toilet soap through the beauty soap, to the hand wash. Lifebuoy total is positioned as a toilet soap endowed with strong germicidal properties that provides all day protection from germs. The positioning strategy used by the brand is benefit positioning. Lifebuoy Care is also positioned on the same grounds but has a brand identity of a gentle soap with germicidal properties and one that is essential for the good health of infants and children. The ad copy shows a young mother taking care of her baby and protecting the infant from germs by using lifebuoy care. The message content element used for positioning is functional.

Lifebuoy handwash also takes off from the same positioning ground but goes a little further and positions itself as the fastest handwash. The advertising copy depicts a classroom scene during recess where a student advices his classmates to wash their hands for complete one minute before any meal, only to be mocked upon by his friends who call his handwash a slow one and suggest the use of lifebuoy handwash. The voice over proclaims "Sabse Tej Handwash! Koi Dar Nahin". Functional element is used in this case as well.

One of the old and successful soap brands from the stable of HUL is Liril. Liril has always been positioned as the original freshness soap with the exciting freshness of lime. The brand uses the strategy of benefit positioning. To depict the benefit of freshness derived from the brand the advertising copy shows a picturesque waterfall with a girl bathing in it and the signature tune of Liril plays in the background. A lively, happy, young girl and a breathtakingly beautiful waterfall epitomizes the hedonistic element of communication. Another well accepted and well entrenched brand of soap from HUL is it glycerin soap 'Pears'. Pears is positioned as a soft and gentle soap for soft skin. The brand identity of the product is a caring soap for the soft , young skin. The positioning strategy is benefit positioning and the benefit of the soft skin and gentle care for the soft skin is shown in the ad copy by depicting the strong bond in the mother daughter relationship whereby the mother takes care of her daughter by pampering her skin with Pears. Love appeal is used overtly/exuberantly in the advertisement copy. The brand name Pears is prefixed with the words 'Masoom' (meaning innocent) to effectively convey the positioning of the brand. An extension of the brand Pears is 'Pears Germshield'. This soap is positioned as being 'Harsh on germs, soft on skin'. This again is a case of benefit positioning. The communication of the brand highlights the special formula for killing germs and the presence of glycerin for soft skin. Thus the functional element is used to convey the brand identity. The voice over in the television commercial claims "Pears Germshield ka Special formula. Kitanu Dho Nikale aur Glycerin Twacha ko Komal Rakhe. Pears germshields Kitanuo pe sakht, Twacha pe Komal Masoom Pears".

The oldest offering amongst soap brands from HUL in the Indian market is Lux. From its inceptions Lux has been positioned as the beauty soap used and preferred by the film stars. Even today it continues with the same positioning. Lux has always associated itself with the top and reigning filmstars of every era. In the recent past the brand has been endorsed by Juhi Chawla, Hema Malini, Shri Devi and Shahrukh Khan. Association with film stars ensures strong brand recall for the brand. Presently the brand is endorsed by filmstars like Aishwaya Rai, Priyanka Chopra and Katrina Kaif each of whom has a strong fan following amongst the Indian audience. Thus the brand heavily relies on celebrity endorsement and makes ample used of celebrity appeal in it advertisements.

Dove, a uniquely positioned soap brand from HUL, stands out from the rest of the soap brands in the market. It has a distinctively different brand identity and is positioned by the company as being different from soap. It is positioned as a bathing bar with one quarter moisturizer. The brand establishes a point of difference with soap and claims "Dove is better than soap". Moreover the advertisement copies for the product loudly proclaim "Dove is different; Enriched with one quarter moisturizer". Dove insists on being called a cream bar and not soap. Even on the pack of the product it is mentioned 'Dove Cream Bar'. Thus the positioning strategy used by the brand is category positioning.

Dettol soap from the stable of Reckitt & Benckiser is positioned completely on health proposition. The company uses benefit positioning whereby the brand is positioned as a product that ensures good health for the entire family. One of the ad copy claims "Jis ghar main dettol rozana istemal hota hai, wahan log kam bimar padte hain" which means that regular use of dettol reduces the incidents of illness in families. Through the ad it is further communicated to the consumers that this claim is endorsed by the Indian medical association. The benefit positioning of the brand is fortified by the punch line "Dettol family, healthy family".

Godrej No.1 from Godrej Consumer Products Ltd. is a strong brand in the Indian market. It is ranked third with a market share of 6.45%. It became the first GCPL brand to cross the. Rs.500/- Crore mark in the year 2009 (Iyer, 2009 c). Godrej No.1 is differentiated from the other brands of soap on the basis of its price. It is a popular market brand targeted towards the mass market. Along with the popular urban market it is also targeted at the rural market. The simple non glossy pack of the product also enhances the brand recall of the product. Thus this brand from Godrej uses a product-price positioning.

Unlike Godrej No.1, one off its variants Godrej No.1 Saffron and Milk cream uses attribute positioning as its positioning strategy. It differentiates itself from other brands by highlighting its natural Ingredients which include natural oils, milk cream, and saffron.

Positioning of Detergent Brands

The size of the detergents market in India is Rs. 13,000/- Crore. In the detergent market about two-third of the sale is contributed by detergent powder and the rest by bars. HUL (with its brands Surf , Wheel and Rin) lead the pack with 37% of the market share. Home grown street fighter Rohit Surfactant (Manufacturer of Ghari and MR-2) has the second largest market share of 17% followed by P & G (with brands Ariel and Tide) at 16% and Nirma at 8%. The detergent market in India is growing at a rate of 5-7% (Source: The Strategist, Nov. 1, 2010). The Indian market for detergent can broadly be broken down into three segments: The premium segment, which is about 15% of the market, the midscale segment that constitutes around 40% of the market and the popular segment contributing around 45% of the market. While HUL straddles all the segments P&G has its presence in the premium segment and the midscale segment, Nirma and Ghari and majorly present in the economy/popular segment. Surf from HUL and Ariel from P&G are the main brands catering to the premium segment. Rin from HUL and Tide from P&G compete in the midscale segment. The economy segment present in the urban as well as the rural market is catered to by the brands Wheel from HUL, Ghari from Rohit Surfactants and Nirma.

 Talking of HUL, the market leader, the company was initially present only in the premium segment of the market with its brand Surf. That was the time when many people had not graduated from soap bars to detergent powder. The entry of Nirma, a low technology small manufacturer at the time, changed the market dynamics. Nirma came in to the market with a new and highly simplified product formulation. The packaging too was incredibly simple and non-sophisticated and the price was way below the price of Surf. This product soon captured the rural market, the semi-urban market and the price sensitive lower income segment. The brand created a dent on the revenues and market share of Surf. In an attempt to protect its market share, HUL (HLL at that time) came up with a new product 'Wheel' that could combat Nirma in the economy segment. The competition facilitated the segmentation of the Indian market, increased the scope of the market and prepared it for different categories of detergent product for different segments.

Today, Surf Excel from HUL, targeted at the premium segment of the market is positioned as a product that removes stains effortlessly. The marketing communication for the brand makes an attempt to allay the fear of stains in the minds of the consumer and assures them that with the presence of the surf excel they need not be afraid of stains. The voice over in the ad copy of the brand says "Dag Lagne se Agar Kuch Accha hota hai toh Daag Acche hai". The positioning strategy being used by the brand is benefit position strategy.

P&G also vies for the same segment of the market with its product Ariel (Oxyblue). Ariel is positioned as a product that removes stains while keeping the clothes new. The ad copies claims "Ariel Oxiblue ka Special formula Kapdon ke Reshon ko smooth Banaye" benefit positioning is used as a positioning strategy and functional element of positioning is used to convey the brand identity.

 Another product Tide from P&G targeted at the Midscale segment plays the whiteness card. The value proposition delivered by the brand is whiteness with floral fragrance. The slogan for the brand "Tide hai toh white hai" (Meaning if tide is there, white is there) conveys the value proposition. Thus benefit positioning is used as the positioning strategy. Functional element is employed as the message content element to convey the brand differentiation and value proposition. The ad copies of the brand are characterized by a strong humour appeal. The humour appeal ensures a strong brand recall amongst the consumers. Unlike Ariel, Tide is targeted at the price sensitive customer. In its initial days the whiteness card was played solely by Rin. However, the whiteness space was later on taken over by Tide in a big way. Today, while trying to the reclaim the position Rin compares itself with Tide and claims to offers a more glowing whiteness. It also highlights its lower price to attract the price sensitive customer in the market. Thus Rin uses both competitor positioning as well as price positioning.

Vying for the economy/popular segment of the market are brands like Wheel, Nirma, and Ghari. Wheel from HUL has moved on from its core price positioning to attribute positioning whereby it talks about the strength of the formulation endowed with the power of lime and the fragrance of flowers. The ad copy mentions "Isme hain Nimbu ki khusboo aur hazaron phoolon ki shakti-Naya Wheel". The use of Salman Khan in the ad copy lends the touch of celebrity appeal to the brand. Sunlight, another offering from HUL, is positioned as a product with colour guard to maintain and protect the colours of the clothes. Benefit positioning strategy is used by the brand. Two important home grown street fighters in the detergent space are Nirma and Ghari Detergent. Both the products are targeted at the economy segment of the market. The target market for Nirma is the small town and lower middle income group. Through its ad copy the brand tries to influence the psyche of the new generation woman in this segment who considers herself smart, intelligent and bold. She has always been the home maker. Today she handles the outside chores also and has grown much smarter and bolder. She is the common Indian woman. 'Hema, Rekha, Jaya and Sushma'. The ad copies and the marketing communication are intelligently designed to appeal to these women. The simple positioning for the brand is 'It fights away the dirt............ boldly'. Today Ghari from Rohit surfactants is a brand worth mentioning and is an important player at the bottom of the market where the real volumelie. It has been able to garner 17% of the market share and has outshined several multinational brands in the country. The main target market of Ghari consists of Villages and small towns. The brand is mainly a price warrior. Though the brand differentiation is not preemptive, it is positioned as a brand that gives value for money.

Positioning of Shampoo Brands

The shampoo story in India is an interesting one. Shampoo used to sell in big bottles only from fancy stores in urban India. This was not considered as a product meant for the rural market. Many rural folks had never used shampoo in their life. The per capita consumption of shampoo even in urban India was very low until the concept of sachet arrived in the Indian market. The sachet concept introduced by a small Indian company revolutionalized the entire shampoo business in the country and brought in an unprecedented vibrancy in a hitherto dull market. The first shampoo brand to be introduced in a sachet was velvette by a company managed by the siblings of C.K. Rangnathan, the Chairman and Managing Director of CavinKare. The brand was later on sold off to Godrej. The sachet concept actually gained popularity when another brand 'Chik' was launched by CavinKare and marketed in the rural markets which were not exposed to this category of product till then. Chik opened up the bottled potential of the rural market, drastically expanded the market and facilitated CavinKare's penetration deeper into the rural market. This encouraged the multinational companies (the main manufactures of shampoo at that time) to follow suit and a number of companies introduced shampoo in sachet and small packs to cater to the small towns, villages and those people who didn't want to purchase shampoo in big bottles. Thus the shampoo market went abuzz with activity. Today the Indian rural market is growing at a pace double that of the urban market (Warrier, 2007).

Today the shampoo market in India is worth Rs. 3000/- Crore with HUL's Clinic Plus being the market leader. The hair conditioner market is estimated at around Rs. 200/- Crore and is growing at around 40-50% a year. (Source: The Business Standard, August 23, 2010). According to AC Neilsen, HUL (with its brands Sunsilk, Clinic Plus and Dove) is the market leader in shampoo with a market share of more than 47.3% followed by P&G at 17.7%. Dabur has a market share of 6.7% (Source: The Hindu Business line, April 10, 2011).

Clinic Plus, the largest selling brand in India is positioned as a product that facilitates the growth of long and healthy hair and helps in maintaining it. The type of positioning is benefit positioning. The brand 'Clinic Plus' was leveraged to launch the anti-dandruff variant which was named Clinic Special, in the year 1980. Its name was later changed to Clinic All Clear in the year 1996. The brand is also present as 'Clear' in fourteen other countries worldwide. To align itself with the international quality standards Clinic All Clear was re-launched in India in 2011 with the name Clear. All Clear has been position as an anti-dandruff shampoo. The brand 'Clear' continues with the same positioning. Clear is positioned not as a simple anti dandruff shampoo but a 'Zero Dandruff shampoo' that also enhances your style quotient and gives you the 'License to wear black'. The type of positioning is again benefit positioning. The ad copies make use of celebrity appeal by getting the brand endorsed by film Stars like, Bipasha Basu, John Abraham, Shilpa Shetty, Asin, and Shahid Kapoor.

Sunsilk is one of the oldest offering from HUL in India. It is available in several variants. Benefit positioning in used as a strategy to position the brand Sunsilk. Sunsilk is positioned as a brand that endows the user with a silky, soft hair. Sunsilk Thick & long is positioned as a product that makes the hair thick and long. Sunsilk black shine is positioned as a brand that endows the user with a gorgeous shiny hair and protects it from the U.V. rays of the sun. The ad copies for the brand appeal to the consumers through the use of expert opinion whereby Hollywood shine expert Jamal Hamadi is made to endorse the brand. An attempt is made to win the trust of the consumers with HUL claiming that the product is Co-created with Jamal Hamadi, a Hollywood shine expert. The brand also banks on celebrity appeal whereby Priyanka Chopra endorses the brand in several of the advertisement copies for the brand.

Panteen from P&G is positioned as a brand that makes the hair strong and smooth by nourishing it from within. The brand uses a benefit position strategy. Functional element of communication is used when the brand communication emphasis smooth hair, hair with no split ends and strong hair through the use of Panteen Pro-V. Physical element of positioning is used when the brand communication highlights the special formula enriched with pro-vitamin that provides nourishment to the hair and strengthens it from root to tip resulting in the benefit of strong and smooth hair. Thus a combination of physical element and functional element of communication is used to communicate the brand identity. To add a touch of celebrity appeal to its advertisement filmstars like Katrina Kaif, Shilpa Shetty, Sushmita Sen, Lara Dutta and Neha Dhupia have been roped in to endorse in the brand.

Another brand from P&G with a strong market presence it is anti dandruff shampoo Head & Shoulders. Head & Shoulders is positioned as an anti dandruff shampoo and claims to be better than other anti dandruff shampoos. The advertisement for this product also claims that it is recommended by 9 out of 10 dermatologists in India. A variant of this brand is Head & shoulders smooth and silky. It is positioned as being an anti dandruff shampoo that makes the hair smooth and silky. It differentiates itself from the other brands of anti dandruff shampoo on the basis of this additional value proposition. Its complete value proposition as well as its positioning is: "Head & Shoulders removes dandruff completely and moisturizes the hair keeping it smooth and silky". Thus it uses benefit positioning strategy. The voice over in the advertisement copy for the brand says "Dandruff free soft Bal, Subah se Rat tak". The brand is endorsed by Priety Zinta. Still another variant of Head & Shoulder is Head & Shoulder Anti Hair fall. This brand claims to remove dandruff by 100% and reduce hair fall by 95%. The additional value proposition offered by the brand is prevention of hair fall. Saif Ali Khan and Kareena Kapoor appear in the ad copy for this product for P&G. Head & Shoulders uses benefit positioning strategy.

L'oreal India has in its kitty several hair care products. Garnier Fructis is the shampoo product from the kitty of L'oreal for the mass market. The different variants of Garnier Fructis are Garnier Fructis Long & Strong, Garnier Fructis Fall fight and Garnier Fructis Shampoo + Oil 2 in 1. Garnier Fructis Long and Strong uses benefit positioning. It offers the benefit of long and strong hair. It promises to "Make Hair up to 5 times stronger and reduce breakage". 'Longer, Stronger, Better' is the value proposition of the brand. As a positioning strategy of Garnier fructis long and strong, in combination with the benefit positioning, a streak of attributes positioning is also used when it claims to be 'enriched with active fruit concentrate and vitamins'. On the other hand Garnier fructis fall fight, offers the value proposition of 'fighting hair fall'. It promises the benefit of "5 times less hair in you brush". The advertisement for the brand sales "New Garnier Fructis fall fight; No one fights hair fall better."

'Garnier shampoo + Oil 2 in 1' is a customized offering for the Indian market. Traditionally the Indian consumer prefers to oil his hair. Oiling the hair has also been a conventional practice after shampooing. In sync with this conventional Indian practice Garnier Shampoo + Oil 2 in 1 has been launched in the Indian market. The brand promises the dual benefit of shampoo and oil. It is differentiated from the other brands on the basic of its composition that consists of 'A blend of shampoo and oil for nourished healthy hair'. Thus the message elements used to communicate the brand identity are physical element (exhibiting the composition, a blend of shampoo and oil) and functional element (reflected in the promised benefit 'Cleanses like shampoo, cares like oil' that makes 'hair so much stronger and shinier').

A premium segment hair care product from L'oreal is L'oreal Total Repair 5. In India the brand is endorsed by Aishwarya Rai. L'oreal Total repair 5 is positioned as a single solution to 5 hair problems. The brand employs the strategy of benefit positioning. The marketing communication for the brand claims that 'its revolutionary ceramide cement repairs hair fall ,dry hair, rough hair, dull hair, and split ends' and ensures 'total repair from root to tip'. Thus the value proposition for the brand is "5 problems one solution" and by virtue of its ability to solve 5 problems, it claims to be superior to other shampoos. Dove from HUL is a premium category product. The dove range of shampoo is named 'Dove damage therapy' and is positioned not just as a shampoo but as a part of a therapy that repairs damaged hair and keeps it strong, healthy and beautiful. Its positioning is 'Expert care for damaged hair'. The dove damage therapy system offers different variants for different needs and hair problems. The different variants from the dove damage therapy range of shampoos are: 'Dove breakage therapy', 'Dove Dryness care shampoo', 'Dove intense repairs shampoo' and 'Dove hair fall rescue system'. Each of these variants has a specific application positioning. The overall positioning for the Dove range of shampoos is benefit positioning.

In line with the natural and Ayurvedic Legacy of Dabur, the different brands of shampoo from Dabur are also positioned using the 'Natural ingredient, Natural Product' platform. Using the same positioning platform, Dabur Vaktika root strengthening shampoo highlights the natural ingredients -almonds and coconut milk in the product. The ad copy to promote the brand categorically mentions the absence of any harmful chemical in the product. The value proposition of the brand is its root strengthening virtue derived from its natural ingredients- almonds and coconut milk. Thus the positioning is a combination of benefit positioning and attribute positioning. Similarly Dabur Vatika black shine uses a combination of attribute positioning and benefit positioning when it highlights the natural ingredients in the product (Black Olive and Amla, sans any harmful chemical) and the resultant ability to make hair naturally black and shiny. Physical element of message used in the marketing communication tool, advertisement to be more precise, conveys the brand identity by overtly highlighting and exhibiting the ingredients of the product.

Just like the other variants of Dabur Vatika shampoo, Dabur Vatika Henna conditioning shampoo also highlights the natural ingredients of the product (Green almonds and Henna conditioning) and the benefit of silky hair derived from the use of the product. The value proposition of the brands is naturally silky hair derived from a natural product. The positioning strategy in this case is also a combination of attribute positioning and benefit positioning.

Positioning of Hair Oil Brands

While moving from the shampoo market to the Indian hair oil market a marked difference could be observed in the nature and type of companies fighting it out in the market and in the brands competing in the market. The Indian hair oil market is characterized by the conspicuous absence of the foreign multinational companies. Unlike that in the other categories of FMCG, the Indian hair oil market is entirely populated by the brands from the domestic companies and homegrown multinationals. Hair oil being a typical hair care product to be used only in the Indian sub continent is not in line with the international portfolio of product of many a multinational. Investing time, effort and money to enter and establish in this segment does not ensure the possibility of international growth and the scope of sustainable diversification and expansion in this sector for such companies. Thus it does not make strong business sense for many of these companies. The major players in this market are Marico, Bajaj Corps, Dabur, Dey's Medical and G.D. Pharmaceuticals (manufacturers of Boroline and Eleen) and Emami. According to AC Nielsen, the hair oil market in India is worth Rs. 4943 Crore and is growing at 13 percent. Of this the coconut oil contributes 52 percent of the market share, Amla oil 14 percent, light or fragrant hair oil 14 percent and cooling hair oil 12 percent (Kar, 2010 d).

Parachute from Marico is the largest selling brand of hair oil. Branded coconut oil in the country is best represented by the brand 'Parachute' with its trademark blue coloured container depicted on which is a coconut tree. Today the brand is positioned as an essential supplement for shampoo for maintaining shiny and gorgeous hair and to prevent dryness. The positioning strategy is that of benefit positioning. Functional element of positioning is used to convey the brand identity.

The second largest selling brand of hair oil in the country is 'Dabur Amla' hair oil. It positions itself against the other Amla oils in the market and claims to be the original Amla oil: 'Asli Amla Dabur Amla' ('Original Amla is Dabur Amla'). Competitor positioning strategy is used by Dabur to position its brand 'Dabur Amla' hair oil. Another widely promoted brand of hair oil from Dabur is 'Dabur Vatika' hair oil. In its positioning, Dabur Vatika highlights the natural ingredients present in the oil (Pure coconut oil, henna, soya, amla and lemon) and the resultant benefit of stopping hair fall, making hair stronger and giving better dandruff control. Thus it is a combination of attribute positioning and benefit positioning. The brand is endorsed by Priety Zinta. The third largest selling brand of hair oil in the market is Bajaj Almond Drops. It is the largest selling brand of the light/fragrant hair oil market with a market share of 51 percent. It is positioned as a light styling oil with the nourishment of Almonds. It compares itself to coconut hair oil and claims to have 300 percent more Vitamin E compared to coconut oil. Thus the positioning strategy is a combination of benefit positioning (nourishment of Almonds and 300 percent more Vit. E) and application/use positioning (styling oil). The voice over in the television commercial for the brand says "Bajaj Almond Drops hair oil- Isme nariyal tel ke muqable jyada vitamin E hai. Yeh balon ko de sampoorn poshan aur kuch bhi karne ka freedom" ("Bajaj Almond Drops Hair oil: it contains more Vitamin E compared to coconut oil. This gives complete nourishment to hair and the freedom to do anything with it").

Hair and Care from Marico is also an important player in the light hair oil category. It tries to occupy the benefit position of "Up to 50 percent less hair fall and style with nourishment". The voice over in the ad copy for the brand says "Hair & Care ke herbal proteins balon ka jharna kare 50 percent tak kam aur de poshan bhara style" ("The herbal protein of Hair & Care reduces hairfall upto 50 percent and give you style enriched with nutrition").

Keo Karpin from Dey's Medical is also a light hair oil with a significant share of the market. It is positioned as a light hair oil with olive oil and Vitamin E. The brand uses attribute positioning. A relatively new player in the light hair oil category is Eleen from Boroline. The brand is positioned as a light hair oil enriched with Amla and Vit. E that gives style and health, stops dandruff and prevents hair fall. The positioning strategy is benefit positioning. The functional element of the product is used to convey the value proposition. The voice over in the ad copy for the brand claims "Amla aur Vitamin E ke double shakti se bhara Eleen. Baal ka jharna kam kare, dandruff roke aur itna halka ki baal rahe style se bhare, sehat se damke". (which means "Eleen filled with the double power of Amla and Vitamin E. Reduces hair fall, stops dandruff and so light that you hair remains enriched with style and shines with health").

Positioning of Hair Colour Brands

A sub category in the hair care segment that is relatively new and is widely gaining acceptance in the Indian market is the hair colour category. Some important brands in this category are L'oreal excellence crème, Garnier colour naturals from L'oreal and Godrej hair colour. Garnier Colour Naturals is positioned as a hair colour with natural ingredients that is easy to apply and gives a long lasting natural colour. The promised benefit/value proposition is natural ingredients (Olive oil) and natural looking colour. The type of positioning is benefit positioning. The advertisement for the brand mentions "Garnier Colour Naturals enriched with natural olive oil; its nourishing cream formula is easy to apply and doesn't drip; Get natural looking hair colour that lasts long".

L'oreal Excellence Crème is a brand of hair colour targeted at the premium segment. It is positioned as a hair colour that doesn't get damaged by sun and makes the hair stronger. The brand positioning is benefit positioning and the value proposition is "Locks out sun damage, locks in colour". The advertisement copy for the brand mentions "New Excellence Crème from L'oreal; it's protection formula locks in colour and protects hair from sun damage". In India the brand is endorsed by the former Miss World and the Indian actress Aiswarya Rai.

Godrej Expert Powder Hair Colour is targeted at the middle class segment. It is positioned as a hair colour that gives a uniform colour and natural looks. The value proposition of Godrej Expert Powder Hair Colour is: colour so natural that it is difficult to make out. The brand positioning is benefit positioning. On the contrary Wella Kolestint hair colour from Wella is positioned as a long lasting hair colour that gets noticed and makes the user get noticed. The benefit promised by the brand is its long lasting effect and the distinctiveness that gets noticed. The type of positioning is benefit positioning. However at the subliminal level the brand compares itself with those brands of hair colours that claim to give a natural look.

Positioning of Coffee Brands

The total coffee market in India is worth Rs. 2000/- Crore (Source: Carvalho, Brian, "New CEO, New HUL", Business Today, April 6, 2008) out of which the instant coffee market is estimated to be Rs. 1300 Crore. Nescafe's share in the instant coffee market is 62 percent followed by that of HUL's Bru at 33 percent. Both the brands together account for 95 percent of the branded coffee sold in the country (Source: Bhattacharjee, Arindam (2010), "A brew for the young", The Strategist, October 4).

The largest selling brand of coffee, Nescafe Classic was initially positioned as an ideal beverage to start your morning and your day. The jingle used in the old advertisement copy for the brand "The taste that gets you started" reinforced this positioning. Later on it was positioned as an integral part of great moments and a good life. The voice over in the advertisement copy said "Come alive to great moments. Nescafe Classic. Coffee at its best". Hedonistic message element was used to effectively communicate this position.

The brand positioning for the brand has recently been tweaked to make the brand more vibrant, energetic and contemporary. The objective is to appeal to the young segment that forms almost half of the country's population. Deepika Padukone, a vibrant, successful and young actress from the Indian cinema has been roped in by the marketing communication team of Nescafe to reflect and communicate the value (Vibrant, energetic, successful) of the brand. The new 'Switch on the best in you' campaign marks a shift from the earlier benefit positioning ('An ideal way to start your day') to a user positioning ('Switch on the best in you').

The other competitor in the market is Bru Instant from HUL. Bru Instant was earlier positioned as being closest to filter coffee. However, today it is positioned as an essential ingredient of good times or as a companion of good times. The jingle in the advertisement copy for the brand 'Bru se hoti hain khushiyan shuru' -which means 'Happiness starts with Bru'- communicates the positioning.

Positioning of Tea Brands

Tea is the most widely consumed beverage in India. The size of the tea market is Rs. 4396 Crore. HUL and Tata Tea (Now Tata Global Beverages) are the major players in the Indian Tea market.

HUL offers several brands targeted at different segments of the market. While it has Taj Mahal Tea in the premium segment, Tazaa in the mid market segment and Red Label in the popular segment, it came up with a new brand Brooke Bond Sehatmand in the economy segment. Similarly Tata Global Beverages offers different brands for the different segments in the Indian market. It has Tata Tea Gold for the premium segment, Tata Tea Premium for the mid market segment and Tata Tea Agni for the economy segment.

Brooke Bond Taj Mahal from HUL is positioned as a premium brand of tea with superior taste and good aroma. The advertisement for the brand uses celebrity. The brand is endorsed by celebrities such as Ustad Zakir Hussain and Saif Ali Khan. HUL offers the brand 'Brooke Bond Tazaa' to target the mid market segment. The brand is positioned as a tea that instills freshness and is stimulating. It uses benefit positioning. The company targets the popular segment with its brand Red Label. The brand used attribute positioning earlier and was positioned as a tea with dark colour, strong flavor and good aroma. The voice over in the ad copy says "Red Label ke liye log kuch bhi karenge kyunki is ke swad mein hai gehri lali, sahi karakpan aur lubhavni mehak" which means that people will do anything to get a cup of Red Label Tea as it had a deep red colour, strong flavor and captivating aroma. Now the positioning of Brooke Bond Red Label has been tweaked to offer a health proposition. The benefit positioning and the sought brand identity is "Improved blood circulation, improved health". In line with its sought identity the punch line in the ad copy for the brand is "Brooke Bond Red Label-Swasth rahein, mast rahein". Enumerating the benefits of the tea the voice over in the television commercial mentions, "Red Label chai healthy hai. Iski khas pattiyon mein hai kudrati flavanoids jo dete hain ise gehri lali; aur healthy flavonoids bhari chai blood circulation improve karne mein madad karti hain jo apke parivar ke liye accha hai" (Red Label tea is healthy. Its special leaves have natural flavonoids that give it a deep red colour; and flavonoids enriched tea improves blood circulation which is good for your family".

Another variant of Brooke Bond Red Label is Brooke Bond Red Label Natural Care. This brand also offers the health benefit and highlights the ayurvedic ingredients of the tea that endows the user with health. Thus the positioning is a combination of attribute and benefit positioning. The television commercial for the brand mentions "Red Label Natural Care chai me hai tulsi aur ashwagandha jaise paanch tatwa jo apko rakhe ander se strong". ("Red Label Natural Care Tea has five ingredients like tulsi and ashwagandha that keep you strong from within"). Functional element is used to convey and communicate the brand identity.

A relatively new offering from HUL is its brand Brooke Bond Sehatmand targeted at the economy segment of the market. The target market for the brand is rural and semi-urban market. The brand competes with Tata Tea Agni which also targets the economy segment. Brooke Bond Sehatmand differentiates itself from its rival by positioning itself as a health supplement (Vit. B supplement to be specific). The company claims that with its breakthrough technology, vitamin is fused into each granule of tea. It is claimed that drinking three cups of the tea ensures 50 percent reference daily intake of important B vitamins. (Iyer, 2010 a). The television commercial for the brand claims "Sirf chai nahi, vitamin yukt nai Brooke Bond Sehatmand.......Iske har pyale me hai vitamin jo aapke sehat ki raksha karne me madad kare". The positioning strategy is benefit positioning.

In its initial days Tata Tea was positioned just as a brand that instills freshness. However with its 'Jago Re' campaign, Tata Tea has embarked on the cause marketing band wagon. Tata Tea now identifies with a social cause through its 'Jago Re' campaign. The social causes with which the brand associates itself are: the awareness of the significance of casting your vote and corruption. It has become a good example of social cause branding.

Tata Tea Premium is also promoted using the same positioning platform. The brand associates itself with the social cause of fighting corruption. The brand positions itself on the basis of its benefit of 'offering a combination of strong taste and aroma (through a blend of small and big leaves)'. The type of branding is cause branding and the positioning is benefit positioning. Tata Tea Premium is targeted at the mid price segment of the market.

Tata Tea Gold is targeted at the premium segment of the market. It is positioned as a good quality tea with rich aroma that comes from the right blend of granules and leaves. Benefit positioning is the type of positioning used for the brand. Hedonistic element is used to communicate the positioning.

Competing for a share of market in the economy segment is Tata Tea Agni. This brand from Tata Global Beverages is targeted at the price sensitive customers. The rural market and the semi urban market majorly constitute the targeted economy segment. The price positioning becomes evident from the slogan in the ad copy for the brand that says "Josh se bhari, dam me khari; Ab sirf tees rupaiye" ("Full of energy, good in price; Now in thirty rupees only"). The ad copy also highlights the price of the product: 250 gm for Rs. 30/-

Unlike other brands of tea, Wagh Bakri uses emotional positioning as a strategy to effectively position and to establish the brand. Functional element of positioning is used to convey the positioning for the brand whereby emotions are depicted in the ad copies by showing the relationships between friends or by illustrating diverse cultures making a united India (Unity in Diversity) or by depicting family relations. In line with its positioning, the punch line in the ad copy mentions "Wagh Bakri Chai; Hamesha rishte banaye" which means "Wagh Bakri Tea; Always makes relations".

Brand Positioning of Soft Drinks

The beverages market in India is worth Rs. 11,500 Crores out of which the aerated drinks constitute Rs. 5,000 Crores (Source: Business Standard, October 17, 2011). Coca Cola and Pepsico are the two major players in this market who battle it out for a greater share of the market. Both these companies have entered into the market after the market liberalized. Before liberalization the major player in the soft drink market was Parle Agro with its brands Thumps Up, Limca and Gold Spot. However, after liberalization, the brands Thumps Up and Limca were acquired by Coca Cola. Thumps Up continues to be the largest selling brand from the stable of Coca Cola. With the young population aggressively taking to products and soft drinks and with the fast changing lifestyle, the soft drink market has grown enormously from the pre liberalization period. The present rate of growth for this market is 10 to 12 percent per annum in case of carbonated drinks, 35-40 percent in case of fruit based beverages and around 25 percent in case of energy drinks.

The brand Pepsi is positioned worldwide as a drink for the young. In India too, it is positioned as the drink for the fun loving, vivacious, young generation with a 'can do' attitude. Thus young film stars with a strong fan following amongst the youth have always been roped in for the advertisement of the brand. Young film stars who have endorsed the brand in the past were Saif Ali Khan, Kareena Kapoor, Priety Zinta, Shah Rukh Khan, Priyanka Chopra and Fardeen Khan. The brand is presently endorsed by Ranbir Kapoor and Deepika Padukone, both young and vivacious youth icons of the day. Hedonistic element is used in the ad copies to effectively communicate the brand identity. The type of positioning is user positioning (The brand identifies with young vivacious people full of life, indulging in innocent mischief and loaded with the 'can do' attitude. The slogans 'Yeh hai youngistan meri jaan' and 'Youngistan ka wow' reinforce the brand identity of Pepsi as a drink for the young people.

Coca Cola entered into the Indian market after Pepsi had already entered and established itself up to some extent in this market. Coca Cola dabbled with its brand positioning in India for quite sometime before it could find a meaningful and relevant position 'Thanda matlab Coca Cola'. Initially the brand tried to position itself as a preferred brand for the youth. Young film stars of that period Aamir Khan, Hritik Roshan and Aishwarya Rai were used as brand ambassadors for Coca Cola. To identify with the carefree and fun loving attitude of the youth, the brand used the slogan 'Jo chahe ho jaye, Coca Cola enjoy'. In order to facilitate the brand recall, Coca Cola played upon its brand association with the colour red, which stands for vibrancy and energy. An ad copy at that point of time highlighted the red colour in various places in the life of various people across various walks of life in India. This advertisement was meant to establish the brand association with the colour red. The association was also shown in a subtle way in the older ad copies as well as the other ad copies for the brand during that period, where the clothes worn by the brand ambassadors Aamir Khan and Aishwarya Rai were Red. The ambience in the setting used for the ad copies also used the red colour liberally. Later on the brand also experimented with its positioning and made an attempt to shift from its positioning 'A drink for the youth' to a new positioning 'A drink for the family'. The ad copy designed to communicate this position, showed the brand ambassador Aishwarya Rai creating a restaurant like ambience in home in Coca Cola. The voice over in the ad copy said 'Kuch pal aise jinhe khass banaye sirf Coca Cola' which means 'Few moments which are made special only by Coca Cola'.

However the brand was able to make a real impact on the psyche of the consumers and was able to occupy a distinctive space in their perceptual space with its campaign 'Thanda matlab Coca Cola'. This was actually the first campaign of Coca Cola that made people sit up and take notice. The brand ambassador for Coca Cola, Aamir Khan was chosen for this ad campaign. Humour appeal was used liberally in the ad copies to appeal to the viewers. This was category positioning in which Coca Cola was positioned as the only synonym of 'Thanda', a generic name used for soft drink in major parts of India. The ad campaign came up with a series of ad copies each with Aamir Khan in it and each packed with humour appeal, to communicate the brand identity of 'Thanda Matlab Coca Cola'. While one of the ad copies showed Aamir Khan as a 'Pahari guide' refusing to accept any other soft drink as 'thanda', another showed Amir Khan asking for 'thanda' from a waiter in a restaurant and telling him 'Thanda matlab Coca Cola'. In another ad copy in that series Amir Khan as a Punjabi farmer offers Coca Cola to three damsels in distress who get stranded because of a puncture in their car tyre and request for 'thanda' to quench their thirst. Another ad copy shows Amir Khan as Manno Bhabhi serving 'thanda' (Coca Cola) to a prospective NRI bridegroom while negotiating an arranged marriage. In another humorous ad copy designed during the pesticide controversy (the controversy in which it was alleged that the water used for manufacturing cold drinks by beverage manufacturers in India was contaminated with pesticides), Amir Khan playing a Bengali gentleman visits a restaurant with his family, consumes Coca Cola to check the authenticity in the allegation, and declares it to be free from any pesticide.

Today Coca Cola is again making an attempt to reinforce its association with the youth. It is being positioned as a companion of good times and as a brand that ushers happiness. The slogans used in the new ad campaign are 'Coke khule to baat chale' and 'Coke opens happiness'. The new brand ambassador selected by the company to appeal to the young consumer is a youth icon of the day, Imran Khan, a young bollywood actor.

The bulk of the sale for Coca Cola India comes from the brand 'Thumps Up'. Thumps Up is positioned as a strong drink for the adventure loving youth. The slogan for the brand 'Thumps UP- Taste the Thunder' conveys the brand identity of Thumps UP- a strong, adventurous and daring brand. The brand ambassador Salman Khan reinforces this brand identity.

Another brand from Coca Cola India is Limca, a lemon flavoured aerated drink. Limca, which earlier used the slogan 'Lime N lemony Limca' is positioned as a refreshing drink that brings good times. The advertisement copies for the brand show a jubiliant young couple indulging in banter and enjoying their time together with Limca. The theme of these advertisement copies exuberate joy. Thus Hedonistic element is used to convey the identity of 'freshness through the refreshing drink'. The punch line in the ad copy mentions "Limca Dubo tazgi mein' ("Limca; Get immersed in freshness') and the slogan is 'Fresh ho jao' which means 'Get refreshed'.

In the 'non aerated soft drink' category, both Pepsico and Coca Cola have their brands of mango drinks. Slice and Mazaa are the brands of mango drinks from Pepsico and Coca Cola respectively. The Slice Aamsutra ad campaign with the hindi film actress Katrina Kaif positions the brand as 'Slice Aamsutra; Pure mango pleasure'. The type of brand positioning is a combination of benefit positioning and attribute positioning (the taste of mango). Hedonistic and experiential element is used to communicate the positioning for the brand. On the other hand the mango drink 'Mazaa' is positioned as a substitute of Mango. Its similarity to mango is exhibited using some humorous story lines in its advertisements designed for the television.

Positioning of Brands of Packaged Fruit Juice

The size of the total fruit juice market in India is Rs. 7000 Crore. Out of this total market, the branded fruit juice market constitutes Rs. 2,500 Crore. (Source: Kar, Sayantani, "Heinz Again", The Strategist, August 9, 2010).

Important players in this market are Dabur (with its range of Dabur Real Active Juice), Coca Cola (with its Minute Maid brand) and Pepsico (with Tropicana 100% fruit juice).

The juice brand Dabur Real Active from the stable of Dabur is positioned on health proposition. The film star Bipasha Basu, who carries an image of a brand conscious celebrity, has been roped in by Dabur to endorse the Dabur Real Active brand. The brand positioning strategy is a blend of attribute positioning ("made up of fresh fruits and vegetables Real Active is a healthy snack") and benefit positioning ("No added sugar. 50% lesser calories"). The advertisement copy for the brand loudly declares "Fresh fruits aur vegetables se bane. Real Active is a healthy snack" (which means "Made up of fresh fruits and vegetables, Dabur Active is a healthy snack") and further adds that the product contains "No added sugar. 50% less calories". Functional element is used as the message content element to communicate the brand identity which is: Real and healthy fruit and vegetable juice with no added sugar. Tropicana 100% from Pepsico also has a similar positioning. It is positioned as a complete and real fruit juice (with no added sugar, no preservative and no added colours) for a nutritious and wholesome breakfast. The advertisement copy for the brand claims that Tropicana 100% offers 100% juice nutrition and fruit nutrition with no added sugar, no preservative and no colours in it.

Minute Maid Pulpy orange from Coca Cola is differentiated from the other fruit juice on the basis of the ingredients (the presence of fruit pulp) in the orange juice. The brand goes for attribute positioning when the marketing communication for the brand emphasizes "New Minute Maid Pulpy Orange- Refreshingly orange, surprisingly pulpy". Also the voice over in the television commercial for the brand declares "It's filled with the goodness of real orange pulp in every gulp".

The other brands of fruit juice worth mentioning here are the brands of lemon juice Minute Maid Nimbu fresh, Nimbooz and LMN from Coca Cola, Pepsico and Parle respectively. Though these brands are not distinctively differentiated from each other, Minute Maid Nimbu fresh can be credited with the use of cultural element (banks on the fact that Nimbu Pani or Shikanji which is a homemade lemon drink is traditionally served in Indian households as a refreshing drink particularly during summers), emotional element (makes a nostalgic appeal and makes the viewer feel nostalgic by reminding him of his childhood days when his mother served him the home made lemon drink) and physical element (exhibits the use of fresh and real lemon that is used to manufacture the product). Thus the type of positioning it uses is a combination of attribute positioning, cultural positioning and emotional positioning.

Brand Positioning of Milk Based Beverages & Health Beverages

Some other brands of beverages in the Indian food and beverage market that merit attention here are the milk based beverages from Amul, Bournvita from Cadbury, Complan from Heinz and Horlicks from GSK. Amul uses the country of origin appeal in its brand positioning strategy. 'The taste of India' campaign of Amul besides highlighting the process of milk collection from the Indian villages also highlights the milk based products typical to Indian tastes and customs and the way the products are consumed in India. Thus the brand uses Local Consumer Culture Positioning. The nature of brand positioning can be called as ethnocentric positioning. Cultural and hedonistic elements are used to communicate the brand identity.

Bournvita from Cadbury has a brand identity and brand perception strongly associated with health and nutrition. Cadbury Bournvita is thus positioned as a health drink for children. Complain from Heinz is targeted at growing children. It is positioned as a necessary health drink for growing children. The brand promises a rapid increase in height. Benefit positioning is used as a positioning strategy by the brand. Functional element in the message content communicates the brand benefit/proposition.

While Complan offers the value proposition of taller height, Horlicks from GSK offers the value proposition of 'Taller, Sharper, Stronger'. Here also the functional element of message content is used to communicate the benefit positioning. Junior Horlicks is a variant of Horlicks targeted at younger children. It claims to be enriched with DHA and essential nutrients that provide complete nutrition for children. Benefit positioning is used as a positioning strategy in this case as well.

Brand Positioning of Noodles

Branded food is a big category in the FMCG sector out of which the instant noodles market has a size of Rs. 1,137 Crore. According to AC Nielsen, the instant noodles market in India is growing at 20 percent per annum. (Source: Kar, Sayantani, "Foodles in the noodle bowl", The Strategist, August 2, 2010). The largest selling brand of Noodles in India is Maggi from Nestle. Other players in the noodles market are Top Ramen from Nissin, Foodles from Glaxo Smithklime in association with Nissin, Sunfeast Yippies from ITC and Knorr Soupy noodles from HUL.

Instant noodle was introduced in India in the year 1984 by Nestle under the brand name Maggi. Since then Maggi has continued to dominate the instant noodles market in India. Even today the brand dominates the market with Maggi Masala flavoured maida noodles having a market share of 91 percent. Other Maggi Noodles products and flavours and all other brands constitute the remaining 9 percent.

Magi 2 minutes noodles was one of the first brands to be systematically positioned in the ready to eat category. The value proposition for the brand is "Cooked and ready to be served in two minutes". However, later on the benefit positioning "Fast to cook; Good to eat" was replaced by the health proposition. Now Nestle instead of positioning the brand Maggi on the 'instant food' characteristics and the time and ease of cooking, positions it as a healthy and tasty food. In line with the new positioning, the product was enriched with vegetables. This new brand identity is reflected in the new slogan for the brand "Taste bhi, health bhi".

To continue with this value proposition further, Nestle launched a new variant Maggi Atta Noodles made up of Atta (wheat flour) instead of maida (processed flour). Aata is considered to be far more healthy and nutritious than maida. The target market for this new product was the health conscious consumer who didn't consider noodles to be a healthy food. This was an attempt by Nestle to reinforce the health proposition of the brand 'Maggi' and to fortify the position of 'Maggi noodles' in the health food space. The type of positioning was benefit positioning. The company then made an attempt to further strengthen its claim on the health proposition by launching another variant Maggi Vegetable Aata Noodles. The product positioning and promotion of this product is in conformance with the new brand positioning of Maggi Noodles ie, "Taste bhi, health bhi". The brand/product claims to deliver the benefits of real vegetables and fibre that makes the product a taste enriched healthy food.

Recently Maggi, on completing twenty five years in the Indian market, was again repositioned. The new brand positioning endeavour was kick started by Nestle Maggi by involving real consumers in the new campaign. The consumers would narrate their stories of first experience or some memorable experience of the product/brand. This story would get published/printed on the pack of Maggi or would be used in the advertising campaign 'Me and my Maggi'. This was envisaged to result in better brand involvement with the consumer. The target audience would be able to associate with the brand because of some similar incidents in their life. The ad campaign would thus have an emotional appeal (a nostalgic appeal) that would strengthen the consumer's bond with the brand. Moreover the advertising campaign would generate an excitement amongst the consumer (who had some past memories associated with the product) as there would be a possibility of their story being aired on the electronic media and published in the print media through the ad copies of Maggi. This positioning strategy is user positioning strategy and the message element used is the emotional element.

Another brand that has been there in the market for quite some time is Top Ramen from Nissin. The company, instead of calling the product as noodles named it 'Top Ramen Smoodles'. The brand was positioned as smooth noodles. It was positioned on the basis of the product attribute (the smooth nature of the noodles). This was attribute positioning. However, with this positioning the brand was unable to make a significant dent on the market share of Maggi. Recently it has been repositioned on health proposition. To communicate and fortify this positioning, Saina Nainwal, the badminton player has been roped in as the brand ambassador for Top Ramen.

Glaxo Smithkline Consumer healthcare has entered the instant noodles market with its brand Horlicks Foodles. Rs. 1500 Crore malted drink Horlicks from GSK is the market leader and is strongly associated with the health proposition. GSK has extended this brand into noodles to leverage the established value proposition of the brand. Foodles from Horlicks is positioned on the health grounds. To leverage the established brand equity of Horlicks, the ad copy clearly mentions "Foodles- the nourishing noodles from Horlicks". A study conducted by GSK showed that instant noodles were not usually considered healthy. "Mothers felt guilty serving instant noodles to children because maida is not as healthy as atta or wholegrain wheat. As a result mothers fortified the noodles with vegetables and eggs." (Kar, 2010 b). GSK went on to exploit this gap in the market. It struck a partnership with Nissin, the makers of Top Ramen, the original challenger to Maggi, and was able to come out with a healthier noodle made from four grains. A tastemaker enriched with minerals was also a result of the product research carried out by GSK in association with Nissin. Thus Foodles, a noodles that stands for nutrition was born. Foodles is positioned as "the more nourishing noodles" that is made up of four cereals/grains and has good food value. The marketing communication for the brand calls it "Four grain noodles with wheat, rice, ragi and corn" and claims "isme hai health maker, power vitamins ke sath" ("it has health maker with power vitamins"). The tag line for the brand says "Foodles- The more nourishing noodles from Horlicks". The brand lays claim on the health benefit delivered by it and supports the claim by highlighting its nutritious ingredients and healthy contents. Thus the brand positioning strategy uses benefit positioning supported by attribute positioning.

ITC also entered into the noodles market in the year 2011 with its brand Sunfeast Yippie Noodles. Unlike the other noodles in the market Sunfeast Yippie noodles are rolled into a round shape, in its uncooked form that opens up to give longer noodles when cooked. The product formulation has been developed in a way that unlike other noodles, it doesn't stick when it becomes cold sometime after it has been cooked. These are the very attributes on the basis of which ITC differentiates Sunfeast Yippie from the other brands of noodles. Thus the type of positioning being used by the company is attribute positioning. The physical elements of the product are highlighted in the marketing communication to differentiate the product and to position it. Thus the message element being used to communicate the brand identity is the physical element.

Similarly HUL also positions its brand of noodles, 'Knorr Soupy Noodles' on the basis of the product attribute (the soupy nature of the noodles). The type of positioning being used here is attribute positioning. The brand name 'Knorr Soupy Noodles' which is in conformance with the positioning of the brand effectively communicates the brand identity. The presence of the bollywood actress Kajol, who is the brand ambassador of Knorr, in the advertisement copies for the brand, adds glamour and celebrity appeal to the advertisement which in turn facilitates the brand recall.

Positioning of Packaged Food Brands

The packaged food market in India is cluttered with a number of brands. Some of the important brands from the stable of multinational companies are: Knorr Soups, Kellogg's Cornflakes, Kellogg's Chocos, Quaker Oats, Lays Kurkure and some brands of edible oils like Saffola and Emami Healthy & Tasty.

The brand Knorr from HUL is known for its packaged food in the Indian market. Knorr Soup is positioned as a healthy snack "with 100% real vegetables". The type of positioning that highlights the vegetable content of the soup is attribute positioning. The Knorr range of soups also includes Knorr Indian Soups. This range of product consists of several varieties and flavours of soups that have been adapted to suit the Indian taste buds. These are Indianised soups that appeal to the specific taste of the Indian consumer. 'Knorr Indian soups' is thus positioned as spicy Indian soup. The type of positioning is Local Consumer Culture Positioning.

A relatively new segment in the food market to be exploited by the multinational companies is the breakfast cereal market. Kellogg's is a well known player in this market with its brands like Kellogg's Chocos, Kellogg's Cornflakes and Kellogg's K. Kellogg's Chocos is a product targeted at the children. The advertisements for the brand highlight the health benefits derived from the fibres, vitamins and minerals present in the wholegrain that forms the main constituents of the brand. The value proposition promised by the brand is 'health and nutrition' for the school going children. The television commercial for the brand declares "Kellogg's chocos ab whole grain ke sath" ("Kellogg's chocos now with whole grain") and claims "Yeh whole grain hai jo de fibres, vitamins, minerals" ("It is the wholegrain that gives fibres, vitamins and minerals"). Kellogg's K on the other hand is a brand of cornflakes targeted at the health conscious and weight conscious consumer, specifically the figure conscious young woman. Thus it is a product that promises a specific benefit and is meant to be used by the figure conscious woman for a specific purpose, the purpose of reducing weight. Thus the type of positioning is use positioning/application positioning. Use positioning becomes amply evident as the specific way of using the product is also communicated to the consumer through the ad copies that have been designed for this purpose. Through these ads, the consumer is urged to 'take the Kellogg's K challenge of 2 bowls 2 meals 2 weeks (ie, 2 bowls of Kellogg's K in 2 meals for 2 weeks) and loose upto 2 ½ Kilos of weight'. The message element that communicates the brand identity is functional element.

The breakfast cereal brand, Quaker Oats is an internationally present brand and is now present in the Indian market as well. Quaker Oats is positioned as a cardio protective food product. It uses a benefit positioning whereby the benefit promised by the brand is a healthy heart and a reduction in cholesterol. To fortify its positioning the company has launched the Quake mission of a healthy heart campaign. To promote the cause of healthy heart, the company has also launched a website by the name www.goodmorningheart.com. This type of branding and brand development effort is an example of cause branding. The brand Quaker Oats has associated itself with the cause of promoting and maintaining a healthy heart and that of reducing the instances of heart ailments. Evidently the brand positions itself on the proposition of health (healthy heart) and uses benefit positioning. Thus the brand Quaker Oats indulges in cause branding and uses benefit positioning.

The branded edible oil market in India is worth Rs. 10,000 Crore. The key players in this market are Marico that sells the brand Saffola, Emami with its brand Healthy & Tasty, the brand Fortune from Adani Group, Sundrop from Agrotech Foods and Dhara from Dhara Vegetable Oil and Foods Company Ltd.

While Saffola and Sundrop battle it out on health grounds, Emami positions itself as both healthy and tasty oil. Dhara on the other hand talks about the quality and purity of its products. Foreign multinational companies do not play a significant role in the edible oil market of India. One of the strongest positioning in the edible oil market is that of Saffola. Marico has positioned Saffola as an edible oil that reduces bad cholesterol and keeps the heart healthy. Through its advertisements the company appeals to the consumers to start using Saffola as it reduces cholesterol and keeps the heart young. The type of positioning is benefit positioning (reduces cholesterol and keeps the heart young). In order to strengthen its association with the cause of keeping the heart healthy, the company set up the Saffola Healthy Heart Foundation in the year 1991. The foundation is actively involved in conducting cardiac camps and free cholesterol checkups. These cardiac camps build awareness about the risks that the modern lifestyle poses to the heart and help people lower those risks. For the family of those recuperating from cardiac ailments, Saffola organizes 'Healthy Hearts' seminars to tell them how to take care of the patients (Kar, 2010 a). Thus Saffola has identified the cause of 'Healthy Heart' and tries to associate itself with it strongly. Saffola is into cause marketing and cause branding.

The company further leverages the brand equity of Saffola by extending it into other functional foods like salt, rice and flour additives. While Saffola oil talks of checking bad cholesterol so as to prevent heart ailments, its salt, rice and flour additives claim to keep under control diseases and problems that increase the probability of the occurrence of heart diseases and diseases such as hypertension, diabetes and lethargy.

Like Marico, Agro Tech Foods Ltd. (an affiliate of Con Agra Foods) also use the health proposition to promote its brand of edible oil Sundrop. Sundrop is positioned as a healthy oil for the health conscious people. The jingle in the television commercial for the brand says "Sundrop Super Refined Sunflower Oil- The healthy oil for healthy people". A variant of the Sundrop refined is Sundrop Super Lite Advanced. It is positioned as a healthy and light oil enriched with vitamins for the health conscious people. Here also benefit positioning is used whereby the brand promises to deliver health benefits. The television commercial for the brand mentions "Sundrop Super Lite Advance ki low absorb technology khane ko banaye light; super light aur less oily" which means "The low absorb technology of Sundrop Super Lite Advance makes the food light, super light and less oily". It further mentions "Low absorb aur Vitamin A, D, E ke sath Sundrop Super Lite Advanced" ("Sundrop Super Lite Advanced with low absorb and with Vitamin A, D and E").

Competing directly with Saffola in the same space "Oil for healthy heart" is a variant of Sundrop called Sundrop Heart. It also offers the same value proposition as Saffola ie, "lowers cholesterol and keeps heart healthy". To support its claim, the marketing communication for the brand talks about the presence of Oryzanol in it which according to research, as mentioned by the company, helps in lowering cholesterol. The type of brand positioning again is benefit positioning.

Emami is a new entrant in the food market. Its brand of edible oil Emami Healthy &Tasty is its first foray into food products. The brand is widely promoted and is positioned on the health and taste proposition. The company claims to refine the oil through seven stages and make it cholesterol free and good for health. Emami Healthy & Tasty is available in six variants-Soyabean, Sunflower, Mustard, Palmolein, Soyabean blend and Palmolein blend. These variants meet the specific needs of the consumers in different parts of the country and deliver them the taste desired by them.

Brand Positioning of Chocolates & Candies

Today, the chocolate market in India stands at Rs. 2000 Crores and unlike the perception the Indian consumer had a couple of decades ago, chocolate is considered to be a product not only meant for kids but a product equally relevant for all ages, a product that marks the celebration of joy, a product that can be gifted. Though there are a number of significant players in this market including companies like Nestle, Perfetti, Parle, Amul, Campco, Godrej & Boyce (Nutrine brand) and off course Cadbury, the credit of bringing this vibrancy and dynamism into the Indian chocolate market goes to Cadbury. Cadbury has single handedly transformed the consumer's perception of chocolate from a product meant 'just for kids' to a product meant for 'the kids in all of us'. Consequently, Cadbury has more than 70 percent of the market share in India and its largest selling and most promoted brand Cadbury Dairy Milk has a market share of 34.3 percent (Source: Iyer, Byravee, "Payday Celebrations", The Strategist, June 30, 2009).

In the story of Cadbury lie hidden the story of evolution of chocolate and that of chocolate consumption in India. Cadbury India Ltd. has been majorly responsible for changing the concept of chocolate in the Indian market and the image of chocolate in the Indian consumer's mind from an alien product in the 40s to a luxury indulgence in the 70s and 80s. The drive to make chocolate an article of regular consumption and a part of the regular snacks of an average Indian was also undertaken by Cadbury in the 1990s that further evolved the Indian chocolate market and transformed the concept of chocolate in the Indian market. It was able to dramatically change the image of chocolate as a 'luxury indulgence' product to a product meant for the masses to be consumed in every occasion that marks the spirit of life.

Cadbury's attempt at driving this transition came in the middle of '90s with its advertising campaign aiming to change the concept of chocolate from 'just for kids' to 'kids in all of us'. 'The real taste of life' campaign which was instrumental in redefining the concept of chocolate in India soon gave way to the 'Kya swad hai zindagi ka' campaign to make it more lingually relevant to the masses. The campaign also marks a turning point for the fortune of chocolate in general and Cadbury in particular in the Indian market. The campaign was executed using different ad copies that captured the exhilarating moments of life and the simple essence of a joyful living. The campaign had many successful executions. However the ad copy that lies etched in the memory of every television viewer is the one showing a young girl dancing vivaciously and exuberantly in a cricket field to express the joy/ ecstasy and celebrate the sixer hit by her friend. Such spontaneous and uninhibited expression of happiness instantly catapulted Cadbury to a unique position and endowed the brand with a sustained and preemptive association with happiness and celebration. This was the first time and 'Asli swad zindagi ka' was the first promotional campaign that targeted a chocolate product to the mass market. The exuberance, the ecstacy and the joy exhibited in the ad copy is a very good example of the use of hedonistic element of communication to convey the brand positioning and brand identity. The campaign went on to be awarded 'The Campaign of the Century' in India at the Abby (Ad Club, Mumbai) awards.

Another ad copy from the same campaign showed a young couple out in a picnic spot. The young man while doing aerobatics on a bicycle, to impress his girl, breaks into a pen by mistake and finds himself being chased by the bull. The couple while seemingly enjoying the chase, escape on the bicycle. The jingle 'kya swad hai zinddagi mein' and the picturesque background establish the association of the brand Cadbury with 'Celebration of life'. Still another ad copy showing a young girl with mehendi on her hands trying to tear open a pack of Cadbury chocolate with her mouth also shows small incidents of joy hidden in very small, seemingly insignificant happenings of life. Hedonistic element of communication was used throughout the campaign (in all the ad copies) not only to position the brand 'Cadbury' as a product that marks the celebration of life but also to redefine chocolate as a category and to expand the market for the entire category.

The 'Asli swad zindagi ka' campaign was followed by the campaign 'Khane walon ko khane ka bahana chahiye' campaign. This campaign marked the attempt of the company to aggressively and rapidly expand the chocolate market. The ad campaign overtly targeted the people of all ages from all walks of life. There was a visible change in the target audience from 'kids' to 'kids in all of us'.

The hedonistic element of communication is conspicuously visible in the jubilance and vibrance exuberated through the theme, storyline and jingle used in the ad copy. The ad copy lends meaning to the slogan "Kya swad hai zindagi mein" chosen by the brand.

This ad campaign soon gave way to those ad campaigns which used the cultural elements of positioning and had a very strong cultural relevance. Local culture came to the aid of the brand in the best possible way when the promotional campaigns associated the brand with festival linked celebrations. The 'Kuch meetha ho jaye' ('let us have something sweet') campaign, associating the brand with celebrations during various local festivals, did an exemplary job in infusing and initiating the chocolate consuming habit into the local culture. The campaign was executed using several different ad copies. This ad campaign which used the Indian cultural element of consuming something sweet ('kuch meetha ho jaye") during celebrations or to mark the moments of celebration was an intelligent extension of the "Khane walon ko khane ka bahana chahiye" campaign. Linking this theme/thought to the cultural and traditional practice of consuming sweets during moments of celebration, the new campaign was designed that urged the consumers to look for new reasons and excuses ('bahana') of celebration in day to day life and celebrate these unconventional moments of celebration with Cadbury (which was offered as "Kuch meetha" meaning something sweet). Thus the campaign 'Khane walon ko khane ka bahana chahiye' got a culturally relevant twist with the new campaign 'Kuch meetha ho jaye'. 'Cadbury' as an essential part of celebration was the new brand identity for Cadbury and was an attempt to substitute the traditional Indian sweet meat ('mithai') which is an integral part of all such celebrations.

Through the use of this cultural element of positioning Cadbury went in for category positioning whereby the product was positioned as 'Not simply a chocolate but a substitute of mithai'. This was a culturally relevant positioning the implied meaning of which was 'Cadbury is an essential part of any celebration and a substitute of mithai in all celebrations'. This was Local Consumer Culture Positioning.

The memorable ad copies from the campaign that were used to establish this positioning were 'Miss Palampur' ad with Amitabh Bachchan in which Amitabh along with the entire village celebrate the victory of a cow in an animal show ('Miss Palampur') with Cadbury. Another advertisement from the same campaign that is worth remembering was the 'Pappu Pass ho gaya' ad in which the entire college comes together to celebrate the success of the resident flunky who finally clears his twelfth class examination. Cadbury chocolate is distributed to mark the celebration. Still another ad copy shows ardent Indian cricket fans celebrating the victory of a lesser known nation, Kenya that has defeated India. Again Cadbury Dairy Milk is distributed to mark this celebration. Humour appeal has been used in all the ad copies throughout this advertising campaign.

Continuing with its 'Kuch meetha ho jaye' positioning, Cadbury India launched a new ad campaign in 2009, that revolved around the celebrations of the pay day. The campaign, conceptualized and executed by Ogilvy and Mather, tries to capitalize on the general euphoria and the upbeat mood of a middle class Indian on the day of the salary. Speaking to Campaign India about the task at hand, Shekhar Jha, creative director, Ogilvy & Mather said, "Generally, the first of every month is the day everyone feels rich and in the mood to indulge. We had to position Cadbury Dairy Milk as something that can be a part of this day of happiness, promises and salaries. Cadbury automatically lends itself to the celebrations" (Lad, 2009). Here the objective was to include the middle class people from smaller towns and cities in the campaign and position the brand effectively by associating it with celebration in their perceptual space. Thus the idea was to capture their moments of happiness and according to Mahesh Gaharth, Senior Creative Director at Ogilvy & Mather 'nothing does it better than salary day".

The next campaign 'Kuch mithas ho jaye' was some sort of continuation of the previous campaign 'Kuch meetha ho jaye' and harped upon the sweetness ('mithas') of relationship. It urges the consumer to celebrate and strengthen relationships with Cadbury Dairy Milk. The campaign urges one to include all relations in the celebration of happiness while making such celebrations special with Cadbury Dairy Milk. This campaign also continues and reinforces the positioning of Cadbury Dairy Milk as 'an essential part of celebration and a substitute of mithai' though laying a little more emphasis on relationships, which again is an integral part of Indian culture. The high degree of importance given to relationships is typical to the Indian culture. The ad copy shows a postman making an attempt to make people happy and to make them interact with each other during Diwali.

The promotional campaign and the brand positioning endeavour for Cadbury celebration makes use of cultural element of positioning. The positioning for the brand builds on emotional bonding and the strength of bonding between relations. Relationships have a special significance in Indian culture. Several festivals like 'Raksha Bandhan' and 'Bhai Duj' mark the celebration of these relationships. Cadbury celebration associates itself with these relationships (between siblings), bonding (between friends, parents and children, etc.) and festivals (Diwali, Raksha Bandhan, etc.). Thus hardcore Local Consumer Culture Positioning is used for the brand positioning of Cadbury Celebration which is also evident in the punch lines "Rishton ki Mithas", "Rishton ka Bandhan" and "Rishtein pakne do" used in the advertising campaign for the brand. Some of the advertising copies from this ad campaign designed for the television are:

a) The ad copy showing Amitabh Bachchan meeting his childhood friend after many years on Diwali and gifting him a pack of Cadbury Celebration.

b) The ad copy showing a brother gifting Cadbury Celebration to his younger sister on Raksha Bandhan.

c) The ad copy showing a younger brother who stays in hostel gifting his elder sister a pack of Cadbury Celebration when she visits him at the hostel.

d) An ad copy showing a couple gifting a conventional gift, a decoration piece, which circulates as a gift from one family to another and finally returns to the couple. The same couple gifts a pack of Cadbury Celebration to the host on some other occasion and the gift is enjoyed and cherished by the host as well as the guest.

Another ad copy with the same theme shows various people gifting Cadbury Celebration packs to strangers and loved ones. Here an emotional element is used to establish a distinctive position for the product 'Cadbury Celebration'. The ad copy exhibits the emotions associated with various relations and positions Cadbury Celebrations as an ideal product to celebrate these relations with. It is a customary practice to give gifts to near and dear ones and to friends and relatives during Diwali. Thus the campaign also uses the cultural element of positioning as Cadbury Celebration is shown as the right gift for Diwali. Local Consumer Culture Positioning is used to develop a suitable position for the brand Cadbury Celebration. As Cadbury Celebration is positioned as a product that can be used as a gift, its positioning can also be called as application positioning (to be used for the purpose gift thus having a specific purpose) as well as Product Category positioning.

To strengthen the claim of Cadbury Dairy Milk as a substitute of sweet meat ('mithai'), the 'khane ke baad meethe mein kuch meetha ho jaye' campaign was launched in the year 2010. The ad theme for this new campaign is about a typical Indian middle class family gathered around the dining table during dinner and Cadbury Dairy Milk being served as dessert after dinner. All the ad copies revolve around a family setting and bring out the sweetness of relations in a typical Indian middle class family. Thus using a family setting and an emotional element the campaign endeavours to position Cadbury Dairy Milk as a dessert. The type of positioning is use positioning/application positioning (Cadbury Dairy milk is not just a chocolate; it is a sweet dish to be consumed as a dessert).

Latest in the series of campaign for Cadbury Dairy Milk is the Cadbury Shubh Arambh campaign. In the Indian culture before embarking on a pious deed or a good job or something new, it is customary to consume some sweets. The campaign exploits this Indian sentiment and offers Cadbury as a sweet to be consumed during such occasions. As an element from the Indian culture has been taken to communicate the positioning of Cadbury Dairy Milk as sweet meat ('mithai'), the positioning strategy being employed to establish the brand identity ('substitute of mithai') is Local Consumer Culture Positioning. As Cadbury Dairy Milk is positioned as a substitute of 'mithai', which is a different product category, this type of positioning is product category positioning. The different ad copies designed for this ad campaign are:

a) A young boy asking a girl standing at a bus stop to give him a bite of Cadbury Dairy Milk before he proposes to drop the girl to her home.

b) An ad copy showing a middle aged woman going out in a pair of jeans for the first time and her husband offering her Cadbury Dairy Milk before she steps out of her house in this dress.

c) The ad copy that shows a young girl ready to elope with her boyfriend is taken by surprise when she finds her parents and family sitting in the boyfriend's car to bless her. They offer her Cadbury Dairy Milk to wish her a happy beginning ('Shubh Arambh').

A relatively new product being offered by Cadbury to the Indian market is Cadbury Bournville. The product is targeted at the premium segment of the market. Here also a cultural element is used to position the brand. The company tries to project the product as a typically British product and the television commercial for the brand talks about a British custom used before eating the product. To give an exotic feel to the brand even the locale in which the advertisement is shot is typically British. Thus the type of cultural positioning in use here is Foreign Consumer Culture Positioning.

A new variant of Cadbury Dairy Milk is Cadbury Dairy Milk Silk. The product is positioned as a smooth creamy chocolate. The brand is positioned on the basis of its physical attribute, its smoothness and its creaminess. The type of positioning used to establish the identity of the brand is attribute positioning. In the advertising campaign, the smoothness of the product is established by comparing it with silk and by focusing on the captivating experience felt by the user on eating Cadbury Dairy Milk Silk. Hedonistic/Experiential element is used to communicate the brand identity.

An attempt to increase the penetration of the brand Cadbury Dairy Milk is made by the company by launching the product Cadbury Dairy Milk Shots. Here the company banks on price as an element of positioning. The product is compared with a lodoo (a type of 'mithai'- sweet ball) and highlights the price of this so called ladoo (2 ladoos for Rs.2/-). This product is positioned on the basis of the constituents of the product (a ladoo made up of chocolate and milk) and its price (two ladoos for Rs.2/-). Thus the positioning strategy is a combination of attribute positioning and price positioning. The advertisement uses humour appeal in it.

Cadbury 5 Star is one of the oldest products of Cadbury in India. It is a caramel chocolate from Cadbury that is positioned on the basis of its constituents and its captivating taste. In its advertisement for Cadbury 5 Star, the company highlights the ingredients of the product which are chocolate, caramel and nuggets. The advertisement claims that the rich chocolate, caramel and nuggets in the chocolate captivate the eater who gets completely lost in its taste. The advertisement says "5 star me hai chocolate, caramel, and nuggets jise khane se log kho jate hain". The type of positioning is attribute positioning as the brand positioning is based on the attribute of the product. Hedonistic/Experiential or sensory element is used in the communication for establishing the positioning of the brand. Humour appeal is liberally used in the advertisement copy. The humour appeals in these funny advertisements facilitate and strengthen brand recall.

Cadbury 5 Star Fruit and Nut is a variant of Cadbury 5 Star, which also uses the same positioning and talks about the constituents of the product. The additional ingredients in this product are cashews, almonds and raisins. Cadbury 5 Star Fruit and Nut being a product extension of Cadbury 5 Star uses the same positioning. Here also the advertisement claims that the rich chocolate, caramel, cashews, almonds and raisins captivate the eater who gets completely enthralled and lost in its taste ("Caramel, chocolate, kaju, badam, kismis itna kuch; Jo khaye kho jaye; Naya Cadbury 5 Star Fruit & Nut").

Cadbury has a well established product in tablet form called Cadbury Eclairs. Attribute positioning is used for this product as well, whereby the physical characteristics of the product are focused upon. The product, Cadbury Eclairs is differentiated and positioned by highlighting its soft chocolaty core of Cadbury Dairy Milk covered by a chewy caramel. The voice over in the ad copy for the product says "Cadbury Eclairs: Ander Cadbury Dairy Milk, bahar chewy caramel" ie, "Cadbury Dairy Milk inside, chewy caramel outside".

The product of Cadbury in the light chocolate segment is Cadbury Perk. In its initial days when the product was just launched, it was positioned as a light and tasty snack that can be used to satisfy the small hunger pangs anywhere, anytime. Priety Zinta was roped in to endorse the brand. The slogan used for the product was "Thodi si pet pooja, kabhi bhi, kahin bhi". The type of positioning was benefit positioning. However, later on benefit positioning gave way to attribute positioning. The product was then positioned on the basis of its crunchier nature and chocolaty constituent. The ad copy designed to communicate the crunchy nature of the product showed Priety Zinta, the brand ambassador in her exercise class biting onto the crunchy Perk and intimidating the instructor with the resultant sound. The voice over in the ad said "Naya crunchier wafer se bana tastier Cadbury Perk; Zabardast crunch, zabardast taste" which means "New Cadbury Perk made up of crunchier wafer; Strong crunch, wonderful taste".

Cadbury Perk has again been repositioned in the year 2011 as a light snack full of glucose energy. In the recent years Nestle Munch from Nestle had compared itself with Cadbury Perk and the point of difference of Cadbury Perk had diluted. This repositioning seems to be an effort to clearly differentiate itself from the other similar products in the market. In its repositioning endeavour the product has been modified and the older package has been changed to blue to symbolize the change to the new benefit, the benefit of glucose energy. Thus a new point of difference has been created through this positioning. This new positioning (a light snack full of glucose energy) as symbolised by the new packing and the new slogan "Perk khao glucose chadao", is clearly benefit positioning. Humour appeal is used in the advertisement which shows an extremely tired young boy, bed ridden and almost unconscious because of fatigue jumps up and rushes on his bicycle after consuming Cadbury Perk. The voice over says "Glucose energy ke sath Cadbury Perk; Perk khao, glucose chadao" which translates to "Cadbury Perk enriched with glucose energy; Eat Perk, be energized with glucose".

Nestle, the country's largest food product company, operates in the chocolate market with its products Nestle Munch, Nestle Kit Kat and Nestle Bar One. While Nestle Bar One competes with the caramel chocolate Five Star from Cadbury, Nestle Munch and Nestle Kit Kat are wafer chocolates (enrobed wafer) competing directly with Cadbury Perk. According to an interview given by a Company spokesman to The Business Standard (for The Strategist, August 25, 2009), the basic proposition of Munch is a light, crunchy and chocolaty treat that is affordable and can be enjoyed any day, anywhere, anytime. The company establishes a point of parity of the brand Nestle Munch with Cadbury Perk by highlighting the crunchiness in Munch. The brand associates itself with fun. The advertisement copies always highlight the fun associated with the consumption of the brand. Hedonistic element (the fun element and the feel good element) is used to communicate the brand identity. In conformance with the brand association, the film actress Rani Mukherjee who is considered to be a vibrant, vivacious and fun loving celebrity was roped in as the brand ambassador of Nestle Munch. Humour appeal is used in all the ad copies to establish the fun association of the brand. The type of positioning is attribute positioning (light and crunchy) also reflected in the slogan "Mera Crunch Mahan".

Nestle Kit Kat is another brand of enrobed wafer from the same company. It is positioned as a light, tasty and chocolaty snack for small breaks. As it is a very light food to be consumed in breaks, the type of brand positioning is use positioning/application positioning. In line with the specific use positioning of the brand, the slogan for Kit Kat says "Kit Kat break banta hai"(meaning Kit Kat break is justified) and "Have a break, have a Kit Kat".

An important player in the Indian confectionary and candy market is the French multinational Perfetti Van Mille. The flagship brand from Perfetti is Alpenliebe. The brand is positioned on the basis of its taste. It is positioned as a candy with an enthralling taste. The use of the film star Kajol in the advertisement designed for promoting the brand adds a touch of celebrity appeal to the ad copy. A distinctive brand of hard boiled candy in the market is Parle Poppins. The main target consumers for hard boiled candies including that of Parle Poppins are children. The product is clearly differentiated from the other brands of hard boiled candies, on the basis of its shape and pack which consists of several flat and round candies heaped together to form a cylindrical pack. Parle Poppins is positioned as a pack of candies with assorted fruit flavours.

A popular and fast growing category of candy product is the mint candy. Several brands of mint candies that compete in the market are Chlormint from Perfetti, Minto Fresh from ITC, Polo from Nestle and Mentos. According to Sameer Suneja, Managing Director Perfetti, Chlormint is targeted at the smokers who want a fresh breath. (Iyer, 2010 b). The humorous ad copies and the slogan "Dubara mat poochna" (Don't ever ask again why Chlormint is consumed) enhance the brand recall of Chlormint.

Minto Fresh from ITC also uses a humour appeal to position itself as a product that gives fresh breath. Nestle Polo uses an attribute positioning and is positioned as "The mint with the hole". Mentos is positioned as a mint candy that opens up your mind and lightens it up with ideas and the slogan says "Mentos-Dimag ki batti jala de". The brands of mint candies are not strongly differentiated from each other. This being an impulsive purchase category, the brand loyalty of the consumers is very low and a brand can be very easily substituted by any other brand. Thus what makes a difference is the availability of the brands at the point of purchase, brand recognition (familiarity with a brand name) and brand recall and this is what the promotional campaign for most of these brands aim for. Thus the brand positioning effort is not that strong in this category.

Most of the promotional campaigns and advertisement copies are designed to enhance brand recognition and brand recall.

Similar is the story in the chewing gum market. This is a market where brand loyalty is not that high but brand recognition (familiarity with the brand) does make a difference. Perfetti and Wrigley are two very important players in this market. Perfetti has four important products in this market-Center Fresh, Center Shock, Big Babol and Happy Dent. Happy Dent is positioned as a chewing gum that whitens the teeth and makes them shiny. The type of positioning is use positioning/application positioning (for making teeth white and shiny). While Happy Dent uses a very specific functional positioning, Center Fresh does not have a clear cut and specific functional positioning. The humorous ad copy and the slogan for the brand 'Zuban pe rakhe lagam' ensure a strong brand recall amongst the target segment i.e., the children and the young people.

Big Babol from Perfetti has a strong point of difference. It is positioned as a cotton candy that changes to bubble gum. A humorous ad copy is used for this brand as well, to strengthen its brand recall.

Brand Positioning of Cosmetics

Personal care is a big business today of which the skin care and cosmetics constitute the major category. The skin care market is India that stood at around Rs. 2,758 Crore in 2008 (Source: Carvalho, Brian, "New CEO, New HUL", Business Today, April 6, 2008) and is worth Rs. 5000 Crore in the year 2011 (Source: Chaturvedi, Anumeha, "Parachuting into Skincare", Business Today, Nov. 13, 2011). The market is currently dominated by Hindustan Uniliver with its brand Lakme, Vaseline, Ponds and Fair & Lovely. "Vaseline and Ponds together occupy more than 50 percent of the market" (Source: Chaturvedi, Anumeha, "Parachuting into Skincare", Business Today, Nov. 13, 2011). The skincare category consists of several sub-categories like facial complexion lighting/fairness cream, body lotions, anti aging creams, sunscreen lotions, moisturizers, fairness cream for men etc. Besides HUL, others important players in the market are Loreal, P&G, Dabur, Emami, Marico, ITC, Cavin Kare and Vicco Laboratories Ltd. With so many stray players of all types i.e., foreign multinational companies, Indian multinational companies and domestic companies, and a number of established brands in this market, the cosmetics market in general and the skin care market in particulars is extremely competitive. So this puts a tremendous pressure on the FMCG companies operating in the personal care and skin care segment to continuously innovate and differentiate their brands from the competing brands present in the market. "The skincare brands are constantly innovating to stay ahead. If Loreal is introducing cheaper variants in smaller packs in a bid to widen the distribution reach of products like Garnier Light, Emami is planning at least three to four variants of Boroplus and Fair and Handsome this year. Dabur too entered the facial care products category in January this year." (Chaturvedi, 2011). The Indian multinational Marico has also entered the skincare market with its product Parachute Advanced Body Lotion which, unlike other competing products that use petroleum jelly, uses 100 percent natural moisturizers. According to Harsh V. Agarwal, Director of Emami "Constant innovation in terms of products, ingredients, marketing, packaging and delivery systems, are critical for success in this market" (Chaturvedi, 2011). With such dynamism in this market and with such aggressive product and marketing innovations by the competing players, it becomes all the more important for companies to look for a non imitable and pre emptive positioning for their brands.

One of the most distinctive positioning is that of Vicco Turmeric by a home grown player Vicco Laboratories Ltd. The company is known for manufacturing and selling Ayurvedic products and brands with Ayrvedic formulations. Vicco Turmeric is positioned as a multipurpose ayurvedic cream. It is differentiated from the others competing skin care products on the basis of its natural ingredients (ie, turmeric and sandal). The company categorically claims that Vicco Turmeric is not a cosmetic but an ayurvedic cream. So it is positioned as in ayurvedic cream, an ayurvedic medicine. The Voice over in the ad copy for the brand claims "Vicco Turmeric- Ek manyata prapt aushadhi" which means Vicco Turmeric is a widely acclaimed medicine. The type of brand positioning is product category positioning (Not a cosmetic but a medicine).

In the Indian cosmetic market one of the best selling brands of mutlipurpose cream is Boroline from GD Pharmaceuticals Pvt. Ltd., a Kolkata based company. It is positioned as an antiseptic cream that is multipurpose in nature (ie, it removes dryness, smoothens skin, heals cracked heels and softens chapped lips). The multipurpose nature of the product implies that Boroline can be used on dry lips, cuts and bruises, dry skin, cracked heels, rough elbows and for general skin problems. The type of brand positioning is use positioning/application positioning. The brand identity of Boroline is a multipurpose cream with medicinal properties (Antiseptic properties). The functional element of the product is used to establish its brand positioning. To leverage the strong brand equity of Boroline the company has gone for a brand extension by launching the sub brand Boroline Suthol. This product from GD Pharmaceuticals is positioned as a multipurpose antiseptic skin shower. Its value proportion is an antiseptic skin shower for prickly heat, itches, skin irritations, cuts, rashes, insect bites, skin infections and other skin related problems. The voice over in the television commercial for the brand claims "Garmi shuru to ghamoriyan, khujli aur rashes bhi; Apnaiye Boroline ka Suthol, India ka pehla antiseptic skin shower" which means "With the onset of summer comes prickly heat, itches and rashes; Use sulthol from Boroline, India's first antiseptic skin shower". The type of brand positioning is benefit positioning.

The direct competition and the strongest rival of Boroline is the antiseptic cream Boroplus from Emami. The brand identity of Boroplus antiseptic cream is a multipurpose cream that prevents dry and chapped checks, chapped lips, cracked heels, protects from dryness during winters and can be applied on nappy rashes, cuts, bruises and burns. Thus the type of brand positioning is use positioning /application positioning. Functional element of the product is used and highlighted to establish the perceptual position of the brand. Celebrity appeal is used in the advertisements of Boroplus by getting the product endorsed by its brand ambassadors Amitabh Bachchan and Kareena Kapoor. Boroplus has gone in for a line extension whereby it has launched Boroplus summer and winter lotions meant to be used specifically during summers and winters respectively. Another product extension is Boroplus Intensive skin care therapy cream. It is specifically meant for keeping elbows, knees and heels smooth and healthy. This is also application positioning. The product is endorsed by the film star Kareena Kapoor. Under the brand Boroplus, Emami has a prickly heat powder called Boroplus Ice prickly heat powder. It is positioned as a talcum powder with the specific use of preventing prickly heat and giving relief from the itching caused due to prickly heat. The type of positioning for the product is also application/use positioning. Like other products from Boroplus, Boroplus Ice is also endorsed by kareena Kapoor.

Vaseline Petroleum Jelly from HUL is positioned as a skin care product that gives a soft and supple skin to the entire family. The voice over in the advertisement claims "Vaseline Petroleum Jelly – Rakhe twacha ka khayaal Banaye rakhe twacha ki raunak" which means "Vaseline Petroleum Jelly- Takes care of the skin. Keeps skin glowing." The brand differentiates itself from other petroleum jellies by highlighting the distinctive design and shape of its container. The type of positioning is benefit positioning (soft and glowing skin is the promised value proportion).

Besides Vaseline, other brands of skin care products from the stable of HUL that are worth mentioning are Lakme and Ponds. Lakme has a number of products that cater to different skin care needs of the consumer. Lakme Fruit blast face wash that is available in three variants (Citrus rain, Berry lush and Melon melt) is positioned as the face wash made up of natural ingredients and containing different real fruits extracts. The advertisement for the brand claim "Lakme fruit blast face washes; Deep clean and rehydrated skin with real mandarin, berries and melon." As the brand of face wash is differentiated and positioned on the basis of the natural ingredients of the product, the type of brand positioning is attribute positioning.

Lakme Peach milk moisturiser is targeted at the young Indian women. The brand promises to make the skin as glowing as when you are in love. Thus the type of positioning is benefit positioning and the advertising appeal in use is love appeal (romance appeal to be more specific).

Like Lakme Peach milk mousturiser, Ponds also makes use of love appeal in its advertisement to promote two of its most well known products: Ponds Cold Cream and Ponds Dreamflower talc. Ponds cold cream promises to make the skin as lovely and soft as that of a child. Thus soft skin is its value proportion and benefit positioning is the type of brand positioning in use. The ad copies show the near and dear ones of the cold cream user being lured to touch her skin and display affection to her. This is where the love appeal comes into play and the feeling of love and the experience of being loved (because of the cheeks made soft by Ponds) communicates the benefit of the brand and the brand identity. This element used to communicate the brand identify is the hedonistic element. In conformance with the identified brand positioning of Ponds Cold cream, the voice over in the television commercial for the brand says "Ponds Cold cream, skin so soft, it says googly, woogly woosh." (Ponds dream flower Tale also uses a love appeal in its advertisements. The brand of talcum powder is positioned on the basis of the fragrance. It promises a freshness that would make you feel loved. The positioning strategy is again benefit positioning.)

In the Indian skin care market, the fairness cream has emerged as a very important category. The size of the fairness cream market is Rs 1700 Crore and the category is growing at a rate of 13 percent to 15 percent per annum. The oldest and the biggest brand in this segment is Fair & Lovely from Hindustan Unilever. Fair and Lovely is the first of its kind to be positioned as a skin lighting cream. It is positioned as a product that lightens the texture of the skin and endows the user with self confidence. The type of positioning is benefit positioning. Though there are a number of other brands of fairness creams in the Indian market, Fair & Lovely has the first mover advantage.

To exploit a gap that existed in the fairness/skin lightening market (a fairness product for men), Emami launched the fairness cream for men Fair and Handsome and targeted it at the young Indian male who used to dip into the dressing table of his wife or sister. Fair and handsome is positioned as a fairness cream for men with a formulation that is specifically suitable for the male skin. Thus the value proportion is fairness and the target market is the young male. Here the type of positioning is benefit positioning (fairness) and category positioning (Men's fairness cream). The success of Emami's Fair & Handsome made HUL to launch a fairness cream targeted at the men. The product is Vaseline Men. The value proportion of the product is fairness and anti spots for men. It is positioned as a Vitamin B3 and triple sunscreen enriched anti spots whitening face cream for men. The type of positioning is benefit positioning. The point of difference from

Emami's Fair & Handsome is that Vaseline Men is not just a fairness cream but an anti spots cream as well. The marketing communication for the brand claims "Vaseline Men mein hai Vitamin B3 aur triple sunscreen jo chehre ko banaye fair aur ghataye paanch tarah ke daag dhabbo ko" which means "Vaseline men is enriched with Vitamin B3 and triple sunscreen that makes you fair and reduces five types of spots."

Hindustan Unilever also has a body fairness cream called Vaseline Healthy white. It is positioned as a Vitamin B3 and triple sunscreen enriched fairness cream for the body. The value proportion of the product is fairness for the body and the type of positioning is benefit positioning (fairness cream) and use/application positioning (fairness cream meant for the body).

Other brands of fairness cream/fairness products are Lakme Perfect Radiance fairness cream and Lakme Perfect Radiance skin ligthening compact from HUL, Ponds white beauty from HUL, Olay Natural white from P&G, L'oreal White Perfect day cream and Garnier Light moisturizer as well as Garnier Men Power Light from L'oreal.

Lakme Perfect Radiance fairness cream is a product from HUL, targeted at the premium segment. It is positioned as a fairness cream that makes the skin radiant. The type of positioning is benefit positioning. Enumerating the benefits of the product the ad copy elaborates "No dark sports, no uneven skin tone, no oiliness and no tanning or dullness; Lakme Perfect radiance fairness cream with white lily and secret lotus extracts. It acts on all signs of skin darkening giving you fairness that's absolutely perfect." A brand extension of Lakme Perfect Radiance is Lakme Perfect Radiance skin lighting compact. It is positioned as a fairness compact with special ingredient that makes the skin two times fairer. The type of positioning is a combination of benefit positioning (skin up to two times fairer instantly) and attribute positioning ("A fairness compact with SPF20, brightening pears and multivitamins").

One of the line extensions/product variants of Ponds, a product of HUL, is Ponds White Beauty. Ponds White Beauty is also a fairness cream. The value proportion of Ponds White Beauty is skin lightening and spot reduction. The product is positioned as a Provitamin B3 enriched cream that reduces spots and lightens skin in just 7 days.

P&G competes in the fairness cream with its product Olay Natural White. Olay Natural white is positioned as a healthy fairness day cream enriched with vitamins and sunscreen. The company claims through its ads that the three nourishing vitamins in Olay Natural white "reduce dark spots, lighten skin tone and give you a glow from within". ("Iske teen nourishing vitamins dark sports kam karein, skin tone lighten karein aur dein andar se glow"). The type of positioning is benefit positioning. The advertising appeal used to promote the band is celebrity appeal whereby the bollywood actress Katrina Kaif endorses the brand.

L'oreal White Perfect day cream from L'oreal Paris uses a combination of attribute positioning and benefit positioning. In its positioning attempt, the company highlights the features of the product like reflecting micro pearls, melano block and UV filters through which it claims to deliver the benefits of instant brightening of the skin, reduction of dark spots and protection from further darkening respectively.

In the skin whiting market, L'oreal Pairs offers another brand, Garnier Light. Garniner Light moisturiser is targeted at women whereas Garnier Men Power Light is targeted at men. Both are positioned on the basis of their functional benefit i.e., fairness that can be measured. The value proportion of both the products is conspicuous fairness that can be seen and measured. To fortify the positioning and to support the claim of measurable result, the packs of Garnier Light and Garnier Men Power light come with fairness scale (a paper strip with a gradient of colour patches that match various skin tones). Garnier Light moisturizer is endorsed by the bolywood actress Genelia D'souza whereas Garnier Men Power Light is endorsed by John Abraham. The voice over in the television commercial for Gariner Light moisturizer claims "Visible results in just 7 days; So confident. It comes with proof. Garnier Light moisturiser Measure and see."

Garnier Light Ultra is positioned as a fairness innovation that offers the benefit of reducing dark spots in size, numbers and intensity and gives a flawless glowing skin. Talking about the innovative technology and the consequent benefits of the product the company says "Its pure lemon essence formula with spot breaker technology reduces dark spots in size, number and intensity thus leaving your skin glowing flawlessly". Thus the brand positioning here is a combination of attribute positioning and benefit positioning.

Fem Herbal bleach cream, though targeting a similar need market (instant fairness), does not have a direct competition from any of the well known brands. It does not compete directly with any of the fairness creams like Fair & Lovely, Fairever or Fair One as these creams promise fairness after weeks of use whereas Fem is about instant fairness. Fem Herbal bleach is specifically targeted to the Indian women who have facial hair. This is not a global phenomenon but a problem typical to the Indian subcontinent. For such women, one way to hide their facial hair is to use a bleach lotion. Since this is not a worldwide problem none of the foreign MNCs have ventured into this product segment and Dabur has some sort of monopoly in this segment. However, there are some lesser known regional players is this market segment.

Women who use a bleach lotion are often concerned about the harmful effects of the product on their skin. To alleviate these fears Dabur has modified the Fem bleach cream and launched Fem Herbal bleach cream with 16 herbs. So the product is now positioned on the basis of the benefit it offers, i.e. instant fairness in a natural way that is safe for the skin and the advertisement for the product claims "15 minutes to fairness naturally". The brand positioning strategy in use is benefit positioning. (Bandari, 2009).

The strong rays of the tropical sun in the Indian subcontinent may cause extensive skin damage and may result in sun burns particularly during scorching summers. Sun tanning caused by solar rays is one of the major reasons of the darkening of the skin. So a specific skin care requirement for the Indian consumer is to protect the skin from the strong tropical sun and prevent the damage caused to the skin by the harmful ultra violet rays of the sun. A number of sunscreens are available in the market to meet this need of the Indian consumer and specifically to meet the need of the complexion conscious Indian women. Besides this need being met by some fairness creams that have sunscreen as an ingredient in them, there are certain products sold as purely sunscreens, which specifically cater to this need. Lakme Sun Expect Ultra Matte Mini is one such product. It is positioned as a non greasy sunscreen. The product is targeted at the modern, urban young Indian woman. It targets the young, urban woman at the premium segment of the market. The Television commercial urges her to use the product and says "Lakme Sun Expert Matte Mini – For non-greasy kissable skin. Stay sun safe on the go". Here the type of brand positioning in use is benefit positioning.

Another product from Lakme that satisfies the same need is Lakme Sunscreen Lotion. It is targeted at the middle class urban and semi urban woman. The value proposition of the product is that it keeps the user sun safe and prevents tanning, spots and wrinkles. The type of positioning is benefit positioning. The television commercial for this brand of sunscreen claims "Sawlapan, daag, jhurryon ko rokey SPF yukt Lakme Sunscreen lotion. Jab aap dhoop mein nikalte hain rahiye sun safe, hamesha", which means "SPF enriched Lakme sunscreen lotion stops skin darkening, spots and wrinkles. When you move out in the sun, remain sun safe, always."

P&G also operates in the sunscreen market with its brand Olay. Olay is targeted at the premium segment of the market and addresses the urban Indian woman in the segment. This brand of sunscreen is endorsed by the bollywood actress Soha Ali Khan. The value proportion of the brand is fighting sun damage and preventing lines, wrinkles and dark spots caused due to sun damage. The brand ambassador Soha Ali Khan appeals to the consumer and says "The summer darkens your skin, par itna hi nahi (ie, not only this); sun damage can also cause lines wrinkles and dark spots; Protect your skin with Olay's SPF range….; This summer try Olay to fight sun damage".

A relatively newer market that has emerged for the companies in the cosmetics and skin care business is the anti-ageing market. Some important brands in the market are Ponds Age Miracle, Olay Total Effects 7 in 1 anti ageing cream and Garnier Age Life.

Ponds Age Miracle is targeted at the women who are 30 years and above. Ponds tries to expand the anti ageing market by urging the 30 years old women to start using the product as this stage when the signs of ageing are not visibly evident. The marketing communication for the brand talks of "delaying the appearance of fine lines, wrinkles and age spots" and urges the 30-35 year old woman to "Start early. Delay ageing". The promised value proportion is the delay of ageing.

Olay Total Effect 7 in 1 Anti-aging Cream from P&G is an anti ageing cream targeted at the women in the premium segment of the market. It is differentiated from the other anti aging creams on the basis of its claimed ability to fight the seven signs of ageing which include dark spots, sagging skin, dull glow-less skin, lines and wrinkles, dry skin, patchy skin and open pores. Thus the benefit positioning for the brand is "7 in 1 anti ageing cream". The brand is endorsed by celebrities like Soha Ali Khan, Shilpa Shetty and Kajol.

Garnier Agelift Triactive from L'oreal is positioned as an anti ageing innovation that smoothens wrinkles, removes dark spots and brings back the lost glow. The benefit positioning of the product talks of delivering three benefits (smoothening of wrinkles, removal of dark spots, removing the dullness and bring back the glow to the skin) delivered through one product.

****

REFERENCES

"How many Cars are Produced in the World Every Year", Retrieved January, 29, 2012 from http://www.worldometers.info/cars/

Bhandari, Bhupesh (2009), "Dabur finds it missing link", *The Strategist* (July 28), p 1

Bhandari, Bhupesh, & Rai, Amit Ranjan (2009), "Munchy Bites", *The Strategist* (August 25), p. 4

Bhandari, Bhupesh, Baggonkar, Swaraj, & Barman, Arijit (2010), "Local Edge, Global Plans", *The Strategist* (August 23), pp. 1-4

Bhattacharjee, Arindam (2010 a), "A brew for the young", *The Strategist* (October 4), p. 3

Bhattacharjee, Arindam (2010 b), "A car for sandeep", *The Strategist* (March 23), pp. 1-4

Carvalho Brian (2008), "New CEO, New HUL", *Business Today* (April 6), pp. 49-58

Chaturvedi, Anumeha (2011), "Parachuting into Skincare", *Business Today* (November), pp. 150-152

DasGupta, Surajeet (2011), "Telecom Policy to allow Spectrum Pooling", *Business Standard* (August 11)

ET Bureau (2011), "Most Trusted Brands 2011: How we did it?", *The Economic Times Brand Equity* (September 28)

Giriprakash, K. (2010), "Ford to stop manufacturing India specific cars", *Business Line* (Sept 14)

Irani, Delshad (2011), "Most trusted brands 2011: How Colgate regained the top spot", *Economic Times* (September 28)

Iyer Byravee (2010 a), "A new brew", *The Strategist* (January 26), p. 3

Iyer Byravee (2010 b), "Gum Power", *The Strategist* (July 05), p. 2

Iyer, Byravee (2009 a), "Back to its roots", *The Strategist* (December 29), pp. 1-4

Iyer, Byravee (2009 b), "Payday Celebrations", *The Strategist* (June 30), p. 3

Iyer, Byravee (2009 c), "Soap Opera", *The Strategist* (August 25), p. 1

Iyer, Byravee (2010 a), "German Designs", *The Strategist* (June 21), pp. 1-4

Iyer, Byravee (2010 b), "Logan's new slogan", *The Stratgist* (July 26), p.3

Kannan, Shanthi (2001), "Rural Market-A World of Opportunity", *The Hindu* (Thursday, October 11)

Kar, Sayantani (2010 a), "A healthy head start", *The Strategist* (March 30), p1

Kar, Sayantani (2010 b), "Foodles in the noodle bowl", *The Strategist* (August 2), pp. 1-4

Kar, Sayantani (2010 c), "Heinz Again", *The Strategist* (August 9), p. 2

Kar, Sayantani (2010 d), "Stretching out in the tight space" *The Strategist* (May 3), pp. 2-3

Khicha, Preeti (2011), "New Improved", *The Strategist* (July 11), pp. 1-4

Kunal L Talgeri, "A passage to America", *Outlook business* (July 10), pp. 40-46

Lad, Mukta (2009), "Cadbury India celebrates pay day with Dairy Milk", Retrieved June 24, 2009, from http://www.campaignindia.in/Article/226532,cadbury-india-celebrates-pay-day-with-dairy-milk.aspx

Madhavan, N. (2008), "India's Detroit", *Business Today* (July 27), pp. 128-130

Malviya, Sagar (2012), "Ghari Moves Out Wheel to be No 1 in Laundry Market", *The Economic Times* (January 10)

Mishra, Arunima (2010). "Watchout the Ghari express", *The Strategist* (Nov. 1), p.1

Mitra, Kushan (2010), "The Zen of Positioning", *Business Today* (August 8), pp. 96-98

Moorthi, Y.S.R. (2002), "We're like this only", Retrieved October 31, 2003, from http://learning.indiatimes.com/bm/guruspeak/moorthi.htm.

Mukherjee, Avinandan (2000), "The Indian Automobile Industry: Speeding into the Future", *Actes du GERPISA*, No. 28 (February), pp. 35-53

Mukund, A., Radhika, A. Neela (2005), "Repositioning Airtel", In Suresh, K (Ed.), *Positioning and Repositioning*, pp. 149-162, Hyderabad: ICFAI University Press

NCAER (1998), 10-year White book- The Indian Consumer Market: 1997-2007

Pandey, Onkar (2011), "Does India have it to give LG the $10 bn?", Retrieved May, 12, 2011 from http://businessandeconomy.org. /12052011/storyd.asp

Prahalad, C.K., & Hart, Stuart L. (2002), "The Fortune at the Bottom of the Pyramid", *Strategy+Business*, Iss. 26 (First Quarter), pp. 1-14

PTI (2011), "LG eyes to improve market share in home entertainment segment", Retrieved April, 26, 2011 from http://www.livemint.com/2011/04/26165756/LG-eyes-to-improve-mkt-share-i.html

PTI (2011), "Rivals eat into HUL's shampoo market share", *The Hindu Business line* (April 10)

PTI (2012), "Car exports rise 34% on non-European nation demand", *Business Standard* (June 11)

Rajagopal (2009), "Branding paradigm for the bottom of the pyramid markets", *Measuring business excellence*, Vol. 13, No. 4, pp. 58-68

Rajan, Rohithari (2007), "Unilever's business in india's subsistence economies", *Product and market development for subsistence marketplaces advances in international management*, Volume 20, 259–277

Sharma, Yogima Seth (2010), "Maruti bets big on new Alto", *Business Standard* (July 25)

Shashidhar, Ajita (2010), "Good to global", *Outlook business* (July 24), pp. 42-53

Warrier, Shobha (2007), "The inspiring success story of CavinKare", Retrieved March, 22, 2007 from http://www.rediff.com/money/2007/mar/22bspec.htm

CHAPTER 3

IMPACT OF SELECTED DEMOGRAPHIC FACTORS ON CONSUMERS' BRAND EVALUATION AND PERCEPTION OF FMCG BRANDS

ABSTRACT

The perception of an individual and his attitude towards an object, besides being influenced by the characteristics of the object is affected by several factors like the culture of the society, social and economic background of the individual, his lifestyle and education level and the environment. The consumer's perception of a brand is also influenced by a complicated mix of social, cultural and economic factors. A proper understanding of these factors and of their influence on the target consumer's brand preference helps the marketer create a favourable brand image and effectively position the brand in the perceptual space of the consumer.

The paper makes an attempt to isolate the importance of social, cultural and economic factors in the consumer's evaluation of an FMCG brand in the Indian market. To get an insight into the influence of the different factors on the Indian consumer's perception of a brand, responses were collected from consumers from five different states of the country. The economic factor was found to be most important in the consumer's evaluation of a brand and in influencing his perception of an FMCG brand. Cultural conformance of a brand is less frequently used as an evaluation criterion for an FMCG brand by the Indian consumer.

Keywords: *Brand Attributes, Brand Positioning, Brand Preference, FMCG, Product Quality.*

INTRODUCTION

Brand Positioning implies finding a valued place for the brand in the mind of the target consumer. The significance of Brand Positioning lies in the fact that it differentiates the company's offer from those of the competitors and establishes a favourable image for the brand in the consumer's mind. Various factors associated with the brand as well as with the consumer influence the consumer's perception of the brand and his eventual preference of the brand. As these factors have a bearing on brand perception and preference, it becomes utmost important for a brand manager to understand these factors and the extent and intensity of their impact on preference. A proper understanding of their impact on brand perception, evaluation and preference would enable the marketer to effectively use the relevant factors in positioning his brand and leverage these factors to create a favourable image and perception of the brand in the minds of the consumer.

LITERATURE REVIEW

Knowledge of the factors that influence the brand perception and brand preference of the consumers help the brand manager in designing the brand positioning strategies. It is a complicated task to predict a consumer's brand preference as several factors influence his brand perception and preference. However, it has been found that consumer's belief about product specific attributes and the relative importance attached to product specific attributes by the consumer influence his brand preference. Hence brand preference can be predicted by "attitude measurement based upon beliefs about and relative importance of product specific attributes" (Bass et al, 1972). It is not only the product attributes that influence the consumer's perception and his preference of a brand. Consumer' purchase motive and his self concept have a significant influence on his brand perception. Study indicates that consumers having a higher public self consciousness have a higher preference for national brand labels whereas those having lower public self consciousness tend to have a higher preference for bargain brand labels (Bushman, 1993). Consumers purchase things only when they are consistent with, enhance or fit well with the conception the consumers have of themselves (Ross, 1971). Research has proved that consumers perceive those brands to be better whose image is in congruence with the self image of the consumer (Jamal et al, 2001). Selection of the right brand concept positively influences the brand image which in turn has an impact on the performance of the brand in the market (Park et al, 1986).

Attitude of a consumer towards a brand and towards consumption besides being affected by other factors also depend on the consumer's motive of consumption. Research suggests that consumer motive is bi-dimensional implying that the motive of consumption may be utilitarian or hedonistic (Batra & Ahtola, 1990 & Voss et al, 2003).
As far as the relationship between brand and consumer perception is concerned, it has been found that "Consumers use brand names as diagnostic and legitimate search attributes" and brand names have an impact on brand perception and preference (Wanke, et al, 2007). Brands offering a greater

variety of compatible (focused and internally consistent) products are perceived to have a greater commitment to the expertise in the category. Such brands are perceived to offer superior quality and experience higher purchase likelihood (Jonah, et al, 2006).

The degree of involvement of a consumer in a product category also influences his decision making process and his response to the products and brands in the category (Lawent, et al, 1985). The consumer's perception of the safety of a product is affected by several product related factors such as price, brand name, promotion channels, source credibility, country of origin, nature of product testing authority and warranty (Tse, et al, 1999). Consumer's experience of a brand can be improved and his perception of the brand can be enhanced if the company offering the brand maintains industry standards in any two of the three value disciplines- operational excellence, customer intimacy and product leadership- and excels in the third value discipline (Treacy, et al, 1993).

A brand's relation to the national culture of a market has significant influence on the perception of the brand in that market. National culture should be taken as an important factor in designing the brand image strategies of the company (Roth, 1995). Country of origin of the brand has a greater influence on the perceived quality of the brand than on the purchase intension of the consumer or on his attitude towards the brand (Verlegh et al, 1999). Research indicates that the effect of the 'Country of Origin' on consumer's brand perception differs across brands and across countries of production (Koubaa, 2008). It has been found that though, the knowledge of the country of origin of a brand influences the belief of the consumer about the brand, it does not have any direct influence on the attitude of the consumer towards the brand. However, as beliefs may be instrumental in shaping the attitude, the consumer's knowledge of the brand's origin may indirectly affect his attitude through the beliefs about the brand emanating out of this knowledge (Erickson et al, 1984).

Though the impact of several factors have been identified on the brand perception and the resulting brand preference of the consumer, a research gap exists as far as measuring the relative degree of impact of social, cultural and economic factors on the brand perception and preference of the consumers.

TYPES OF FACTORS AFFECTING BRAND PERCEPTION

How the consumers perceive a brand depend not only on the characteristics of the brand or the company that offers the brand but also on the demographic, psychographic and behavioural characteristics of the consumer.

All factors affecting brand positioning as well as the brand preference of the consumer can broadly be classified as:

1. Consumer Related Factors.
2. Competition (Competing brands) Related Factors and
3. Factors related to the brand characteristics and virtues of the company (Company Related Factors)

Besides the consumer related factors, competition related factors and product related factors, the positioning strategy for a brand is also affected by the organisational culture and management system. Research indicates that many successful firms are those which become outstanding in one of the three value disciplines ie, Operational Excellence, Customer Intimacy or Product Leadership while maintaining industry standards in the other two value disciplines. The value discipline chosen by a company is done so by taking into account the capabilities of the company, its culture and the strength of the competitors. These leaders "align their entire operating model- that is, the company's culture, business processes, management systems and computer platforms- to serve one value discipline".

As their focus for achieving outstanding excellence is on one of the three value disciplines, it is this chosen value discipline that guides their operation and marketing activities. It can thus be concluded that it is this specific value discipline that guides the positioning of the company's brand and becomes an important factor influencing the brand positioning strategy as well as the perception and preference of the brand by the consumer.

Each of the above mentioned categories of factors that influence the consumer's brand preference ie, Consumer related factors, Product related factors, Competition related factors and Company related factors can be subdivided into several sub-categories. A summary of the various factors affecting consumers' brand perception and brand preference, organised into their respective categories and sub-categories, is represented in Table 3A.

Table 3A: Factors Affecting Consumers' Brand Perception			
	Categories	**Sub Categories**	**Factors**
1.	**Consumer Related Factors**	Demographic Characteristics	Age, Gender, Occupation, Income, Education, Family Size and Family Life Cycle, Socioeconomic Factors
		Geographic Characteristics	rural or urban background, nationality, the region to which the consumer belongs, etc.
		Psychographic Characteristics & Consumer Perception	values and beliefs, culture, tradition, lifestyle, Cultural Factors
		Behavioural Characteristics	purchase habits, frequency of purchase, usage habits, patterns of consumption and media habits of the consumer.
2.	**Product Related Factors**	Product Class	Existing or new product category, Relevance of product category in the market.
		Brand Attribute	Unique Characteristics of the brand & product, Technological superiority, Functional characteristics of the brand, Emotional associations of the brand

		Brand Positioning Strategy	Positioning Strategies of the competitors, Positions occupied by competing brands, Gaps left by the competing brands
3.	**Competition Related Factors**	Strength of the Competitor	Capabilities of the competitors, Strengths of the competitors, Weaknesses of the competitors
4.	**Company Related Factors**	Company's Objectives	Company's Vision and Mission, Company's Overall Objectives
		Marketing Strategy	Corporate Strategy, Marketing Strategy.
		Value Discipline	Value Discipline chosen and implemented by the company

OBJECTIVES OF THE STUDY

1. To understand the degree of impact of the social, cultural and economic factors on consumer's brand perception (of FMCG brands).
2. To find out if the factors considered for evaluating an FMCG brand by the consumer vary with the gender of the consumer.
3. To find out if the importance attached to the social, cultural and economic factors in evaluating an FMCG brand change with the occupational background of the consumer.
4. To find out if the factors considered for evaluating an FMCG brand by the consumer vary with the age of the consumer.

METHODOLOGY

The empirical study is based on the responses gathered from 250 consumers spread across five different states of India. The respondents included housewives, working professionals, businessmen and students (pursuing graduation and post graduation). Consumers were selected for the study through judgemental sampling. A structured questionnaire with non disguised questions was administered to the respondents. The questions based on likert scale were designed to measure the impact of the social, cultural and economic factors in the consumers' evaluation of an FMCG brand and their impact on the consumers' brand perception.

t-test was used to figure out if the impact of the factors vary across the genders and ANOVA was used to establish how the impact of the different types of factors vary across consumers from different ages and occupational backgrounds.

DATA ANALYSIS & DISCUSSION

Impact Of Social, Cultural & Economic Factors On Consumer's Brand Perception

To understand which factors the consumers deem important to categorise a brand as a good brand and to find out on which parameters consumers base their evaluation of brands, consumers were asked to rate how importance certain parameters would be in a brand to enable him to rate the brand as a good brand. Six parameters were taken in all. Two of the parameters are culture related parameters, two of the parameters are related to the social factor and two parameters are related to the economic factors.

The parameters which relate to the cultural factor are: 'The brand's conformance to the consumer's culture and tradition' and 'Brands reflecting Indian Values'. The parameters related to the social factor are: 'The brand being closely related and associated with local life and people' and 'The brand's conformance to the consumer's lifestyle'. The parameters related to the economic factor are: 'The brand being friendly to the pocket' (Despite being affordable, the price of some brands may be on the higher side) and 'The Brand being affordable' (Price of brand should not be out of reach of the consumer).

The frequency table (See Table 3.1) reveals that a larger number of respondents deemed the 'affordability' factor and the brand being 'pocket friendly' as either essential or very essential in their evaluation of a brand and its categorisation as a good brand. Largest number of the respondents (57.6 %) considered the 'affordability' factor as being very essential for a good brand of Fast Moving Consumer Good. Many of the respondents also considered the 'conformance of the brand to their lifestyle' as being very essential for a good brand.

Table 3.1: Parameters Considered Essential by the Consumer in Evaluating a Brand

	Absolutely Unessential	Somewhat Unessential	Somewhat Essential	Very Essential
The brand should conform to your culture & tradition	6.0	21.6	35.6	36.8
The brand should reflect Indian values	6.4	24.0	41.6	28.0
Brand should be closely related to the life of the local people	10.8	22.0	30.4	36.8
The brand should conform to your lifestyle	7.2	14.4	24.0	54.4
The brand should be friendly to the pocket	4.4	13.6	28.4	53.6
The brand should be affordable	6.4	8.8	27.2	57.6

To get a clear picture of the extent up to which the cultural, social and economic factors in totality vary in the importance attached to them by consumers of different sexes, different occupations and different ages while evaluating the brands, the response obtained from the respondents were re-coded. The scale parameters 'Absolutely Unessential' and 'Somewhat Unessential' were grouped together and coded as 'Unessential'. The scale parameters 'Somewhat essential' and 'Essential' were grouped together and coded as 'Essential'. Thus the responses were divided into two categories 'Essential' and 'Unessential'. The six variables were then grouped into three new variables. The variables 'Brand's conformance to the consumer's culture & tradition' and 'Brands reflecting Indian Values' were grouped together into a new variable 'Culturally Relevant Factor'. The variables 'Brand being closely related to local life' and 'Brand's conformance to the consumer's lifestyle' were grouped together to form a new variable 'Socially Relevant Factor' and the variables 'Brand being pocket friendly' and 'Brand being affordable' were grouped together into the new variable 'Economically Relevant Factor'.

Analysis shows that though all the factors ie, Cultural, Social and Economic factors are considered by the consumers to be playing an important role in the evaluation of a brand, Economic factor emerges out as the most important factor, considered essential by the largest percentage of respondents (92.4%) followed by Social factor which is considered essential by 91.6 % of the respondents. Relatively lesser percentage of respondents (82.8%) considers cultural factors to be essential in the evaluation of FMCG brands (See Table 3.2).

Table 3.2: Essential Factors in Evaluating a Brand

Factors/Relevance in Brand Evaluation	Not Essential	Essential
Cultural Factor	17.2	82.8
Social Factor	8.4	91.6
Economic Factor	7.6	92.4

Thus the economical factor emerges as the most important factor in the consumers' evaluation of a Fast Moving Consumer Good brand.

To ascertain if the importance attached to these factors for brand evaluation changes with the gender of the consumer, t-test was conducted (See Table 3.3). In the table the p value for the variable 'conformance of the brand with the consumer's culture & tradition' appears as 0.000 which is

much less than 0.05. The results of the t-test indicate that there is no gender based difference in the importance attached to any of the parameters used by the respondents in evaluating the brands

Table 3.3: Independent Sample T-Test

		Levene's Test for Equality of Variances		t-test for Equality of Means		
		F	Sig.	t	df	Sig. (2-tailed)
The brand should conform to your culture & tradition	Equal variances assumed	1.106	.294	3.841	248	.000
The brand should reflect Indian values	Equal variances assumed	2.843	.093	.419	248	.676
Brand should be closely related to the life of the local people	Equal variances assumed	1.178	.279	-1.079	248	.282
The brand should conform to your lifestyle	Equal variances assumed	2.954	.087	-1.259	248	.209
The brand should be friendly to the pocket	Equal variances assumed	.029	.865	-1.053	248	.293
The brand should be affordable	Equal variances assumed	.395	.530	.070	248	.944

except that attached to the parameter 'conformance of the brand with the consumer's culture & tradition'.

A look at the frequency table reveals that most of the males attach a higher importance to this parameter than the females (See Table 3.4). 44.6 % of the male respondents consider this to be a very essential virtue of a good brand as compared to just 23.7 percent of their female counterparts.

Table 3.4: Gender wise Comparison of the Importance attached to 'Brand's Conformance to Consumer Culture & Tradition' in Brand Evaluation

	Gender	Absolutely Unessential	Somewhat Unessential	Somewhat Essential	Very Essential
Brand's conformance to consumer culture & tradition	Male	3.2%	18.5%	33.8%	44.6%
	Female	10.8%	26.9%	38.7%	23.7%

To check whether the importance attached to the various cultural, social and economic parameters while evaluating a brand changes with the occupation of the consumer, ANOVA was applied. As shown in Table 3.5, the homogeneity of variance condition was not satisfied for the variables 'Conformance of the brand with the consumer's culture and tradition' and 'Pocket friendliness of the brand'. So for these two variables, Robust test of equality of means (Welch test and Brown Forsythe test) was used.

Table 3.5: Test of Homogeneity of Variances

	Levene Statistic	df1	df2	Sig.
The brand should conform to your culture & tradition	7.050	4	245	.000
The brand should reflect Indian values	.799	4	245	.527
Brand should be closely related to the life of the local	1.381	4	245	.241
The brand should conform to your lifestyle	.895	4	245	.468
The brand should be friendly to the pocket	2.632	4	245	.035
The brand should be affordable	.638	4	245	.636

The results of ANOVA in Table 3.6 show that p value for the variable 'the brand should conform to the consumer's lifestyle' is 0.041 (less than 0.05). It indicates that the importance given to the parameter 'conformance of the brand with the consumer's lifestyle' changes with the occupation of the respondent. Similarly, the Welch Test and Brown Forsythe Test for Robust Test of equality of means show that the p value for the variable 'Brand's conformance with the consumer's culture & tradition' is less than 0.05 indicating that the importance attached to this parameter in evaluating a brand changes with the consumer's occupation (See Table 3.7).

Table 3.6: ANOVA

		Sum of Squares	Df	Mean Square	F	Sig.
The brand should reflect Indian values	Between Groups	3.844	4	.961	1.251	.290
	Within Groups	188.220	245	.768		
	Total	192.064	249			
Brand should be closely related to the life of the local people	Between Groups	3.246	4	.811	.793	.531
	Within Groups	250.598	245	1.023		
	Total	253.844	249			
The brand should conform to your lifestyle	Between Groups	9.037	4	2.259	2.532	.041
	Within Groups	218.579	245	.892		
	Total	227.616	249			
The brand should be affordable	Between Groups	2.307	4	.577	.724	.576
	Within Groups	195.293	245	.797		
	Total	197.600	249			

Table 3.7: Robust Tests of Equality of Means

		Statistic[a]	df1	df2	Sig.
The brand should conform to your culture & tradition	Welch	2.874	4	72.644	.029
	Brown-Forsythe	3.331	4	140.842	.012
The brand should reflect Indian values	Welch	1.186	4	73.240	.324
	Brown-Forsythe	1.220	4	144.226	.305
Brand should be closely related to the life of the local people	Welch	.742	4	76.386	.566
	Brown-Forsythe	.839	4	173.216	.502
The brand should conform to your lifestyle	Welch	2.343	4	73.867	.063
	Brown-Forsythe	2.536	4	150.415	.043
The brand should be friendly to the pocket	Welch	1.142	4	74.660	.344
	Brown-Forsythe	1.152	4	147.718	.335
The brand should be affordable	Welch	.814	4	77.773	.520
	Brown-Forsythe	.797	4	186.345	.528

a. Asymptotically F distributed.

The Post Hoc test points out that housewives attribute a higher average importance to the 'conformance of the brand with the consumer's lifestyle' whereas businessmen attribute a lesser importance to this parameter while evaluating a brand (See Table 3.8).

Table 3.8: Post Hoc Test for 'The brand's conformance with the consumer's lifestyle

| | Occupation of Respondent | N | Subset for alpha = 0.05 | |
			1	2
Tukey HSD[a]	Business	28	2.86	
	Education	53	3.09	3.09
	Working Professionals	71	3.34	3.34
	Student	81	3.36	3.36
	Housewife	17		3.59
	Sig.		.168	.179
Waller-Duncan[a]	Business	28	2.86	
	Education	53	3.09	3.09
	Working Professionals	71	3.34	3.34
	Student	81	3.36	3.36
	Housewife	17		3.59

Table 3.8: Post Hoc Test for 'The brand's conformance with the consumer's lifestyle

	Occupation of Respondent	N	Subset for alpha = 0.05	
			1	2
Tukey HSD[a]	Business	28	2.86	
	Education	53	3.09	3.09
	Working Professionals	71	3.34	3.34
	Student	81	3.36	3.36
	Housewife	17		3.59
	Sig.		.168	.179
Waller-Duncan[a]	Business	28	2.86	
	Education	53	3.09	3.09
	Working Professionals	71	3.34	3.34
	Student	81	3.36	3.36
	Housewife	17		3.59

Means for groups in homogeneous subsets are displayed.

The Post Hoc Test also shows that the importance attached to the parameter 'Brand's conformance to the consumer's culture & tradition' is significantly different in case of students and Education professionals. The average importance attached to this parameter while evaluating a brand is more in case of students and relatively much less in case of people working in the education sector (See Table 3.9)

Table 3.9: Post Hoc Test for 'The conformance of the brand to the consumer's culture & tradition

	Occupation of Respondent	N	Subset for alpha = 0.05	
			1	2
Tukey HSD[a]	Education	53	2.66	
	Housewife	17	2.94	
	Business	28	3.00	
	Student	81	3.12	
	Working Professionals	71	3.24	
	Sig.		.050	
Waller-Duncan[a]	Education	53	2.66	
	Housewife	17	2.94	2.94
	Business	28	3.00	3.00
	Student	81	3.12	3.12
	Working Professionals	71		3.24

Means for groups in homogeneous subsets are displayed.

ANOVA was also applied to test if the importance attached to the different parameters while evaluating a brand, vary with the varying age groups of the consumers. Levene's test was used to check the homogeneity of variance and the homogeneity of variance condition was found to be fulfilled (See Table 3.10).

Table 3.10: Test of Homogeneity of Variances

	Levene Statistic	df1	df2	Sig.
The brand should conform to your culture & tradition	2.628	2	238	.074
The brand should reflect Indian values	.730	2	238	.483
Brand should be closely related to the life of the local people	.174	2	238	.840
The brand should conform to your lifestyle	.282	2	238	.754
The brand should be friendly to the pocket	1.373	2	238	.255
The brand should be affordable	.322	2	238	.725

The results of ANOVA show that the p value for all the variable is more than 0.05, indicating that the degree of importance attached to none of the parameters changes with the age group of the consumers (See Table 3.11).

Table 3.11: ANOVA

		Sum of Squares	df	Mean Square	F	Sig.
The brand should conform to your culture & tradition	Between Groups	.173	2	.087	.108	.898
	Within Groups	191.412	238	.804		
	Total	191.585	240			
The brand should reflect Indian values	Between Groups	.026	2	.013	.017	.983
	Within Groups	180.314	238	.758		
	Total	180.340	240			
Brand should be closely related to the life of the local people	Between Groups	1.338	2	.669	.658	.519
	Within Groups	242.164	238	1.017		
	Total	243.502	240			
The brand should conform to your lifestyle	Between Groups	2.826	2	1.413	1.545	.216
	Within Groups	217.705	238	.915		
	Total	220.531	240			
The brand should be friendly to the pocket	Between Groups	1.744	2	.872	1.159	.316
	Within Groups	179.011	238	.752		
	Total	180.755	240			
The brand should be affordable	Between Groups	1.620	2	.810	1.067	.346
	Within Groups	180.770	238	.760		
	Total	182.390	240			

FINDINGS

The study indicates that out of all the factors, the economic factors particularly the affordability factor of an FMCG brand plays an important role in positively influencing the consumers preference for the brand. The economic characteristics of a brand is considered as an important parameter by most of the consumer in evaluating brands of Fast Moving

Consumer Goods followed by the social characteristics like conformance of the brand to the lifestyle of the consumer. In general consumers purchasing FMCG brands in India are relatively less particular about the conformance of the brand to their culture and tradition. Cultural conformance of a brand is less frequently used as an evaluation criterion for an FMCG brand by the Indian consumer. However as compared to their female counterparts, males seem to attach a higher importance to the 'conformance of the brand with the consumer's culture & tradition'.

There are some distinctive differences in the way an FMCG brand is evaluated by consumers from different occupational backgrounds. Amongst all types of consumers, Housewives attribute a higher average importance to the 'conformance of the brand with the consumer's lifestyle' whereas businessmen attribute a much lesser importance to this parameter while evaluating a brand. Similarly the 'Brand's conformance to the consumer's culture & tradition' as an evaluation criterion has a greater significance for the students than other category of consumers.

Age of the consumer does not have any significant influence on the way the different factors are used for evaluating a brand and on the way these factors impact the consumers' brand perception.

IMPLICATIONS OF THE STUDY

While positioning FMCG brands in the Indian market, suitable emphasis on the economic characteristics of the brand would increase the chances of the brand being included in the consideration set of the consumer. When targeting a brand to the housewives the positioning strategy and the message strategy for marketing communication should highlight the 'economic benefit' and 'lifestyle conformance' characteristics of the brand.

****

REFERENCES

Bass, Frank M. and Talarzyk, W. Wayne (1972), 'An Attitude Model for the Study of Brand Preference', *Journal of Marketing Research,* Vol. IX (February), pp. 93-96.

Batra, Rajeev, and Olli, T. Ahtola (1990), 'Measuring the Hedonic and Utilitarian Sources of Consumer Attitudes', *Marketing Letters,* Vol. 2, No. 2, pp. 159-170.

Berger, Jonah, Dragansha, Michaela and Simonson Itamar (2006), 'The Influence of Product Variety on Brand Perception and Choice', Research Paper Series Stanford Graduate School of Business, May 2006.

Bushman, Brad J. (1993), 'What's in a Name? The Moderating Role of Public Self-Consciousness on the Relation Between Brand Label and Brand Preference', *Journal of Applied Psychology*, Vol. 78, No.5, pp. 857-861.

Erickson, Gary M., Johansson, Johny K., Chao, Paul (1984), 'Image Variables in Multi-Attribute Product Evaluations: Country-of-Origin Effects', Journal of Consumer Research, Vol. 11 (September), pp: 694-699.

Jamal, Ahmad and Goodke, Mark M.H. (2001), 'Consumers and Brands: A Study of the Impact of Self Image Congruence on Brand Preference and Satisfaction', *Marketing Intelligence and Planning*, Vol. 19, Issue 7, pp. 482-492

Koubaa, Yamen (2008), 'Country of Origin, Brand Image Perception, and Brand Image Structure', Asia Pacific Journal of Marketing and Logistics, Vol. 20, Issue 2, pp.139 – 155.

Lawent, Gilles and Kapferer, Jean Noel (1985), 'Measuring Consumer Involvement Profiles', *Journal of Marketing Research*, Vol. XXII (February), pp. 41-53.

Park, C. Whan, Bernard, J. Jaworski, and Deborah, J. MacInnis (1986), 'Strategic Brand Concept-Image Management', *The Journal of Marketing*, Vol. 50, No. 4 (October), pp. 135-145.

Ross, Ivan (1971), 'Self Concept and Brand Preference', *The Journal of Business*, Vol. 44, No. 1 (January), pp. 38-50.

Roth. Martin S. (1995), 'The Effects of Culture and Socioeconomics on the Performance of Global Brand Image Strategies', *Journal of Marketing Research*, Vol. XXXII (May), pp. 163-175.

Treacy, Michael and Wiersema, Fred (1993), 'Customer Intimacy and Other Value Disciplines', *Harvard Business Review*, (January-February), pp. 84-93.

Tse, Alan Ching Biu (1999), 'Factors Affecting Consumer Perceptions on Product Safety', *European Journal of Marketing*, Vol. 33, Issue 9/10, pp. 911-925.

Verlegh, Peeter W.J and Steenkamp, Jan-Benedict E.M. (1999), 'A Review and Meta Analysis of Country of Origin Research', *Journal of Economic Psychology* (20), pp:521-546.

Wanke, Michaela, Herrmann, Andreas and Schaffner, Dorothea (2007), 'Brand Name Influence on Brand Perception', *Psychology and Marketing*, Vol. 24, Issue 1 (January), pp. 1-24.

Voss, Kevin E, Eric, R. Spangenberg, and Bianca, Grohmann (2003), 'Measuring the Hedonic and Utilitarian Dimensions of Consumer Attitude', *Journal of Marketing Research*, Vol. 40, No. 3 (August), pp. 310-320.

CHAPTER 4

A STUDY OF THE INFLUENCE OF BRAND ATTRIBUTES ON CONSUMERS' PREFERENCE OF FMCG BRANDS IN INDIA

ABSTRACT

A consumer's preference for a brand is influenced by a complicated mix of several factors and determinants like the demographic and socioeconomic characteristics of the target market, the lifestyle of the consumer, characteristics of the brands available in the market, level of technological development in the market, nature of competitors and purchase motive of the consumer. Besides several other factors that influence the consumer's brand preference, the product related factors and the brand attributes also play a significant role in shaping the consumer's attitude towards the brand and his preference for the brand. Identifying those brand attributes that form an important part of the consumer's evaluation criteria for a brand and those that favourably influence his brand preference helps a marketer in inculcating those attributes into his brand and leverage such attributes for effectively positioning the brand in a way that it forms a part of the consumer's consideration set. The paper makes an attempt to identify those brand attributes that significantly influence the consumer's preference of FMCG (Fast Moving Consumer Goods) brands in the Indian market. The paper also examines if the influence of brand attributes on consumer's preference of FMCG brands vary with the age, gender and occupation of the consumer. The empirical study has been conducted by analysing the response collected from consumers spread across five states of India. Findings indicate that the consumer's choice of an FMCG brand is most strongly influenced by the technology used in the product and the perceived quality of the brand.

Keywords: *Brand Attributes, Brand Positioning, Brand Preference, FMCG, Product Quality.*

INTRODUCTION

Brand Positioning aims at creating a distinctive and valued place for the brand in the mind of the consumer. The place that a brand occupies in the consumer's perceptual space is carefully created and etched out by company engineered communication strategies and marketing strategies. Though advertisement and marketing communication play a significant role in chalking out the image for a brand, there are a number of other factors that significantly influence the image and consumer perception of the brand (Park, et al, 1986).

Whether a brand forms a part of the consumer's consideration set or not also depends on a number of such factors. The characteristics of the brand and specific brand attributes are also some of the factors that influence the consumer's preference of a brand. Understanding the extent of influence of these factors helps the marketer in designing an appropriate offer for the consumer and in formulating effective brand positioning strategies.

Such effective brand positioning designed after a careful assessment of the factors influencing brand image formation and brand preference, goes a long way in ensuring sustainability and survival for the brand.

NEED/IMPORTANCE OF THE STUDY

Identification of the research gap that exists in the measurement of the influence of brand attributes on consumer preference of FMCG brands in the Indian market has prompted the research. An assessment of the dimensions and attributes of an FMCG brand that favourably influences the consumer's perception of the brand, would establish the possibility of leveraging these attributes and using them for effectively positioning an FMCG brand in India.

TYPES OF FACTORS AFFECTING BRAND POSITIONING

It is an arduous task to predict the brand preference of a consumer as the consumer's preference is influenced by a number of different factors. However, all the factors that influence the brand preference of a consumer can be broadly categorised into the following four categories:

4. Product Related Factors
5. Consumer Related Factors.
6. Competition (Competing brands) Related Factors and
7. Factors related to the brand characteristics and virtues of the company (Company Related Factors)

Corresponding to these factors, the four essentials to be considered while deciding the positioning concept of a brand and while formulating its positioning strategy are Product Class, Consumer Segmentation, Consumer Perception of the brand in relation to its competitors (which lead to perceptual mapping) and Brand Attributes (translated into and expressed as consumer benefits) (Subroto Sengupta, 1997).

OBJECTIVES OF THE STUDY

1. To study the influence of brand attributes on consumer's brand perception (of FMCG brands).
2. To find out if the influence of brand attributes on consumers' preference of FMCG brands vary with the gender of the consumer.
3. To identify how the influence of brand attributes on consumers' preference of FMCG brand vary with the occupational background of the consumer.
4. To study if the influence of brand attributes on consumers' preference of FMCG brand vary with the age of the consumer.

METHODOLOGY

The empirical study is based on the responses gathered from 250 consumers spread across five different states of India. The respondents included housewives, working professionals, businessmen and students (pursuing graduation and post graduation). Consumers were selected for the study through judgemental sampling. A structured questionnaire with non disguised questions was administered to the respondents. The questions based on Likert scale were designed to measure the impact of product related factors (brand characteristics) on the consumers' preference of an FMCG brand.

Student's t-test was used to figure out how the impact of the factors vary across the genders and ANOVA was used to understand if the impact of the different types of factors vary across consumers from different ages and occupational backgrounds.

DATA ANALYSIS & DISCUSSION

In product related factors, product quality/technology is the most influencing factors in affecting the consumers' preference of brands. As indicated in Table 4.1, consumers show the highest average preference (Mean: 5.28 & Mode: 6.0) for brands with improved quality.

Table 4.1: Consumers' Preference of Brand Attributes & Characteristics

	Brands with improved quality (Indicating better technology)	Brands that have some unique characteristics	Brands originating from India	Brands which have their origin in some foreign country	Brand sold only in India (Local Brands)	Brands also present in other parts of the world (global brands)
Mean	5.28	4.67	3.68	3.20	2.57	3.42
Mode	6	5	5	2	1	4

Table 4.2 shows that 56.7 percent of respondents have rated 'improved quality brands' (indicative of better technology) to be having the highest degree of influence on brand preference.

Table 4.2: Preference of Brands with improved quality

Degree of Preference	Lowest Preference	Next to lowest Preference	Fourth highest Preference	Third highest Preference	Next to highest Preference	Highest Preference
Frequency	3	5	10	28	60	144
Percent	1.2	2.0	4.0	11.2	24.0	57.6

Table 4.3 shows a comparison of the degree of influence of the various product related factors on the brand preference of the consumers.

Table 4.3: Degree of Influence of Product Related Factors on Consumers' Brand Preference

Product Related Factors / Degree of Preference (in percentage)	Lowest Preference	Next to lowest Preference	Fourth highest Preference	Third highest Preference	Next to highest Preference	Highest Preference
Brands with improved quality	1.2	2.0	4.0	11.2	24.0	57.6
Brands with some unique characteristics	2.4	4.0	12.8	16.8	32.8	31.2
Brands originating from India	6.8	20.8	20.0	15.2	24.0	13.2
Brands which have their origin in some foreign country	14.0	24.0	20.0	18.8	16.8	6.4
Brand sold only in India (Local Brands)	35.6	19.6	17.6	11.2	11.6	4.4
Brands also present in other parts of the world (global brands)	17.6	17.2	14.8	23.6	9.6	17.2

T-TEST TO JUDGE THE GENDER BASED DIFFERENCES IN THE FACTORS INFLUENCING BRAND PREFERENCE

To judge if the influence of the product related factors on the brand perception and brand preference of the consumers vary with the gender of the consumers, the independent sample t-test was applied (See Table 4.4). As the p value for all the factors is more than 0.05, it implies that there is no significant difference in the mean of the degree of influence of these factors on brand preference. Thus the statement that there is no difference in the mean of the degree of influence of the product related factors on brand preference in male and female respondents is accepted.

Therefore it can be concluded that the influence of the brand attributes on brand perception and preference do not vary with gender.

Table 4.4: Independent Sample T-Test to Judge the Gender Based Differences in the Factors Influencing Brand Preference

		Levene's Test for Equality of Variances		t-test for Equality of Means		
		F	Sig.	t	df	Sig. (2-tailed)
Brands with improved quality	Equal variances assumed	.001	.979	-1.633	248	.104
Brands that have some unique characteristics	Equal variances not assumed	4.842	.029	-1.424	210.250	.156
Brands originating from India	Equal variances assumed	.040	.841	1.430	248	.154
Brands which have their origin in some foreign country	Equal variances assumed	.622	.431	.020	248	.984
Brand sold only in India (Local Brands)	Equal variances assumed	.235	.629	-.267	248	.790
Brands also present in other parts of the world (global brands)	Equal variances assumed	1.864	.173	-1.542	248	.124

ANOVA TO JUDGE WHETHER THE INFLUENCE OF THE PRODUCT RELATED FACTORS ON BRAND PREFERENCE VARY WITH OCCUPATION

To test if there is any difference in the influence of product related factors on brand perception and preference amongst the consumers of different occupations, One Way ANOVA was applied.

Homogeneity of Variance in all the occupational categories was checked using Levene Statistics (See Table 4.5). For all the factors except for 'Brands with improved quality' and for 'Brands that have some unique characteristics', no difference in variances was found in the various occupational categories (the homogeneity of variance condition was fulfilled).

Table 4.5: Test of Homogeneity of Variances

	Levene Statistic	df1	df2	Sig.
Brands with improved quality	5.123	4	245	.001
Brands that have some unique characteristics	4.632	4	245	.001
Brands originating from India	.572	4	245	.683
Brands which have their origin in some foreign country	1.482	4	245	.208
Brand sold only in India (Local Brands)	.701	4	245	.592
Brands also present in other parts of the world (global brands)	.210	4	245	.933

Thus the difference in the influence of these factors on consumers from different occupation can be judged through ANOVA (See Table 4.6).

Table 4.6: ANOVA (To Compare the Mean of Influence of Factors on Consumers of Different Occupations)

		Sum of Squares	df	Mean Square	F	Sig.
Brands originating from India	Between Groups	30.571	4	7.643	3.420	.010
	Within Groups	547.465	245	2.235		
	Total	578.036	249			
Brands which have their origin in some foreign country	Between Groups	5.558	4	1.390	.626	.644
	Within Groups	543.838	245	2.220		
	Total	549.396	249			
Brand sold only in India (Local Brands)	Between Groups	9.709	4	2.427	1.005	.405
	Within Groups	591.635	245	2.415		
	Total	601.344	249			
Brands also present in other parts of the world (global brands)	Between Groups	17.424	4	4.356	1.526	.195
	Within Groups	699.476	245	2.855		
	Total	716.900	249			

To judge whether the factors 'Brands with improved Quality' and 'Brands that have some unique characteristics' have varying influences on the consumers from different occupational backgrounds, Welch statistic (for Robust Test of Equality of Means) was applied (See Table 4.7).

Table 4.7: Robust Tests of Equality of Means (Welch Test)

	Statistic[a]	df1	df2	Sig.
Brands with improved quality	8.937	4	96.601	.000
Brands that have some unique characteristics	1.165	4	82.728	.332
Brands originating from India	3.313	4	73.571	.015
Brands which have their origin in some foreign country	.632	4	75.789	.641
Brand sold only in India (Local Brands)	.897	4	73.340	.470
Brands also present in other parts of the world (global brands)	1.395	4	73.244	.244

a. Asymptotically F distributed.

Table 4.6 indicates that the F value for 'Brands originating from India' is 3.420 and the p value is 0.010. As the p value is less than 0.05, it implies that there is a significant difference in the preference of 'Indian origin brands' amongst the consumers from different occupations. In other words the influence of 'Indian Origin Brands' on brand preference is significantly different amongst consumers from different occupational backgrounds.

Similarly, Table 4.7 indicates that the F value for 'Brands with improved quality' is 8.937 and the p value is 0.000. As the p value is much less than 0.05, it implies that there is a highly significant difference in the preference of 'Brands with improved quality' amongst the consumers from different occupations. In other words the influence of 'Improved Technology and Improved Quality' factor on brand preference is significantly different amongst consumers from different occupational backgrounds.

Post Hoc test was conducted to check in which of the category of respondents the mean of these factors significantly varied. It was found that the influence of the 'brands originating from India' on the brand preference of housewives was significantly different from that of businessmen (See Table 4.8). The influence of the 'Indian origin of brand' on brand preference is significantly higher in case of businessmen.

Similarly, it was found that the influence of the 'brands with improved quality' on the brand preference of housewives was significantly different from that of students as well as that of those in the Education profession (See Table 4.9). The influence of 'brands with improved quality' on brand preference is significantly higher in case of housewives.

Table 4.8: Post Hoc Test for Brands originating from India

Occupation of Respondent		N	Subset for alpha = 0.05	
			1	2
Tukey HSD[a]	Housewife	17	3.24	
	Student	81	3.27	
	Education	53	3.79	
	Working Professionals	71	4.01	
	Business	28	4.11	
	Sig.		.102	
Waller-Duncan[a]	Housewife	17	3.24	
	Student	81	3.27	3.27
	Education	53	3.79	3.79
	Working Professionals	71	4.01	4.01
	Business	28		4.11

Means for groups in homogeneous subsets are displayed.

Table 4.9: Post Hoc Test for Brands with improved quality

| | Occupation of Respondent | N | Subset for alpha = 0.05 | |
			1	2
Tukey HSD[a]	Student	81	5.17	
	Education	53	5.21	5.21
	Working Professionals	71	5.28	5.28
	Business	28	5.32	5.32
	Housewife	17		5.88
	Sig.		.977	.061
Waller-Duncan[a]	Student	81	5.17	
	Education	53	5.21	
	Working Professionals	71	5.28	5.28
	Business	28	5.32	5.32
	Housewife	17		5.88

Means for groups in homogeneous subsets are displayed.

ANOVA TO JUDGE WHETHER THE INFLUENCE OF THE PRODUCT RELATED FACTORS ON BRAND PREFERENCE VARY WITH AGE

To test if there is any difference in the influence of product related factors on brand perception and preference amongst the consumers of different age groups, One Way ANOVA was applied.

Homogeneity of Variance in all the age groups was checked using Levene Statistics (See Table 4.10). For all the factors except for the factor 'Brands originating from India', no difference in variances was found in the various age categories (the homogeneity of variance condition was fulfilled).

Table 4.10: Test of Homogeneity of Variances

	Levene Statistic	df1	df2	Sig.
Brands with improved quality	.667	2	238	.514
Brands that have some unique characteristics	.620	2	238	.539
Brands originating from India	5.135	2	238	.007
Brands which have their origin in some foreign country	.447	2	238	.640
Brand sold only in India (Local Brands)	.500	2	238	.607
Brands also present in other parts of the world (global brands)	.477	2	238	.621

Thus the difference in the influence of all these factors on consumers of different ages can be judged through ANOVA (See Table 4.11).

Table 4.11: ANOVA (To Compare the Mean of Influence of Factors on Consumers of Different

		Sum of Squares	df	Mean Square	F	Sig.
Brands with improved quality	Between Groups	.498	2	.249	.215	.807
	Within Groups	275.428	238	1.157		
	Total	275.925	240			
Brands that have some unique characteristics	Between Groups	1.133	2	.566	.340	.712
	Within Groups	396.967	238	1.668		
	Total	398.100	240			
Brands originating from India	Between Groups	34.866	2	17.433	7.906	.000
	Within Groups	524.794	238	2.205		
	Total	559.660	240			
Brands which have their origin in some foreign country	Between Groups	3.129	2	1.564	.708	.494
	Within Groups	525.652	238	2.209		
	Total	528.780	240			
Brand sold only in India (Local Brands)	Between Groups	14.506	2	7.253	3.058	.049
	Within Groups	564.474	238	2.372		
	Total	578.979	240			
Brands also present in other parts of the world (global brands)	Between Groups	1.773	2	.887	.300	.741
	Within Groups	702.733	238	2.953		
	Total	704.506	240			

To judge whether the factors 'Brands originating from India' has varying influences on the consumers of different ages, Welch statistic (for Robust Test of Equality of Means) was applied (See Table 4.12).

Table 4.12: Robust Tests of Equality of Means (Welch Test)

	Statistic[a]	df1	df2	Sig.
Brands with improved quality	.297	2	22.716	.746
Brands that have some unique characteristics	.311	2	20.938	.736
Brands originating from India	14.365	2	24.903	.000
Brands which have their origin in some foreign country	.616	2	20.804	.550
Brand sold only in India (Local Brands)	2.786	2	20.988	.085
Brands also present in other parts of the world (global brands)	.310	2	21.291	.737

a. Asymptotically F distributed.

Table 4.11 indicates that the F value for 'Brands sold only in India' is 3.058 and the p value is 0.049. As the p value is less than 0.05, it implies that there is a significant difference in the preference of 'Local Brands' (Brands sold only in India) amongst the consumers of different age groups. In other words the influence of 'Local brands' on brand preference is significantly different amongst consumers of different ages.

Similarly, Table 4.12 indicates that the F value for 'Brands originating from India' is 14.365 and the p value is 0.000. As the p value is much less than 0.05, it implies that there is a highly significant difference in the preference of 'Brands originating from India' amongst the consumers of different ages. In other words the influence of 'Indian origin' factor on brand preference is significantly different amongst consumers of different age groups.

Post Hoc test was conducted to check in which of the category of respondents the mean of these factors significantly varied. It was found that the influence of the 'brands sold only in India' on the brand preference of respondents belonging to different age groups was not significantly different from each other (See Table 4.13).

Similarly, it was found that the influence of the 'brands originating from India' on the brand preference of consumers in the age group 16-35 was significantly different from that of consumers in the age group 56-75 (See Table 4.14). The influence of 'Indian origin brands' on brand preference is significantly higher in case of senior citizens and elderly people ie, consumers belonging to the age group 56-75 years.

Table 4.13: Post Hoc Test for Brands sold only in India (Local Brands)

	Age of Respolndent	N	Subset for alpha = 0.05
			1
Tukey HSD[a]	16 - 35	170	2.42
	36 - 55	62	2.87
	56 - 75	9	3.33
	Sig.		.119
Waller-Duncan[a]	16 - 35	170	2.42
	36 - 55	62	2.87
	56 - 75	9	3.33

Means for groups in homogeneous subsets are displayed.

Table 4.14: Post Hoc Test for Brands originating from

	Age of Respolndent	N	Subset for alpha = 0.05	
			1	2
Tukey HSD[a]	16 - 35	170	3.46	
	36 - 55	62	4.15	4.15
	56 - 75	9		4.89
	Sig.		.269	.215
Waller-Duncan[a]	16 - 35	170	3.46	
	36 - 55	62	4.15	4.15
	56 - 75	9		4.89

a. Uses Harmonic Mean Sample Size = 22.536.

FINDINGS

The most influential characteristics of a brand influencing the brand preference of consumers purchasing FMCG brands in the Indian market is the technology used in the brand and the resulting perceived superior quality of the brand. The study found that gender does not have a significant impact on the degree of influence of brand characteristics on the consumer's preference of a brand. Technology used in the product and the quality of the product is a factor considered most essential in the evaluation of an FMCG brand by consumers of both the sexes.

Businessmen in India seem to have a higher preference for 'Made in India' brands as compared to other consumers. Their preference of Indian origin brands is significantly different from the modern Indian housewife who has a relatively higher preference for a brand originating from a foreign country. Indian housewives also have a significantly higher preference for improved quality brands of Fast Moving Consumer Goods and brand perceived to be using superior technology.

It was also found that as compared to consumers in other age groups, senior citizens and elderly people belonging to the age group 56-75 years are more ethnocentric in their preference and prefer to use brands of Fast Moving Consumer Goods made in India.

IMPLICATIONS OF THE STUDY/CONCLUSION

Quality of the brand and technological superiority seems to be an important element that can be effectively used for differentiating an FMCG brand from its competitors. Leveraging the technological superiority, that favourably influences the consumer's perception and preference of a brand, can result in effective positioning for the brand in the perceptual space of the consumer. However, further research needs to be conducted to establish on what parameters, the Indian consumer assesses the quality and technological superiority of an FMCG brand.

****

REFERENCES

Bass, Frank M. and Talarzyk, W. Wayne (1972), "An Attitude Model for the Study of Brand Preference", *Journal of Marketing Research*, Vol. IX (February), pp. 93-96.

Batra, Rajeev and Olli T. Ahtola (1990), "Measuring the Hedonic and Utilitarian Sources of Consumer Attitudes", *Marketing Letters,* Vol. 2, No. 2, pp. 159-170.

Berger, Jonah, Dragansha, Michaela and Simonson, Itamar (2006), "The Influence of Product Variety on Brand Perception and Choice", *Research Paper Series Stanford Graduate School of Business* (May), pp.2-20.

Bushman, Brad J. (1993), "What's in a Name? The Moderating Role of Public Self-Consciousness on the Relation Between Brand Label and Brand Preference", *Journal of Applied Psychology*, Vol. 78, No.5, pp. 857-861.

Erickson, Gary M, Johansson, Johny K, Chao, Paul (1984), "Image Variables in Multi-Attribute Product Evaluations: Country-of-Origin Effects", *Journal of Consumer Research*, Vol. 11, (September), pp: 694-699.

Jamal, Ahmad, Goodke, Mark M.H. (2001), "Consumers and Brands: A Study of the Impact of Self Image Congruence on Brand Preference and Satisfaction", *Marketing Intelligence and Planning*, Vol. 19, No. 7, pp. 482-492.

Koubaa, Yamen (2008), "Country of Origin, Brand Image Perception, and Brand Image Structure", *Asia Pacific Journal of Marketing and Logistics*, Vol. 20, No. 2, pp.139 – 155.

Lawent, Gilles and Kapferer, Jean Noel (1985), "Measuring Consumer Involvement Profiles", *Journal of Marketing Research*, Vol. XXII (February), pp. 41-53.

Park, C. Whan, Bernard, J. Jaworski and Deborah J. MacInnis (1986), "Strategic Brand Concept-Image Management", *The Journal of Marketing*, Vol. 50, No. 4 (October), pp. 135-145.

Park, C. Whan, Jaworski, J. and MacInnis, Deborah J. (1986), "Strategic Brand Concept-Image Management", *Journal of Marketing*, Vol. 50 (October), pp. 135-145.

Ross, Ivan (1971), "Self Concept and Brand Preference", *The Journal of Business*, Vol. 44, No. 1 (January), pp. 38-50.

Roth, Martin S. (1995), "The Effects of Culture and Socioeconomics on the Performance of Global Brand Image Strategies", *Journal of Marketing Research*, Vol. XXXII (May), pp. 163-175.

Sengupta, Subroto (1997), *"Brand Positioning Strategies for Competitive Advantage"*, Tata McGraw-Hill Publishing Company Ltd., New Delhi.

Strebinger, Andreas (2002), "B.A.S.E.- A Brand Architecture Strategy Explorer", *International Business & Economics Research Journal*, Vol. 1, No. 11, pp. 115-124.

Treacy, Michael and Wiersema (1993), "Three Paths to Market Leadership- Customer Intimacy and Other Value Disciplines", *Harvard Business Review*, January-February 1993, pp. 84-93.

Tse, Alan Ching Biu (1999), "Factors Affecting Consumer Perceptions on Product Safety", *European Journal of Marketing*, Vol. 33, No. 9/10, pp. 911-925.

Verlegh, Peeter W.J, Steenkamp, Jan-Benedict E.M. (1999), "A Review and Meta Analysis of Country of Origin Research", *Journal of Economic Psychology, Vol.* 20, pp. 521-546.

Wanke, Michaela, Herrmann, Andreas and Schaffner, Dorothea (2007), "Brand Name Influence on Brand Perception", *Psychology and Marketing*, Vol. 24, No. 1 (January), pp. 1-24.

CHAPTER 5

INFLUENCE OF SELECTED PSYCHOGRAPHIC FACTORS ON CONSUMERS' PREFERENCE OF FMCG BRANDS

ABSTRACT

Human behaviour is complex and is dependent on a number of factors and variables like the situation to which he is subjected to, the environment in which he lived and in which he has grown, his experience with life, the education and teachings he has received and the values and beliefs that has been inculcated in him by his parents, family and the society. Like human behaviour in general, the purchase behaviour and consumption behaviour of an individual is also a function of a myriad of factors.

It is a known fact that as we move from one region to another, there is a change in the purchase pattern and consumption behaviour of the people. An important reason behind this change may be the difference in the culture, values and beliefs of the people across the regions. Moreover, people living even in the same geographical area may exhibit a difference in purchase preference based on their lifestyle.

The paper undertakes to address the inquisitiveness regarding the extent of influence of values, faith, religion and lifestyle on the Indian consumers' preference of FMCG brands.

Keywords: *Brand Positioning, Brand Preference, FMCG, Psychographic Factors, Lifestyle, Values, Faith, Belief, Culture.*

INTRODUCTION

Brand Positioning is all about creating a distinctive place for the brand in the minds of the consumers. The consumer's mind and the competing brands constitute the frame of reference for positioning a brand. As numerous factors are at play within the consumer's mind that influence the consumer's choice of brands, his perception of various brands and his preference for some specific brands, it is always in the interest of the brand manager to properly understand the influence of various factors on the consumer's perception and preference of brands.

Like human behaviour in general, the purchase behaviour of an individual is also dependent on a myriad of factors. It is a known fact that as we move from one region to another, there is a change in the purchase pattern and consumption behaviour of the people. An important reason behind this change may be the difference in the culture, values and beliefs of the people across the regions. Moreover, people living even in the same geographical area may exhibit a difference in purchase preference based on their lifestyle.

LITERATURE REVIEW

A number of factors may influence the consumers' buying behaviour and their brand preference. Amongst the several factors that influence the consumers' buying behaviour and preference of goods, services and brands are the cultural factors, social class, values and beliefs, lifestyle and personality. These factors are jointly referred to as the psychographic factors (Kotler, 1996). The Values and Lifestyle (VALS) typography developed at SRI International by Mitchell, 1983 has been used as a base for segmentation by several companies and researchers. Similarly the List of Values (LOV) construct has been put forward as an important psychographic base for developing marketing strategies (Kahle & Kennedy, 1989).

It has been established that the differential value orientation leads to variations in preferences for products and brands (Vinson, et al, 1977). Though brand preference is not directly influenced by the consumer's value structure, the importance given to choice criteria for brands has been found to depend on the value structure of the consumer (Pitts & Woodside, 1983). A study conducted in China and Korea found that self directed values had a greater impact as compared to social affiliation values on the consumer's decision of the needs to be satisfied and his choice of brands (Kim, et al, 2002). Another study conducted in the Chinese market showed that the lifestyle of the consumer has a significant influence on his perception of advertising, buying behaviour and consumption preferences (Wei, 1997). The degree of psychological involvement of a consumer in a product category also influences his decision making process and his response to the products and brands in the category (Lawent, et al, 1985).

With increased globalization, increased affluence and enhanced education, people across the world have become more aware and sensitized towards their history and civilization and hence accord greater relevance towards their civilizational identity. Thus there is an increased influence of their culture and tradition on the consumers' brand preference and brand choice (Mooig, 2010). Even taste of food is an expression of cultural capital and the preference of food taste and the consumption of food by an individual is strongly influenced by his culture (Wright, et al, 2001). As brand's relation to the national culture of a market has significant influence on the perception of the brand in that market, National culture should be taken as an important factor in designing the brand image strategies of the company (Roth, 1995). Also adherence to a particular religious faith and religious value system significantly influences the purchase decisions and shopping behaviours of the consumers (Esso, et al, 2004).

A study conducted in the Indian market concluded that while preparing brandiing strategies for the Indian market, it is immensely important that the brand manager takes into consideration the Indian culture and value dimension (Banerjee, 2008). In order to target the rural markets in India, the key elements of rural marketing strategy are culture, lifestyle, standard of living, disposable income, consumption pattern and communication facilities (Rao, 2000).

A number of studies have indicated that influence of different psychographic factors on consumer decision making and the choice of products and brands and have talked about the use of these factors on segmentation variables. Studies have however not been conducted to compare the extent of influence of these factors on consumers' preference of brands. The present study undertakes to understand the comparative degree of influence of some selected psychographic factors on consumers' preference of FMCG brands and to study whether the influence varies with the gender, occupation and age of the consumers.

OBJECTIVES:

1. To study whether culture & tradition, values, faith & belief, religion or lifestyle influence a greater number of consumers in their preference of FMCG brands.
2. To understand if the influence of culture & tradition, values, faith & belief, religion and lifestyle vary with the gender of the consumer.
3. To find out if the influence of culture & tradition, values, faith & belief, religion and lifestyle vary with the occupation of the consumer.
4. To find out if the influence of culture & tradition, values, faith & belief, religion and lifestyle vary with the age of the consumer.

METHODOLOGY:

To study the influence of culture and tradition, values, faith and belief, religion and lifestyle on consumers' preference of FMCG brands, response was sought from two hundred fifty consumers from different age groups. Respondents were selected from five different states of the country using judgemental sampling. These respondents included housewives, working professionals, businessmen and students (pursuing graduation and post graduation). A structured questionnaire was administered to the respondents and whether the different values and lifestyle related factors influence consumers' preference of FMCG brands, was recorded using a close ended, multiple choice question (Yes, No, Can't Say).

Chi Square Test was used to judge if the influence of the various factors on consumers' preference of FMCG brands vary with the gender, occupation and age of the consumer.

INFLUENCE OF PSYCHOGRAPHIC FACTORS ON CONSUMERS' PREFERENCE OF FMCG BRANDS

While studying the influence of the selected psychographic factors on brand preference of the consumers, it was found that most of the consumers (78.4% of respondents) have a higher degree of preference for brands that conform to their lifestyle. An almost equal proportion of respondents (77.6%) also have a high degree of preference for such brands that conform to their value system (See Table 5.1).

Table 5.1: Influence of Selected Psychographic Factors on Brand

Consumer Related Factors	Responses (N)	Percent	Percent of Cases
Brands that conform to the consumer's value system	194	17.3%	77.6%
Brands that reflect the consumer's culture & tradition	136	12.1%	54.4%
Brands that conform to the consumer's faith & belief	160	14.3%	64.0%

Brands that conform to or reflect the virtues of the consumer's	97	8.6%	38.8%
Brands that conform to the consumer's lifestyle	196	17.5%	78.4%
Total	1122	100.0%	448.8%

Chi Square test has been used to ascertain if there is a relationship between the gender of the consumer and the degree of influence of the different psychographic factors on his/her brand perception. Table 5.2 shows that the chi square value for the association between the attributes 'Gender' and each of the selected factors is less than the table value of chi square (5.99) at level of significance 0.05 and degree of freedom 2 and the p value for each of the factors is more than 0.05, it indicates that there is a no association between the sex of the consumer and the impact of various psychographic factors on the consumers' brand preference.

Table 5.2: Association of Gender and the Influence of Selected Psychographic Factors on Brand Preference

Consumer Related Factors	Gender	Yes	No	Can't Say	d/f	Chi Square (p Value)
Brands that conform to the consumer's value system	Male	77.1%	9.6%	13.4%	2	.971 (.615)
	Female	78.5%	11.8%	9.7%		
Brands that reflect the consumer's culture & tradition	Male	53.5%	35.7%	10.8%	2	1.678[a] (.432)
	Female	55.9%	29.0%	15.1%		
Brands that conform to the consumer's faith & belief	Male	65.0%	20.4%	14.6%	2	.306[a] (.858)
	Female	62.4%	20.4%	17.2%		
Brands that conform to or reflect the virtues of	Male	43.3%	39.5%	17.2%	2	4.171[a] (.124)

the consumer's religion						
	Female	31.2%	44.1%	24.7%		
Brands that conform to the consumer's lifestyle	Male	74.5%	17.8%	7.6%	2	4.844a (.089)
	Female	84.9%	12.9%	2.2%		

To check if there is any association between the influence of psychographic factors on brand perception and the occupation of the consumer, Chi Square test has been used (See Table 5.3). The result of the Chi Square Test in Table 5.3 shows that the p value for the variable 'Brands that conform to consumer's faith & belief' is 0.030. The p value being less than 0.05 signifies that the occupation of the respondent has some relation with the degree of influence that 'Brands conforming to consumer's faith & belief' has on his brand preference. A look at the response of the consumers reveal that more than 70% of the students prefer such brands that conform to their faith and belief. Also close to 70% of the consumers in the education profession are influenced by this factor in their brand preference.

As evident from Table 5.3, another factor whose influence on the consumers' brand preference varies with the occupation of the consumer is the 'conformance of the brand with the consumer's lifestyle'. The p value for this variable (0.025) being less than 0.05 indicates a relationship between the consumer's occupation and the influence of this factor. More than 88% of housewives are influenced in their brand preference by this factor. Students are close followers with 87.7% of students indicating a preference for brands that conform to their lifestyle.

Table 5.3: Association of Occupation and the Influence of Selected Psychographic Factors on Brand

	Occupation	Yes	No	Can't Say	d/f	Chi Square (p Value)
Brands that conform to the consumer's value system	Professional	78.9%	7.0%	14.1%	8	5.387a (.716)
	Education	81.1%	11.3%	7.5%		
	Business	85.7%	7.1%	7.1%		
	Housewife	64.7%	17.6%	17.6%		
	Student	74.1%	12.3%	13.6%		
Brands that reflect the consumer's culture & tradition	Professional	47.9%	39.4%	12.7%	8	5.030a (.754)
	Education	54.7%	30.2%	15.1%		
	Business	46.4%	39.3%	14.3%		
	Housewife	58.8%	35.3%	5.9%		
	Student	61.7%	27.2%	11.1%		
Brands that conform to the consumer's faith & belief	Professional	59.2%	18.3%	22.5%	8	17.058a (.030)
	Education	69.8%	11.3%	18.9%		
	Business	50.0%	42.9%	7.1%		
	Housewife	58.8%	29.4%	11.8%		
	Student	70.4%	18.5%	11.1%		
Brands that conform to or reflect the virtues of the consumer's religion	Professional	36.6%	46.5%	16.9%	8	10.337a (.242)
	Education	32.1%	49.1%	18.9%		
	Business	53.6%	25.0%	21.4%		
	Housewife	47.1%	17.6%	35.3%		
	Student	38.3%	42.0%	19.8%		
Brands that conform to the consumer's lifestyle	Professional	78.9%	11.3%	9.9%	8	17.554a (.025)
	Education	69.8%	24.5%	5.7%		
	Business	60.7%	32.1%	7.1%		
	Housewife	88.2%	11.8%	.0%		
	Student	87.7%	9.9%	2.5%		

Table 5.4: Association of Age and the Influence of Selected Psychographic Factors on Brand Preference

	Age	Yes	No	Can't Say	d/f	Chi Square (p Value)
Brands that conform to the consumer's value system	16-35 Years	77.6%	10.6%	11.8%		
	36-55 Years	74.2%	11.3%	14.5%	4	.383[a] (.984)
	56-75 Years	77.8%	11.1%	11.1%		
Brands reflecting consumer culture & tradition	16-35 Years	52.9%	34.7%	12.4%		
	36-55 Years	54.8%	32.3%	12.9%	4	2.552a (.635)
	56-75 Years	77.8%	22.2%	.0%		
Brands that conform to the consumer's faith & belief	16-35 Years	61.8%	22.9%	15.3%		
	36-55 Years	62.9%	17.7%	19.4%	4	3.973a (.410)
	56-75 Years	88.9%	11.1%	.0%		
Brands that conform to or reflect the virtues of the consumer's religion	16-35 Years	36.5%	42.9%	20.6%		
	36-55 Years	45.2%	37.1%	17.7%	4	2.874[a] (.579)
	56-75 Years	22.2%	44.4%	33.3%		
Brands that conform to the consumer's lifestyle	16-35 Years	81.8%	14.1%	4.1%		
	36-55 Years	72.6%	16.1%	11.3%	4	7.317[a] (.120)
	56-75 Years	66.7%	33.3%	.0%		

Chi Square Test was also conducted to find our if the influence of the chosen psychographic factors on brand preference has some kind of relationship with the age group of the consumers (See Table 5.4). As shown in Table 5.4, the p value for none of the variables tested in the Chi

Square Test was less than 0.05. Thus the tested hypothesis that influence of none of the consumer related factor has a relationship with the age group of the consumer is accepted. The result indicates that all the studied factors have the same influence across all age groups.

FINDINGS

The study found that a vast majority of the consumers preferred those FMCG brands that conform to their value system and those that conform to their lifestyle. It was found that the brand preference of housewives was majorly influenced by their lifestyle. Similarly the brand preference of most of the students is influenced by their lifestyle followed by their faith and belief. Faith and belief also influence the brand preference of education professionals. The influence of the various factors on consumers' brand preference was not found to vary with the age and gender of the consumer.

****

REFERENCES

Banerjee, Saikat (2008), "Dimensiions of Indian Culture, Core Cultural Values and Marketing Implications-An Analysis", *Cross Cultural Management: An International Journal*, Vol. XV, No. 4, pp. 367-378

Esso, Nitin & Dibb Sally (2004), "Religious Influence on Shopping Behaviour: An Exploratory Study", *Journal of Marketing Management*, Vol. XX, Issue 7-8, pp. 683-712

Kahle, Lynn R., Kennedy, Patricia (1989), "Using the List of Values (LOV) to Understand Consumers", Journal of Consumer Marketing, Vol. VI, Issue 3, pp. 5-12

Kim, Jai-OK, Forsyth, Sandra, Gu, Quingliang & Moon, Shook Jae (2002), "Cross Cultural consumer Values, Needs and Purchase Behaviour, *Journal of Consumer Marketing*, Vol XIX, Issue 6, pp. 481-502

Kotler, Philip (1996), *Marketing Management-Analysis, Planning, Implementation and Control*, 8th ed., PHI (New Delhi), pp. 173-188, 273-274

Lawent, Gilles and Kapferer, Jean Noel (1985), "Measuring Consumer Involvement Profiles", *Journal of Marketing Research*, Vol. XXII (February), pp. 41-53.

Mitchell, A. (1983), "The Nine American Lifestyles: Who Are We and Where Are We Going", New York: Warner Communications

Mooig, Maricke de (2010), *Consumer Behaviour and Culture: Consequences for Global Marketing and Advertising*, Ed. 2nd, Sage Publication Ltd (London)

Pitts, Robert E. & Woodside, Arch G. (1983), "Personal Value Influences on Consumer Product Class and Brand Preference", *The Journal of Social Psychology*, Vol. 119, Issue 1, pp. 37-53

Rao, S.L. (2000), "India's Rapidly Changing Consumer Markets", *Economic & Political Weekly*, Vol. XXXV, No. 4 (September 30-October 06), pp. 3570-3572

Roth, Martin S. (1995), "The Effects of Culture and Socioeconomics on the Performance of Global Brand Image Strategies", *Journal of Marketing Research*, Vol. XXXII (May), pp. 163-175.

Vinson, Donald E., Scott, Jerome E. & Lavont, Lawrence M. (1977), "The Role of Personal Values in Marketing and Consumer Behaviour, *Journal of Marketing*, Vol. XLI, No. 2 (April), pp. 44-50

Wei, Ran (1997), "Emergiing Lifestyles in China and Consequences for Perception of Advertising, Buying Behaviour and Consumption Preferences", *International Journal of Advertising*, Vol. XVI, Issue 4 (November), pp. 261-275

Wright, Lee Tiu, Nancarrow, Clive, Kwok, Pamela M.H. (2001), "Food Taste Preference and Cultural Influences on Consumption, *British Food Journal*, Vol. 103, No. 5, pp. 348-357

CHAPTER 6

USE OF COMMUNICATION ELEMENTS BY MULTINATIONAL COMPANIES FOR POSITIONING THEIR FMCG BRANDS IN THE INDIAN MARKET

ABSTRACT

Brand positioning involves communicating the brand identity to the consumer so as to create a desired and distinctive image about the brand in his mind. Communicating this identity requires the use of certain communication elements that conform to the brand concept.

The paper attempts to identify the use of these communication elements, by MNCs, in positioning their FMCG brands in India. To understand the type of communication elements being used to position these FMCG brands, the advertisement copies of several brands were analysed for their content.

Functional elements of communication was found to be the most commonly used element for positioning a brand across all categories of FMCG products in the Indian market.

Keywords: MNCs, Brand Identity, Brand Image, Communication Elements, FMCG, Element of Brand Positioning

INTRODUCTION:

The differential effect that the brand knowledge has on the consumer's response to the marketing of the brand is known as Customer Based Brand Equity. Thus it can be stated that brand knowledge is the key to creating a Customer Based Brand Equity. A brand is said to be strong if it has strong brand equity. Marketing communication in general and advertisement in particular incessantly endeavour to strengthen the brand by creating strong customer based brand equity. For this the advertisements use various elements derived from the brand concept so as to effectively communicate the brand identity, create the right brand image and embed the right kind of brand knowledge into the minds of the customer.

LITERATURE REVIEW:

The strength of a brand can be measured in terms of its brand equity. According to Kevin Lane Keller "Customer Based Brand Equity is defined as the differential effect of brand knowledge on consumer response to the marketing of the brand." Thus the key element that affects brand equity is the brand knowledge which comprises of the two constituents brand awareness and brand image (Keller 1993). "Conveying a brand image to a target market is a fundamental marketing activity" and a fundamental responsibility of a brand manager. Research also suggests that a well communicated image helps establish a brand's position and insulate it from competition (Park et al, 1986). A brand image can be developed by properly understanding the brand concept. Thus the brand concept guides the brand positioning and the brand image. The three brand concepts that guide the brand positioning and brand image are functional, symbolic and experiential (Park et al, 1986). Besides these three concepts another brand concept is the emotional concept that finds its application in the marketing communication and image developing activity for a number of brands (Strebinger, 2002).

A detailed explanation of these brand concepts was given by Andreas Strebinger. According to the explanation given by him, functional brand concept is all about the utilitarian benefit of the product delivered through technical superiority, greater durability or reliability.Symbolic brand concepts "enable the buyer to express personality, values and status and help to improve self esteem and social self presentation". Experiential brand concept refers to the sensory experience with the brand, which involves the use of the five sense organs and builds up association of some kind with the five senses. "Experiential brand concepts aim to evoke hedonism and pleasure through a sensual product experience". The emotional brand concept is about emotions evoked by some generally accepted social values and emotional conditioning through music, pictures, nostalgic associations, etc.Strebinger pointed out that "Emotional brand concepts try to evoke an emotional attachment to the brand as well as to the community and to impart a sense of familiarity with the brand. While talking of the symbolic brand concept, a study by Chang is worth mentioning. The study found that advertisements depicting consumer culture did not have a significant influence on the response of the consumers towards the brand being advertised but a congruency between the values portrayed in the advertisements and the consumer's personal values significantly affected the consumer response (Chang, 2006).

Research indicates that eight categories of consumption objects can be identified in terms of the primary meanings that the consumers attach to different products (Fournier, 1991). The proposed categories are objects of utility, objects of action, objects of appreciation, objects of transition, objects of childhood, ritual enhancers, objects of personal identity and objects of position and role. A similarity is exhibited between the brand concepts and the proposed consumption objects based on product meaning. As found by Strebinger these brand concepts can be applied to most of the products and product categories.However certain product categories are inherently more suitable candidates for the use of some specific brand concepts. Another finding categorically points out that many brands do not use a 'pure' form of these brand concepts but a mixture or combination of more than one of these concepts (Strebinger Andreas, 2002).This finding is reinforced by the finding of another study that concludes that a brand can be positioned successfully as both a functional as well as a symbolic brand (Bhat & Reddy, 1998).

A brand's value proposition emerges from a combination of the elements of brand concept ie, functional, symbolic and experiential. The value proposition of the brand is a statement of the functional benefits, symbolic benefits (self expressive benefit) and emotional benefit delivered by the brand (Godeswar, 2008). According to Godeswar "Functional benefits are the most common basis for a value proposition, based on a product attribute that provides functional utility to the customer and relate directly to the functions performed by the product for the customer". This research on brand identity indicated that a brand identity based on the emotional element of the brand concept and on the self expressive benefit is able to establish a strong connect and relationship of the brand with the consumer (Godeswar, 2008). Research also indicates an emerging use of culture for developing brand identity and the emergence of the concept of cultural positioning whereby culture is used as an element of positioning and as a communication element to convey the brand identity. The three types of brand positioning based on culture have been identified as Local Consumer Culture Positioning (LCCP), Foreign Consumer Culture Positioning (FCCP) and Global Consumer Culture Positioning (GCCP) (Steenkamp et al, 1999).

One of the objectives of marketing communication is to influence the attitude of the consumer towards the brand and its consumption.Attitude of a consumer towards a brand and towards consumption besides being affected by other factors also depend on the consumer's motive of consumption. Research suggests that consumer motive is bi-dimensional implying that the motive of consumption may be utilitarian or hedonistic (Batra& Ahtola, 1990& Voss et al, 2003). "Hedonic consumption designates those facets of consumer behaviour that relate to the multisensory, fantasy and emotive aspects of one's experience with products". These multisensory experiences are not only afferent (eg. A product taste test) but also efferent (that interprets the external stimuli by associating it with some historic imagery or fantasy imagery) (Hirschman & Holbrook, 1982). Marketing literature further indicates that product categories that have a higher consumer involvement during the consumption process generate a hedonic response. Also stimuli that is more involving for the consumer result in a more intense and greater hedonic response from the consumers(Spangenberg et al, 1997). A combination of both utilitarian benefit and hedonistic benefit together shape the general attitude of the consumer towards the product or the brand (Ahtola, 1985).

It has been observed that the consumer oriented advertising in India have relatively few information cues and generate more of emotional associations than rational ones. The advertising themes use traditional Indian themes that generate local cultural associations (with the brand), themes with foreign association that generate foreign cultural association as well as themes that create association with hedonism, self esteem and individualism (Srivastava & Schoeebachler). The fact that the Indian consumer rates high on ethnocentricism yet has a higher esteem for the quality of foreign brand and the technology used in them (Kinra, 2006), point towards the requirement of using a brand concept and developing a brand identity that would appease this aspect of the Indian consumer's attitude.

Management literature clearly point out the impact of a well communicated brand image on brand positioning and focuses on the relationship between brand concept and brand identity. Studies also show that in the absence of conformance between brand concept, brand identity and brand image, positioning would be ineffective and brand gap would be created. However, no study has been conducted either to identify the elements of communication that can be used to communicate the brand image and establish the right kind of brand positioning, or to evaluate the effectiveness of various communication elements in positioning a brand. The identified research gap calls for a study on the use of communication elements in brand positioning. In other words, the study aims to identify the elements of brand positioning being used by the MNCs to position their FMCG brands in India, and to find out which type of communication element for positioning is preferred to be used by the MNCs dealing in FMCG in India.

CONCEPTUAL FRAMEWORK:

It is a pressing need for the marketer in general and the brand executive/manager in particular to understand how the right kind of brand knowledge can be embedded into the minds of the customer (through maketing communication, advertisement and company engineered stimuli).[1]

126

Brand knowledge can be thought of as consisting of two components: brand awareness and brand image. While brand awareness is the trace of the brand in memory, brand image refers to the consumer's perception about the brand, formed as a result of the brand associations held in the consumer's memory.

A proper understanding of the brand identity prism of the brand gives an idea to the brand manager regarding the brand associations that should be developed and strengthened. Kapferer's brand identity prism talks about the various facets of brand identity. As shown by Kapferer (2004), the different dimensions of brand identity represented as different facets of the brand identity prism are: brand physique, brand culture, reflection, self image and brand relations. Brand physique is the physical attribute and appearance of the brand or of the product that goes under the brand name. In the brand identity prism, brand personality refers to the characteristics of the brand that include the functional and non functional benefits of the brand. Some brands bring with them a certain culture; promise a certain cultural benefit and the satisfaction of being associated with the cultural value through the use of the brand. This is referred to as brand culture. A relationship exists between the brand and its user. The quality and strength of this relationship nourishes the brand. This emotional bonding offered by the brand and this relationship on which the brand gets rooted is referred to as the brand relation in the brand identity prism. Self image refers to how the user sees himself, the image that the user carries for himself. A brand stands to benefit if it glorifies the self image of its user and makes him feel good about himself. Reflection on the other hand refers to how the user of the brand would be seen or perceived by others and how the consumer thinks that the use of the brand would make him appear.

Brand associations may be developed through marketing communication in conformance with these facets of brand identity. Thus the elements used to communicate the positioning of the brand and to establish the desired brand associations have to have a relationship with the relevant facets of brand identity. To develop and strengthen these brand associations that are derived from the analysis of the facets of brand identity prism suitable elements of communication need to be identified and used. The different elements (derived from the brand concept and having relation to the brand identity) that can be used are:

1) The Physical Element: It talks about the physical attribute of the product and the physical features of the brand that differentiate it from the competitor's products and the competing brands. The physical element facilitates the development of the brand association that corresponds to the physique facet of the brand identity.

2) The Functional Element: It talks about the performance and performance efficiency of the product as well as the functional and utilitarian benefits offered by the brand to the consumer.

   This element proves to be instrumental in developing those brand associations in the consumer's memory that correspond to the personality facet of brand identity and the functional brand concept.

3) The Cultural Element: Culture of the consumer or a foreign culture admired by the consumer may be used to communicate the positioning of the brand. The cultural element talks about the cultural values with which the brand is associated and subtly or overtly exhibit the cultural benefit derived from the brand. The cultural element when used to communicate the positioning of the brand develops a brand association that corresponds to the brand culture facet of brand identity.

4) The Emotional Element: It includes the various emotions that may be used to communicate the positioning of the brand. Emotional element when used effectively in marketing communication develops emotional association with the brand. This type of association corresponds with the relation facet of brand identity.

5) The Hedonistic Element: The purpose of the use of hedonistic element in communication is to develop a feel good association with the brand. This type of association corresponds with the reflection and self image facet of brand identity.

These elements of communication shape up the brand associations (information nodes in consumer's memory) in the mind of the consumer and become instrumental in crafting the brand image in the consumer's mind space. These are the elements that are used to communicate the positioning of the brand to the consumer. These elements that find use in the advertisements and in marketing communication, become an important component and an underlying fabric of the brand positioning construct. These elements derived from the brand concept and used in marketing communication, are important elements that may influence the cognitive, conative and affective components of the consumer's attitude.

METHODOLOGY

To identify the communication elements for brand positioning being used by the multinational companies to position their FMCG brand in the Indian market, content analysis of the advertisements of various FMCG brands (from the stable of multinational companies) was conducted. Ten categories of FMCG products were selected for the study. The categories taken for the study were Oral Care Products, Toilet Soap, Detergent, Shampoo, Soft Drinks, Packaged Fruit Juice, Food & Beverage, Noodles, Chocolates and Cosmetics. For the analysis television commercials of these brands were collected from the internet. A total of 53 advertisement copies were analysed.

ANALYSIS OF ADVERTISEMENT CONTENT TO IDENTIFY THE ELEMENTS USED FOR COMMUNICATING BRAND IDENTITY AND BRAND POSITIONING OF FAST MOVING CONSUMER GOODS

BRAND	HIGHLIGHT/EXPLANATION	ELEMENT
ORAL CARE BRANDS		
Colgate Active Salt	The ad poses the question "Kya aapke toothpaste mein namak hai?" and associates the brand with the germicidal benefit of salt.	Physical & Emotional Element
Colgate	All the ad copies talk about the ability of the brand to effectively fight tooth decay. Dentists demonstrate the reason of tooth decay using a model of the teeth and propose Colgate as a solution.	Functional Element
Colgate Total	The ad emphasises on the ability of the product to fight twelve tooth related ailments.	Functional Element
Close Up	The ad promises the benefit of the confidence to get close and talks about a 'feel good' feeling because of fresh breath.	Hedonistic Element
TOILET SOAP		
Lifebuoy Care	The ad copies try to create an association of 'protection against germs' with the brand. The product is presented as being essential for the good	Functional Element

	health of infants and children.	
Lifebuoy Handwash	Presented as the 'fastest handwash' ie, fights germs fastest.	Functional Element
Lifebuoy (The ad featuring a small boy and a puppy)	The ad talks about all day protection from germs.	Functional Element
Liril	The ads create an imagery of fresh feeling that comes from bathing in a waterfall and presents the product as the original freshness soap. The imagery aims to create fantasy and hedonism.	Hedonistic Element
Pears	The ad exhibits the beautiful and loving relationship between a mother and a daughter. It associates the brand with the innocence of a child and presents the brand as one that is most suitable for soft skin. The advertisement calls the brand 'Masoom Pears'.	Emotional Element
Dettol	The ads highlight the association of the brand with health. It says "Jis ghar mein dettol rozana istemal hota hai, wahan log kam bimar padte hain". Punchline: Be 100% Sure.	Functional Element
Dove	The ads continually claim that one quarter moiisturiser in Dove keeps the skin soft and supple.	Functional Element
Lux	The advertisements always associate the brand with film stars and the fantasy of looking beautiful.	Hedonistic Element.
DETERGENT		
Tide	The ads talk about the whiteness benefit and associate the brand with whiteness.	Functional Element
Ariel	The ads talk about the benefit of being gentle on clothes and protecting them while cleaning.	Functional Element

Surf Excel	The marketing communication highlights the stain removing capability of the brand. Ads try to create an association with 'remover of stains' by saying 'Daag acche hain'.	Functional Element
Sunlight	The ads promise the benefit of protecting and maintaining the bright colours of the clothes.	Functional Element
SHAMPOO		
Sunsilk	The ads talk about the benefit of gorgeous, shiny hair and thick and long hair. The ad for 'Sunsilk black shine with UV protector' also talk about protecting the hair from the harmful effects of ultra violet rays.	Functional Element
Clinic Plus	The ads communicate and focus on the benefit of long hair.	Functional Element
Clear	Highlights the dandruff fighting efficiency	Functional Element
Pantene	The ads communicate the benefit of healthy and strong hair.	Functional Element
Head & Shoulder Anti Hairfall	The ad claims "Removes hairfall by 95%".	Functional Element
Garnier Fructis Long & Strong	The ads demonstrate the hair strengthening benefit of the shampoo through some unusual images of heavy loads being pulled by long hair strengthened by Garnier Fructis.	Functional Element
Garnier Shampoo+Oil 2 in 1	The ad copy communicates the content of the product and the resulting benefit by calling the product as "A bend of shampoo and oil for nourished healthy hair".	Physical & Functional Element
SOFT DRINKS		

Pepsi	No functional benefit promised or shown in marketing communication for the brand. The ads talk about the youthful attitude of the user and make the viewer relate himself to the young protagonist in the ad and thus make him feel young. Slogan: 'Yeh hai youngistan meri jaan' and 'Youngistan ka wow'.	Fun Element/ Hedonistic Element
Coca Cola	The ads don't promise any functional or emotional benefit but promises fun and happiness. Punchline: 'Coke khule to baat chale' and 'Coke opens happiness'.	Hedonistic Element
Limca	The imagery iin the ads, the visual stimuli and the audio stimuli that promises freshness aims to transform the viewers to a fantasy world. Punchline: 'Limca Dubo taazgi mein' and 'Fresh ho jao'	Hedonistic Element
Slice (Aamsutra Campaign)	The ads promise Pure mango pleasure. The marketing communication mentions "Slice Aamsutra: Pure mango pleasure".	Hedonistic Element
PACKAGED FRUIT JUICE		
Coca Cola Minute Maid Pulpy Orange	The ad talks about the presence of fruit pulp in the product and highlights the ingredients of the product.	Physical Element
Tropican 100%	The ads talk about the nutrition benefit and food value of the product.	Functional Element
FOOD & BEVERAGES		
Complan	The advertisements show that children who consume complain grow taller, faster.	Functional Element
Horlicks	The ads claim that Horlicks makes children 'Taller, Stronger, Sharper'	Functional Element
NOODLES		

Maggi	The ads talked about the health and taste benefit.	Functional Element
Maggi ('Me & My Maggi' Campaign)	The ads would involve the viewer and the consumer by inviting stories of their first experience with Maggi. The ads generate a nostalgic feeling.	Emotional & Hedonistic Element
Kellog's Chocos	The ad talks about the health and nutrition proposition of the brand and says 'Yeh whole grain hai jo de fibres, vitamins, minerals'.	Functional Element
Kellog's K	The ads communicate the benefit of reduced weight by following the regimen of 2 bowls, 2 means, 2 weeks.	Functional Element
Quaker Oats	The ads communicate the benefit of healthy heart and reduced cholesterol through the use of Quaker Oats.	Functional Element
CHOCOLATES		
Cadbury Classic Ad (Girl dancing in the cricket after a sixer by the batsman)	The ad highlights the happiness and enjoyment in the smaller things in life and associates the brand with this enjoyment. Punchline: 'Cadbury's Dairy Milk-Asli swad zindagi ka'.	Hedonistic Element
Cadbury (Another classic ad-'Asli swad zindagi ka' Campaign)	The ad showed a young couple out in a picnic spot. The young man while doing aerobatics on a bicycle, to impress his girl, breaks into a pen by mistake and finds himself being chased by the bull. The couple while seemingly enjoying the chase, escape on the bicycle. The jingle 'kya swad hai zinddagi mein' and the picturesque background establish the association of the brand Cadbury with 'Celebration of life'	Hedonistic Element
Cadbury (Kuch meetha ho jaye campaign)	The ad copies present Cadbury Dairy Milk as a substitute of 'mithai' (sweet meat) to be consumed during any celebration.	Cultural Element

Cadbury Celebration	The ad copies present Cadbury celebration as an ideal gift to be given to friends, relatives and near and dear ones during celebration of various festivals like diwali, raksha bandhan, etc. An association is established with these Indian festivals. The ads also show the warmth, bonding and celebration of relations, a part of the Indian culture.	Emotional & Cultural Element
Cadbury ('Khane ke baad khane mein kuch meetha ho jaye' campaign)	The ads show a typical Indian middle class family gathered around the dining table during dinner and Cadbury dairy milk being served as a dessert after dinner. The theme of the ads revolve around a family setting and bring out the sweetness of relations in a typical middle class family.	Emotional Element
Cadbury (Shubh Arambh Campaign)	The ads associate the brand with the custom of consuming sweets before embarking on something pious or some pious deed.	Cultural Element
Cadbury Dairy Milk Silk	The ad talks about the captivating feel experienced by consuming a rich, smooth and creamy chocolate.	Hedonistic Element
Cadbury Five Star	The ads highlight the captivating experience and the lost feeling experienced by the consumer after consuming Cadbury Five Star Chocolate.	Hedonistic Element
Cadbury Perk	The ad presents the product as a fun snack and also highlights the benefit of glucose derived from the product.	Hedonistic & Functional Element
Nestle Munch	The product is presented in the advertisements as a fun snack and the ads highlight the fun in consumption.	Hedonistic Element
COSMETICS		
Vaseline Petroleum Jelly	The advertisements talk about the ability of Vaseline to give a healthy, shiny and glowing skin.	Functional Element

Vaseline Men	The ad talks about the anti spots and whitening benefit for men. The advertisement claims "Vaseline Men mein hai Vit. B3 and triple sunscreen jo chehre ko banaye fair aur ghataye paanch tarah ke daag dhabbon ko".	Functional Element
Lakme Fruit Blast face wash	The ad highlights the natural fruit ingredients of the product and the cleaning and rehydrating benefit to the skin.	Physical & Functional Element
Ponds Cold Cream	The ads exhibit the happiness of the consumers and her loved ones because of her soft skin. The ads use a love appeal.	Hedonistic Element
Ponds Age Miracle	The ad addresses the fear of wrinkles and signs of ageing in an ageing woman and presents Ponds Age Miracle as a solution.	Functional Element
Olay Total Effects 7 in 1 Anti Ageing Cream	The ad draws the attention of the consumer towards the 7 signs of ageing and presents the product as a solution or as a means of alleviating these signs.	Functional Element
Garnier Age Lift	The advertisement highlights the utilitarian benefit of the product and focuses on the triple benefit i.e., smoothening of wrinkles, removal of dark spots and bringing glow to the skin.	Functional Element

FINDINGS

The important findings from the analysis are as follows:

1) The most commonly used communication element by the MNCs for positioning a brand across all categories of FMCG products in the Indian market was the functional element of positioning.

2) As rational appeal is a part of the functional communication element for brand positioning, it can be concluded that the MNCs dealing in FMCG in India believe that rational appeal

attracts most of the consumers to a brand. In other words, consumers are thought to be most influenced by the use of functional element.

3) Unlike other categories of FMCG brands, soft drink brands predominantly use the hedonistic element of positioning.

4) Chocolate brands were also found to differ in the use of communication elements in their positioning efforts. It was found that the chocolate brands from MNCs used more of cultural element and hedonistic element of brand positioning.

CONCLUSION

The present study successfully found out the communication elements being used by MNCs to position different types and categories of FMCG brands in the Indian market. It identified the functional element of positioning to be the most commonly used communication element for positioning FMCG brands and one that is believed to have the greatest influence on the Indian consumers of Fast Moving Consumer Goods.

The study was only limited to identifying the communication elements used for positioning FMCG brands in India and no attempt was made to examine their degree of effectiveness in positioning a brand or in creating a desired brand image. Further investigation may be carried out to analyse the efficacy of communication elements in positioning different types of FMCG and non FMCG products and for different segments of consumers.

****

NOTE:

1. *At this point it is important to appreciate that brand image is not affected by a firm's marketing communication alone (Park et al, 1986). Nonetheless marketing communication and advertisement do have a significant influence on the brand image.*

REFERENCES

Ahtola, Olli T. (1985), "Hedonistic and Utilitarian Aspect of Consumer Behaviour: An Attitudinal Perspective", *Advances in Consumer Research*, Volume 12, pp. 7-10

Alden, Dana L., Jan-Benedict EM Steenkamp and Rajeev Batra (1999), "Brand Positioning Through Advertising in Asia, North America and Europe: The role of global consumer culture", *Journal of Marketing*, Vol. 63 (January), pp. 75-87

Andreas, Strebinger (2002), "B.A.S.E.- A Brand Architectute Strategy Explorer", *International Business & Economics Research Journal*, Volume 1, Number 11, pp. 115-124.

Batra, Rajeev, and Olli T. Ahtola (1990), "Measuring the Hedonic and Utilitarian Sources of Consumer Attitudes", *Marketing Letters 2:2*, pp. 159-170

Bhat, Subodh, and Srinivas K Reddy (1998), "Symbolic and Functional Positioning of Brands", *Journal of Consumer Marketing*, Vol. 15, Iss:1, pp. 32-43

Chang, Chingching (2006), "Seeing the small Picture: Ad Self Versus Ad-Culture Congruency in International Advertising", *Journal of Business and Psychology*, Vol 20, No.3 (Spring), pp. 445-465

Fournier, Susan (1991), "A Meaning Based Framework for the Study of Consumer-Object Relations", *Advances in Consumer Research*, Volume 18, pp. 736-742

Ghodeswar, Bhimrao M. (2008), "Building Brand Identity in Competitive Markets: A Conceptual Model", *Journal of Brand Management*, pp. 4-12

Hirschman, Elizabeth C. and Morris B. Holbrook (1982), "Hedonic Consumption: Emerging Concepts, Methods and Propositions", *The Journal of Marketing*, Vol. 46, No. 3 (Summer), pp. 92-101

Kapferer, Jean Noel (2004), *The New Strategic Brand Management: Creating and Sustaining Brand Equity Long Term*, First South Asian Ed.(New Delhi: Kogan Page India Pvt. Ltd.), p. 106-113

Keller, Kevin Lane (1993), "Conceptualising, Measuring and Managing Customer Based Brand Equity", *The Journal of Marketing*, Vol. 57, No.1 (January), pp. 1-22

Keller, Kevin Lane (2008),*Strategic Brand Management: Building, Measuring and Managing Brand Equity*, 3rd Ed. (Pearson Education Inc.), p.70-81

Kinra, Neelam (2006), "The effect of country of origin on foreign brand names in the Indian Market", *Marketing Intelligence and planning*, Vol. 24, Number 1, pp. 15-30

Park, C. Whan, Bernard J. Jaworski and Deborah J. MacInnis (1986), "Strategic Brand Concept-Image Management", *The Journal of Marketing*, Vol. 50, No. 4 (Ocober), pp. 135-145

Spangenberg, Eric R, Kevin E. Voss and Ayn E. Crowley (1997), "Measuring the Hedonic and Utilitarian Dimensions of Attitude: A Generally Applicable Scale", *Advances in Consumer Research*, Vol. 24, pp. 235-241

Srivastava, Tanuja and Denise D. Schoeebachler (2000), "An Examination of the Information and Thematic Content of Consumer Print Advertising in India", *Journal of International Consumer Marketing*, Volume 12, Issue 2, pp. 63-85

Voss, Kevin E, Eric R. Spangenberg and Bianca Grohmann (2003), Measuring the Hedoniic and Utilitarian Dimensions of Consumer Attitude", *Journal of Marketing Research*, Vol 40, No. 3 (August), pp. 310-320

CHAPTER 7

EFFECTIVENESS OF MESSAGE STRATEGY ELEMENTS IN BRAND POSITIONING OF FAST MOVING CONSUMER GOODS IN INDIA

ABSTRACT

Brand positioning involves communicating the brand identity to the consumer so as to create a desired and distinctive image about the brand in his mind. Communicating this identity requires the use of certain elements of the advertising message strategy that conform to the brand concept.

The paper attempts to understand the use of the message elements in positioning FMCG brand in India and to study the effectiveness of these elements in positioning brands of Fast Moving Consumer Goods. To get an insight into the type of elements more preferred by the brand managers while positioning their brands in the Indian market and to understand their perception of the effectiveness of these elements, a structured questionnaire was administered to selected brand managers. The effectiveness of the elements was judged by measuring the consumer response to various elements through another questionnaire.

Emotional and Functional elements of the message strategy were found to significantly impact consumer response and brand recall and hence were more effective in positioning a brand. Brand managers too have a higher preference for the use of these elements.

Keywords: Brand Association, Brand Identity, Brand Image, Brand Recall, FMCG

INTRODUCTION

One of the most important tasks at hand for a brand manager is to conceptualise the brand identity and effectively communicate the conceptualised identity to the consumer so as to efficaciously position the brand in the minds of the consumer and endow the brand with a distinctive image in his conceptual space. Marketing communication tools in particular and advertisement in general have always been important instruments at the disposal of the marketer to achieve this objective

A judicious use of marketing communication tools and incorporation of the right concoction of elements of the message strategy in the brand campaigns helps put across an envisaged identity of the brand to the existing and prospective customer. The challenge for a brand manager is to identify and use such message elements for positioning that would conjure up the desired feelings, thoughts, emotions, images and perception about the brand and evoke the right kind of experience of the customer with the brand or its marketing activities.

CONCEPTUAL FRAMEWORK

To embed a brand strongly in the minds of the consumer, the consumer's knowledge of the brand has to be influenced. According to the 'Associative Network Model', the consumer's brand knowledge may be thought of as consisting of two components: the brand awareness (which refers to the consumer's ability to identify the brand) and pieces of brand related information with the consumer. Brand related information may include actual attributes and virtues associated with the brand and perceived brand associations. These pieces of brand related information and associations combine together to form the consumer's image of the brand.

A brand manager, by using the marketing communication tools and advertising messages would try to create and influence some of these brand information and associations so as to create a favourable image of the brand in the consumers' mind. It is at this point that the brand manager needs to explore and select the right message elements which would be able to create and influence the brand associations and information and consequently the brand image in a desirable way.

Message Elements:

The different elements of the message content strategy that can be used for effectively positioning a brand are the physical elements, functional elements, cultural elements, emotional elements and hedonistic elements (Van den Putte, 2002, 2009). These message elements correspond to the different brand concepts and have relation to the different facets of brand identity. A brief explanation of these elements of message content strategy is given below:

6) The Physical Element: It talks about the physical attribute of the product and the physical features of the brand that differentiate it from the competitor's products and the competing brands.

7) The Functional Element: It talks about the performance and performance efficiency of the product as well as the functional and utilitarian benefits offered by the brand to the consumer. This element proves to be instrumental in developing those brand associations in the consumer's memory that correspond to the 'personality' facet of brand identity and the functional brand concept.

8) The Cultural Element: Culture of the consumer or a foreign culture admired by the consumer may be used to communicate the positioning of the brand. The cultural element talks about the cultural values with which the brand is associated and subtly or overtly exhibit the cultural benefit derived from the brand. The cultural element when used to communicate the positioning of the brand develops a brand association that corresponds to the 'brand culture' facet of brand identity.

9) The Emotional Element: It includes the various emotions that may be used to communicate the positioning of the brand. Emotional element when used effectively in marketing communication develops emotional association with the brand. This type of association corresponds with the 'relation' facet of brand identity.

10) The Hedonistic Element: The purpose of the use of hedonistic element in communication is to develop a feel good association with the brand. This type of association corresponds with the 'reflection' and 'self image' facet of brand identity.

As the different message elements can be used to create, influence and fortify the brand information that combine together to form the brand image, the use of these message elements in advertising appeals and in company engineered brand associations may have some impact on brand positioning. The present empirical research has been carried out to measure the extent of this impact.

OBJECTIVES OF THE STUDY

The objectives of the study are:

1. To study the impact of the use of various message elements on consumers' response to the brand.
2. To compare the impact of different message elements on consumers' brand recall.

3. To check the brand manager's perception regarding the effectiveness of the various message elements in positioning brands of Fast Moving Consumer Goods.

4. To find out which type of message element is preferred to be used in brand positioning by the brand managers of MNCs dealing in FMCG in India.

5. To identify the elements of the message strategy that are more effective in positioning brands of Fast Moving Consumer Goods in the Indian market.

METHODOLOGY

The data for the study was collected using two separately designed questionnaires for the consumers and the brand managers. To understand the effectiveness of the message elements used for brand positioning, a questionnaire was administered to 250 consumers. Consumers were selected for the study through judgemental sampling. The respondents were selected from five different states of India and included housewives, working professionals, businessmen and students (pursuing graduation and post graduation). Questions were designed to measure up to what extent the different message elements are able to attract the consumers to a brand and to measure the effectiveness of these elements in facilitating brand recall.

Another questionnaire was administered to brand managers and assistant brand managers working for Indian or Foreign Multinational companies operating in India and dealing in FMCG. Thirty respondents were selected from different multinational companies selling FMCG brands in India. The product categories for which the study was conducted are: Food & Beverage, Confectionary, Soaps & Detergents, Cosmetics and Home Care products.

The questions administered to the brand managers were designed to understand the perception of the brand managers regarding the impact of the use of different message elements on consumer response towards the advertised brands. The questionnaire also had questions to study the manager's perception regarding the impact of message elements on brand recall. As elements of the message strategy for communicating positioning are encrypted in advertising appeals and get reflected in brand associations projected through advertisements, two questions were framed to judge the perceived impact of these elements on brand recall. One of these questions measured the impact of different advertisement appeals (having different message elements encrypted within) on brand recall as perceived by the brand managers. The other question measured the impact of different brand associations on brand recall as perceived by the brand managers.

The rationale of treating the impact of brand association as a direct impact of message element was based on the relationship between brand concept (from which the message element for communicating brand positioning is drawn) and brand association (Park et al, 1986, & Strebinger, 2002).

Rationale of using brand recall and consumer's response as indications of the strength of brand positioning: The strength of a brand identity can be measured in terms of the top of mind awareness of the brand, brand recall and the consumer's response to the brand which refers to the likelihood that the brand will be in the consumer's consideration set (Keller, 1993). As brand positioning is all about the brand identity as perceived by the consumer (Kapferer, 2004), the strength of brand positioning can also be measured in terms of the extent of brand recall and in terms of the consumer's purchase response to a brand. Based on this concept the present study has taken brand recall as an indication of the strength of brand positioning.

ANALYSIS OF DATA COLLECTED FROM BRAND MANAGERS

The data obtained from the brand managers was analysed to get an insight into the brand managers' perception regarding the effectiveness of the various communication elements in positioning brands of Fast Moving Consumer Goods and to identify the communication element that is preferred to be used by a brand managers dealing in FMCG in India. The analysis has been discussed under the headings:

1. Elements of Message Strategy (Encrypted in Advertisement Appeal) that Generate a Better Response from the Consumer
2. Elements of Message Strategy (Encrypted in Advertisement Appeal) that Ensure a Stronger Brand Recall
3. Message Elements (When Reflected in Brand Association) that are Believed to Ensure a Better Brand Recall
4. The Message Elements that the Brand Managers Dealing in FMCG Prefer to Use While Positioning Brands

1) Elements of Message Strategy (Encrypted in Advertisement Appeal) that Generate a Better Response from the Consumers

An analysis of the brand managers' opinion regarding the consumers' response to message elements (concealed within advertisement appeals) indicate that 46.7% of the managers believe that a combination of functional and emotional element ensures a better response from the consumers (See Table 7.1).

Table 7.1 Advertisement Message Elements and Consumer Response

APPEAL	Responses (N)	Percent	Percent of Cases
Functional Element (as rational appeal)	3	6.4%	10.0%
Emotional Element (as emotional appeal)	1	2.1%	3.3%
Cultural Element (as cultural appeal)	3	6.4%	10.0%
Hedonistic Element (as hedonistic appeal)	3	6.4%	10.0%
Rational & Emotional Element Combined (As combination of rational & emotional appeal)	14	29.8%	46.7%
Rational & Cultural Element Combined (as combination of rational & cultural appeal)	5	10.6%	16.7%
Rational & Hedonistic Element Combined (as combination of rational & hedonistic appeal)	2	4.3%	6.7%
Emotional & Cultural Element Combined (as combination of emotional & cultural appeal)	9	19.1%	30.0%
Emotional & Hedonistic Element Combined (as combination of emotional & hedonistic appeal)	6	12.8%	20.0%
Cultural & Hedonistic Element Combined (as combination of cultural & hedonistic appeal)	1	2.1%	3.3%
Total	47	100.0%	156.7%

Table 7.2 Association of Message Elements and Consumer Response

	YES	NO	d/f	Chi Square (p value)
Functional element gives better consumer response	3	27	1	19.20 (.000)
Emotional element gives better consumer response	1	29	1	26.13 (.000)
Cultural element gives better consumer response	3	27	1	19.20 (.000)
Hedonistic element gives better consumer response	3	27	1	19.20 (.000)
A combination of rational & emotional element gives better	14	16	1	0.13 (.715)
A combination of rational & cultural element gives better	5	25	1	13.33 (.000)
A combination of rational & hedonistic element gives better	2	28	1	22.53 (.000)
A combination of emotional & cultural element gives better	9	21	1	4.80 (.028)
A combination of emotional & hedonistic element gives better	6	24	1	10.80 (.001)
A combination of cultural & hedonistic element gives better	1	29	1	26.13 (.000)

Chi Square analysis also exhibits the influence of the combination of functional and emotional element on the response from the consumers (Refer Table 7.2).

145

As the calculated chi square value for the item 'combination of functional and emotional element giving better consumer response' (0.13) is lesser than the table value of chi square (3.84) at level of significance 0.05 and degree of freedom 1, the statement that "A combination of Functional and Emotional element gives better consumer response" is not rejected.

From the analysis of this question it can be inferred that brand managers dealing in FMCG in India believe that the combination of functional element and emotional element of communication have a significant impact on consumer response.

2) Elements of Message Strategy (Encrypted in Advertisement Appeal) that Ensure a Stronger Brand Recall

A study of the brand managers' perception regarding the type of message element that strengthens the brand recall reveals that 30% of the brand managers believe that emotional element ensures a stronger brand recall. It was also found that 30% of the respondents believe that a combination of functional and emotional element ensured a stronger brand recall (See Table 7.3).

Table 7.3 Elements of Message Strategy and Brand Recall

APPEAL	Responses (N)	Percent	Percent of Cases
Functional Element (as rational appeal)	2	4.5%	6.7%
Emotional Element (as emotional appeal)	9	20.5%	30.0%
Cultural Element (as cultural appeal)	2	4.5%	6.7%
Hedonistic Element (as hedonistic appeal)	3	6.8%	10.0%
Rational & Emotional Element Combined (as combination of rational & emotional appeal)	9	20.5%	30.0%
Rational & Cultural Element Combined (as combination of rational & cultural appeal)	3	6.8%	10.0%
Emotional & Cultural Element Combined (as combination of emotional & cultural appeal)	8	18.2%	26.7%
Emotional & Hedonistic Element Combined (as combination of emotional & hedonistic appeal)	8	18.2%	26.7%
Total	44	100.0%	146.7%

However Chi Square analysis does not indicate any significant influence of any of the message elements on brand recall (Refer Table 7.4).

Table 7.4 Association of Message Elements and Brand Recall

	YES	NO	d/f	Chi Square (p value)
Rational element ensures strong brand recall	2	28	1	22.533 (.000)
Emotional element ensures strong brand recall	9	21	1	4.800 (.028)
Cultural element ensures strong brand recall	2	28	1	22.533 (.000)
Hedonistic element ensures strong brand recall	3	37	1	19.200 (.000)
A combination of rational & emotional element ensures strong brand recall	9	21	1	4.800 (.028)
A combination of rational & cultural element ensures strong brand recall	3	27	1	19.200 (.000)
A combination of rational & hedonistic element ensures strong brand recall	0	30		
A Combination of emotional & cultural element ensures strong brand recall	8	22	1	6.533 (.011)
A Combination of emotional & hedonistic element ensures strong brand recall	8	22	1	6.533 (.011)
A combination of cultural & hedonistic element ensures strong brand recall	0	30		

As the calculated chi square value for none of the statements regarding the influence of message elements (within advertising appeals) on the brand recall of the consumers is lesser than the table value of chi square (3.84) at level of significance 0.05 and degree of freedom 1, all the statements that claim that different message elements (within corresponding advertisement appeals) ensure strong brand recall are rejected.

3) Message Elements (When Reflected in Brand Association) that are Believed to Ensure a Better Brand Recall

On seeking an opinion from the brand managers regarding the type of message element (as reflected in brand association) that ensures a stronger brand recall it was found that 46.7% of the brand managers believe that hedonistic/experiential element (reflected in the association of a brand with special experience) ensure a stronger brand recall. At the same time 43.3% of the respondents believe that emotional element (reflected through celebrity association) ensure a stronger brand recall (See Table 7.5).

Table 7.5 Brand Association and Brand Recall

Association	Responses (N)	Percent	Percent of Cases
Celebrity association (reflecting emotional element)	13	24.1%	43.3%
Health association (reflecting functional element)	6	11.1%	20.0%
Association with festivals & events (reflecting cultural element)	8	14.8%	26.7%
Association with culture & tradition (reflecting cultural element)	6	11.1%	20.0%
Performance association (reflecting functional element)	7	13.0%	23.3%
Association with special experience (reflecting hedonistic element)	14	25.9%	46.7%
Total	54	100.0%	180.0%

The calculated chi square values for the items 'celebrity association ensuring better brand recall' and 'association with special experience ensuring better brand recall' are 0.5333 and 0.133 respectively. Both the values being lesser than the table value of chi square (3.84) at level of significance 0.05 and degree of freedom 1, the statements that "Emotional Element (reflected in celebrity association) ensures a better brand recall" and that "Hedonistic Element (applied as association with some special experience) ensures a better brand recall" are not rejected (Refer Table 7.6).

Table 7.6 Relationship between Brand Association and Brand Recall

	YES	NO	d/f	Chi Square (p value)
Emotional Element as celebrity association ensures better brand recall	13	17	1	.533 (.465)
Functional Element as health association ensures better brand recall	6	24	1	10.800 (.001)
Cultural Element as association with festivals & events ensure better brand	8	22	1	6.533 (.011)
Cultural Element as association with culture & tradition ensures better brand	6	24	1	10.800 (.001)
Functional Element as performance association ensures better brand recall	7	23	1	8.533 (.003)
Hedonistic Element as association with special experience ensures better	14	16	1	.133 (.715)

From the analysis it can be inferred that a majority of the brand managers dealing in FMCG believe in the ability and effectiveness of hedonistic element to strengthen brand recall and thus believe in its importance in brand positioning. Similarly it can be inferred that a good percentage of brand managers (43.3%) consider the emotional element of positioning important for brand recall and thus consider it effective for brand positioning.

4) The Message Elements that the Brand Managers Dealing in FMCG Prefer to Use While Positioning Brands

The frequency table showing the type of communication elements that the brand managers prefer to use, while positioning their brands, reveals that most of the brand managers (46.7%) of MNCs dealing in FMCG brands in the Indian market prefer to use the sensory/experiential element followed by the emotional element as well as the functional element (as indicated in 43.3% of the cases) while positioning their FMCG brands (See Table7.7).

Table 7.7 Brand Managers' Preference of Communication Elements

Association	Responses (N)	Percent	Percent of Cases
physical elements	12	20.3%	40.0%
functional elements	13	22.0%	43.3%
cultural elements	7	11.9%	23.3%
emotional elements	13	22.0%	43.3%
sensory/experiential elements	14	23.7%	46.7%
Total	59	100.0%	196.7%

The calculated chi square values for the items 'preference of physical elements', 'preference of functional elements', 'preference of emotional elements' and 'preference of experiential/hedonistic elements' are 1.200, 0.533, 0.533 and 0.133respectively (Refer Table 7.8). All these values are lesser than the table value of chi square (3.84) at level of significance 0.05 and degree of freedom 1. Hence, the statement "Brand Managers prefer to use physical elements while positioning", "Brand Managers prefer to use functional elements while positioning", "Brand Managers prefer to use emotional elements while positioning" and "Brand Managers prefer to use experiential/hedonistic elements while positioning" are not rejected.

Table 7.8 Use of Communication Elements for Positioning

	YES	NO	d/f	Chi Square (p value)
Preference of Physical Elements in	12	18	1	1.200 (.273)
Preference of Functional Elements	13	17	1	0.533 (0.465)
Preference of Cultural Elements in	7	23	1	8.533 (.003)
Preference of Emotional Elements	13	17	1	.533 (.465)
Preference of Sensory/	14	16	1	.133 (.715)

However as the calculated chi square value for the item 'preference of cultural elements' (8.533) is greater than the table value of chi square (3.84) at level of significance 0.05 and degree of freedom 1, the statement that "Brand Managers prefer to use cultural elements while positioning" is rejected.

Inference From the analysis of the data collected from the brand managers of various multinational companies dealing in FMCG, it can be concluded that the brand managers consider the functional element and a combination of functional element and emotional element as the most important message elements to communicate the positioning of FMCG brands to the consumers and to establish a distinctive position for the brand in the minds of the consumers.

The response from the brand managers also indicate that the most commonly used and most preferred message elements for positioning the FMCG brands in the Indian market are hedonistic element/experiential element followed by the emotional element and functional element. Use of cultural element is least preferred while positioning the FMCG brands.

ANALYSIS OF DATA COLLECTED FROM CONSUMERS

The data collected from the consumers was analysed to understand which type of communication element is actually more effective in positioning a Fast moving Consumer brand in the Indian market. The analysis has been discussed under the headings:

1. Elements of Message Strategy (Encrypted in Advertisement Appeals) that Attract the Consumer Towards a Brand
2. Elements of Message Strategy (As Reflected in Brand Associations) that Facilitate Brand Recall

1) Elements of Message Strategy (Encrypted in Advertisement Appeals) that Attract the Consumer Towards a Brand

Table 7.9 Message Elements that Attract Consumers

Association	Responses (N)	Percent	Percent of Cases
Functional Element (as rational appeal)	100	25.9%	40.8%
Emotional Element (as emotional appeal)	59	15.3%	24.1%
Cultural Element (as cultural appeal)	42	10.9%	17.1%
Hedonistic Element (as hedonistic appeal)	39	10.1%	15.9%
Rational & Emotional Element Combined (As combination of rational & emotional appeal)	45	11.7%	18.4%
Rational & Cultural Element Combined (as combination of rational & cultural appeal)	25	6.5%	10.2%
Rational & Hedonistic Element Combined (as combination of rational & hedonistic appeal)	31	8.0%	12.7%
Emotional & Cultural Element Combined (as combination of emotional & cultural appeal)	23	6.0%	9.4%
Emotional & Hedonistic Element Combined (as combination of emotional & hedonistic appeal)	11	2.8%	4.5%
Cultural & Hedonistic Element Combined (as combination of cultural & hedonistic appeal)	11	2.8%	4.5%
Total	386	100.0%	157.6%

An analysis of the consumer opinion pertaining to the ability of a message element to attract the consumers towards a brand showed that 40.8% of the consumers selected for the study were attracted towards a brand because of the use of functional element (See Table 7.9).

It can be concluded that the consumers are most influenced by the use of the functional element of message strategy used by a company for positioning its brands

2) Elements of Message Strategy (As Reflected in Brand Associations) that Facilitate Brand Recall

A study of the frequency table exhibiting the response of the consumers, regarding the type of message element (reflected in brand association) that makes it easy for them to remember a brand, shows that emotional element (as in celebrity association) is the most effective message element that facilitates brand recall amongst the consumers (See Table 7.10). A majority of the consumers (43.6%) stated that brands that have some celebrity association are easy to remember and recall followed by those FMCG brands that use performance association (constituted of the functional element of the message strategy) for their positioning.

Table 7.10 Message Elements in Brand Associations that Facilitate Brand Recall

Association	Responses (N)	Percent	Percent of Cases
Celebrity association (reflecting emotional element)	109	26.7%	43.6%
Health association (reflecting functional element)	50	12.3%	20.0%
Association with festivals & events (reflecting cultural element)	46	11.3%	18.4%
Association with culture & tradition (reflecting cultural element)	48	11.8%	19.2%
Performance association (reflecting functional element)	97	23.8%	38.8%
Association with special experience (reflecting hedonistic element)	58	14.2%	23.2%
Total	408	100.0%	163.2%

As celebrity association hints at the use of emotional element of communication for brand positioning, it can be inferred that emotional element used in marketing communication has an impact on consumer's brand recall and brand positioning. Similarly as performance association hints at the use of functional element of communication for brand positioning, it indicates that functional element also effectively facilitates the brand recall and establish the positioning of the brand.

Inference From the analysis of the data collected from the users of Fast Moving Consumer Goods, it can be inferred that the functional element of communication is most effective in influencing the consumers' brand preference as well as in facilitating brand recall and the emotional element of communication has a significant influence on brand recall. Thus the functional element and the emotional element of communication emerge to be more effective in positioning a Fast Moving Consumer Goods brand than the other elements of communication used for brand positioning.

FINDINGS

The important findings from the analysis are as follows:

5) Brand Managers believe that a combination of functional and emotional element of the advertising message strategy is most effective in affecting the response from the consumer and is thus important for positioning the brand.

6) None of the message elements when present as a constituent of different advertising appeals has a distinctively stronger influence on brand recall. However, the brand managers feel that the use of hedonistic element as part of the special experience association facilitates brand recall. Emotional element (reflected through celebrity association) is believed to be the second most effective element in facilitating brand recall. Thus brand managers tend to believe that hedonistic element is most effective in influencing brand recall followed by the emotional element.

From Finding (1) and from this Finding, it can be concluded that emotional element, hedonistic element and a combination of emotional and functional elements are thought to be most important by the brand managers in influencing the positioning of a brand.

7) Somewhat in conformance with the belief of the brand managers regarding the importance and influence of the communication elements on brand positioning (Refer to Finding 1 and Finding 2), the most preferred message element for positioning an FMCG brand by the

brand managers in the Indian market is the hedonistic element followed by the emotional element and the functional element.

8) As indicated from the response of the consumers surveyed, consumers are most influenced by the use of functional element. This is in conformance with the perception of the brand managers regarding the effectiveness of the communication elements (See Finding 1).

9) Proving the belief (regarding the impact of message elements on brand recall) of the brand managers fairly correct (See Finding 2), emotional element of message (projected in the form of celebrity association) is found to be most influential in facilitating brand recall followed by the functional communication element (in the form of performance association). Hedonistic element that is regarded by brand managers to be very significant in influencing brand recall is not so potent in reality. The response of the consumers clearly indicates that emotional element of communication is most effective in influencing and facilitating brand recall followed by the functional element.

From the response of the consumers it can be concluded that the message elements that have the most significant impact on the consumers' perception of the brand and his ensuing response to it are the emotional element and the functional element.

IMPLICATION OF THE RESEARCH

The study indicates a conformance between the brand managers' perception of the impact of emotional and functional elements of the message strategy on brand positioning and the actual impact of these two elements on brand positioning (manifested and noted as the consumers' perception of the brand). However an undue importance seems to be given by the brand managers to the hedonistic message element for positioning brands of Fast Moving Consumer Goods. Mellowing down the intensity of use of the hedonistic element and stepping up the use of the functional and emotional message elements may be considered by a brand manager to strengthen the positioning of a brand of FMCG product in the Indian market.

****

REFERENCES

Ahtola, Olli T. (1985), "Hedonistic and Utilitarian Aspect of Consumer Behaviour: An Attitudinal Perspective", *Advances in Consumer Research*, Vol. 12, pp. 7-10

Alden, Dana L., Jan-Benedict EM Steenkamp, and Rajeev Batra (1999), "Brand Positioning Through Advertising in Asia, North America and Europe: The role of global consumer culture", *Journal of Marketing*, Vol. 63 (January), pp. 75-87

Bahl, Pooja, Bobby B. Pandey, and Manoj Sharma (2012), "A Study of the Impact of Celebrity Endorsement on Brand Positioning of Different Product Categories", *International Journal of Research in IT & Management*, Vol. 2, No.3, pp. 31-43

Batra, Rajeev, and Olli T. Ahtola (1990), "Measuring the Hedonic and Utilitarian Sources of Consumer Attitudes", *Marketing Letters,* Vol. 2, No. 2, pp. 159-170

Bhat, Subodh, and Srinivas K Reddy (1998), "Symbolic and Functional Positioning of Brands", *Journal of Consumer Marketing*, Vol. 15, No.1, pp. 32-43

Chang, Chingching (2006), "Seeing the small Picture: Ad Self Versus Ad-Culture Congruency in International Advertising", *Journal of Business and Psychology*, Vol. 20, No.3 (Spring), pp. 445-465

Ghodeswar, Bhimrao M. (2008), "Building Brand Identity in Competitive Markets: A Conceptual Model", *Journal of Brand Management*, Vol. 17, No. 1, pp. 4-12

Hirschman, Elizabeth C., and Morris B. Holbrook (1982), "Hedonic Consumption: Emerging Concepts, Methods and Propositions", *The Journal of Marketing*, Vol. 46, No. 3 (Summer), pp. 92-101

Kapferer, Jean Noel (2004), *The New Strategic Brand Management: Creating and Sustaining Brand Equity Long Term*, 1st South Asian ed. (New Delhi: Kogan Page India Pvt. Ltd.), pp. 106-113

Keller, Kevin Lane (1993), "Conceptualising, Measuring and Managing Customer Based Brand Equity", *The Journal of Marketing*, Vol. 57, No.1 (January), pp. 1-22

Keller, Kevin Lane (2008), *Strategic Brand Management: Building, Measuring and Managing Brand Equity*, 3rd ed. (New Delhi: Pearson Education Inc.), pp.70-81

Kinra, Neelam (2006), "The Effect of Country of Origin on Foreign Brand Names in the Indian Market", *Marketing Intelligence and planning*, Vol. 24, No. 1, pp. 15-30

Park, C. Whan, Bernard J. Jaworski, and Deborah J. MacInnis (1986), "Strategic Brand Concept-Image Management", *The Journal of Marketing*, Vol. 50, No. 4 (October), pp. 135-145

Spangenberg, Eric R, Kevin E. Voss and Ayn E. Crowley (1997), "Measuring the Hedonic and Utilitarian Dimensions of Attitude: A Generally Applicable Scale", *Advances in Consumer Research*, Vol. 24, pp. 235-241

Srivastava, Tanuja, and Denise D. Schoeebachler (2000), "An Examination of the Information and Thematic Content of Consumer Print Advertising in India", *Journal of International Consumer Marketing*, Vol. 12, No. 2, pp. 63-85

Strebinger, Andreas (2002), "B.A.S.E.- A Brand Architecture Strategy Explorer", *International Business & Economics Research Journal*, Vol. 1, No. 11, pp. 115-124.

Van den Putte, Bas (2002), "An Integrative Framework for Effective Communication", in Bartels, G & W. Nellissen (ed.s), *Marketing for Sustainability: Towards Transactional Policy Making,* (Amsterdam: IOS Press), pp. 83-95

Van den Putte, Bas (2009), "What Matters the Most in Advertising Campaigns? The Relative Effect of Media Expenditure and Message Content Strategy", *International Journal of Advertising*, Vol. 28, No. 3, pp. 669-690

Voss, Kevin E, Eric R. Spangenberg, and Bianca Grohmann (2003), Measuring the Hedonic and Utilitarian Dimensions of Consumer Attitude", *Journal of Marketing Research*, Vol. 40, No. 3 (August), pp. 310-320

CHAPTER 8

USE OF HOST COUNTRY CULTURAL ELEMENT IN BRAND POSITIONING OF MULTINATIONAL BRANDS

ABSTRACT

An important element of brand positioning is the cultural component used therein. Whether a company adapts a local culture to position its brand in a host country or goes for acculturation depends on the type of International Orientation of the company. This paper makes an attempt to find out if the companies that use Local Consumer Culture Positioning (LCCP), have a competitive advantage as compared to those which don't (or those which use GCCP) and to find out the extent by which the companies can build in a strong consumer preference by introducing some elements of a foreign culture (Acculturation).

Keywords: Cultural Positioning, LCCP, FCCP, GCCP, FMCG

INTRODUCTION

Brands have conventionally established their identity in the minds of the consumers by positioning themselves on the basis of product attributes, benefits, uses, price or users. However the culture of the consumer in whose mind the brand is to be positioned forms an equally important or perhaps a more important element while going for a brand positioning strategy in the international market. An MNC that indulges in cultural positioning may have three brand positioning strategies at its disposal for positioning its brand- Local Consumer Culture Positioning (LCCP), Foreign Consumer Culture Positioning (FCCP) and Global Consumer Culture Positioning (GCCP). (Dana L. Alden, Jan- Benedict EM Steenkamp & Rajeev Batra). The type of cultural positioning strategy a company may use will depend, upto a certain extent, on the international orientation of the company. An MNC with an ethnocentric orientation would have a propensity to use its domestic cultural element in all the markets where it operates whereas a polycentric company would prefer to adapt its positioning strategy in accordance with the culture of the market where it operates. However international orientation of the company is not the only determinant that decides the use of a specific cultural positioning strategy.

LITERATURE REVIEW

While positioning a brand, culture forms an important element. The culture based positioning strategies may be classified as Global Consumer Culture Positioning (GCCP), Local Consumer Culture Positioning (LCCP) and Foreign Consumer Culture Positioning (FCCP). (Dana L. Alden, Jan- Benedict EM Steenkamp & Rajeev Batra,1999). Many MNCs are making a deliberate effort to position their brands as 'global brands' as such a step may yield economies of scale and increase the scope in R&D besides increasing its strategic appeal because of the development of some similar taste and preferences among the consumers throughout the globe. Moreover it also speeds up the brand's time to market by reducing the time consuming local modifications. It has also been found that 'perceived brand globalness' may provide a significant source of competitive strength: the higher a brand's perceived globalness, the higher is its perceived quality, prestige and purchase likeliness. (Jan Benedict EM Steenkamp, Rajeev Batra and Dana L Alden, 2003).

Though Global Positioning has certain advantages, local positioning is also being used advantageously by certain companies and brands. Many local brands taking advantage of the knowledge of the local culture and making proper use of the cultural capital are giving a tough competition to the global brands. For such a positioning the companies need to inculcate a unique mix of value into their brands and thoroughly understand and exploit the cultural capital of the country. (Kippenberger, 2000). FCCP is also seen to exist alongside GCCP and LCCP. There are many products/ brands that take on some elements of a foreign culture while positioning the brands. Foreign branding i.e., the strategy of using a foreign name while branding or pronouncing or spelling a brand name in a foreign language triggers cultural stereotypes and influences product perception and attitude. (France Leclerc, Bernd H. Schmitt and Laurette Dube, 1994) However which category of products would get a good response from the consumers by using such a positioning strategy and the extent of benefit of such a positioning remains to be studied.

A particular Study has revealed that individuals with higher Consumer Ethnocentrism exhibit higher level of 'Domestic Country bias' (DCB) and hence are less favourably disposed towards foreign products. (George Balabanis & Adamantios Diamantopoulos, 2004). While taking a peep at the Indian market and looking at the Indian buyer it can be said that by and large Indians are also ethnocentric in nature. But at the same time they don't have any strong negative feeling about the foreign brands. They would prefer to patronize the 'Made in India' goods but at the same time believe that 'Foreign brands' are of superior quality. At least one study highlights in its findings that the Indian consumers rate high on ethnocentrism, which might indicate a positive bias towards local brands and a preference towards indigenous manufacturers. Despite this fact it was found that the quality of the foreign brands and the technology used therein was perceived to be generally higher and superior to that of the local brands. (Neelam Kinra, 2006). However no study has been done regarding how effectively LCCP can be used in such a situation and what would be the impact of ethnocentric positioning on consumer preference in such a situation.

It is not only the country of origin that plays an important role in shaping the consumer perception of a brand but a more important role is played by the 'culture of origin' of the brand. Brand origin is a useful concept for marketing a brand in an emerging economy like India. But if any company wants to attach a positive value to its brand via brand origin association it calls for a very careful navigation and a well chalked out strategy. (Zongqui Jin, Bal Chansarkar and N.M. Kondap, 2006). In a study conducted in Singapore it was found that the consumers can more readily identify the cultural origin of brands over their country of origin. The study proposed that the Culture of Brand Origin (COBO) has replaced the Country of Origin (COO) as the most important origin influence in the consumer's perception of brands. (Kenny Lim and Aron O' Cass, 2001).

Local brands provide a link between economic nationalism and individual well being. On the other hand, at times, Foreign brands may be thought of as a threat to the local culture. "In the mind of the ethnocentric consumer, global brands pose not only an economic but also a cultural threat." "Ethnocentric consumers may even be willing to sacrifice 'objective' gain to enjoy the psychological benefit of avoiding contact with the outgroup (i.e., the global culture) by purchasing local brands." (Jan Benedict EM Steenkamp, Rajeev Batra and Dana L Alden, 2003). This fact may raise a query regarding the possibility of the Multinational brands of gaining the confidence of the consumers in the host country by using some elements of the foreign culture for their positioning. Thus the competitive strategy for brands may have to be adapted or changed in accordance with the customer characteristics and preferences. A brand may have to be repositioned in response to the evolving needs of the buyers. Competitive advantage can be achieved "by constantly adapting to and instigating change" (Allan D. Shocker, Rajendra K. Srivastava and Robert W. Ruekert, 1994).

INTERNATIONAL ORIENTATION AND CULTURAL POSITIONING

The culture of a nation is the composite of the values, beliefs, customs, language and religion of its people. It has a strong influence on the perception and attitude of the people and their predisposition towards any object, product or a brand. If a brand is able to reflect the beliefs and values of a certain population and conform to its culture, it is likely to experience a favourable impact on its brand acceptability and brand preference.

Thus while going for a brand building exercise in a host country, the Multinational Companies either inculcate some local cultural elements in their brand or make a serious effort to bring in certain elements of a foreign culture (which is inherent in the brand) into the host country. The latter is the process of acculturation.

Whether a company adapts a local culture to position its brand in a host country [Local Consumer Culture Positioning (LCCP)] or goes for acculturation [Foreign Consumer Culture Positioning (FCCP) OR Global Consumer Culture Positioning (GCCP)] depends on the type of International Orientation of the company. For example a company like Dabur, having a very strong ethnocentric orientation with its core competence enshrined in its product formulations that make use of Ayurvedic formulations and traditional products of Indian origin, would invariably use the concept of foreign consumer culture positioning to establish itself in a foreign market. On the other hand a company like Hindustan Unilever Ltd. or any other company with a polycentric orientation or regiocentric orientation adapts its products, marketing communication and marketing strategy according to the requirement of the specific country into which they enter. Such multi-domestic companies try to imbibe elements of local culture into the product that they sell and the communication that they use to promote and sell their products. Such companies make use of Local Consumer Culture Positioning for their product in each of the host country in which they operate. Companies with a geocentric orientation that consider the entire world as a single market make an attempt to figure out some cultural elements that have a global appeal and rope in such global cultural elements for chalking out a standardized marketing strategy to be used across the world. The following table shows which type of Positioning a company is likely to go for:

ORIENTATION	COUNTRY OF OPERATION	POSITIONING	EXAMPLES
Ethnocentric	Home	LCCP	Amul
	Host	FCCP	Sumeet mixers
Polycentric	Home	LCCP	Colgate &
	Host	LCCP	Ponds
Geocentric		GCCP	Coca Cola & Pepsi

Some examples of brands, from the stable of multinational companies, using local cultural elements in brand positioning are Cadbury's, Maggi (2 minutes Noodles & Maggi Atta Noodles), ICICI Prudential, Colgate (Toothpowder, Herbal Toothpaste & Active Salt Toothpaste), Mcdonald's, Pizza Hut, Pillsbury (Chakki Fresh Atta), AT&T (Idea) etc. Similarly some examples of brands, from the stable of domestic companies, using local cultural elements in brand positioning are Amul, Dhara, Vicco, Bajaj, Shalimar Coconut Oil, etc.

COMMUNICATION ELEMENTS AND CULTURAL POSITIONING

The subtle element in any communication that play a pivotal role in conveying the thoughts and the ideas to the receiver are the language, the words, the modulation and the pitch of the voice, expressions and gestures. Without these elements or without the effective use these elements communication fails to achieve its objective. The same holds true for marketing communication. If these elements are used in the same way as the listener uses them or is familiar to, the marketer finds it easy to drive the point across to the target audience. If these elements in the marketing communication match the communication elements commonly used by the consumer and is in conformance with the values, beliefs and customs of the target audience it is able to convey a desired meaning effectively and is able to carve out a position for the product or the brand in the mind of the target consumer. Thus ICICI Prudential Life Insurance Policy drives home a strong point with the use of 'sindoor' that symbolically emphasizes and ensures a long, happy and safe life. The gesture of applying 'sindoor' effectively conveys an array of meanings laced with positivity, hope and benefit to the Indian consumer. The same advertisement, instead of communicating such positivity, would lead to an utter confusion in the consumer's mind and would go absolutely waste if aired in the European, American or any other market. The obvious reason would be the culture specific use of the communication element that has a strong relation to the Indian culture but would be meaningless in all other cultures. Thus Foreign consumer culture positioning would not be feasible with such an element that is so strongly related to the lifestyle of a specific culture.

The fact can be conveniently demonstrated with the example of Cadbury and its role in the evolution of the chocolate consumption in the Indian market. Cadbury has been there in the Indian market since 1946 and has been synonymous with chocolate consumption in India. However for a long period of time chocolate has been considered as a product for the kids, a very specific market segment. The product was considered to be a sophisticated and costly product affordable by the upper class or the upper middle class. The perception made the market segment not highly specific but very limited. Chocolate was not something that was traditionally consumed in the Indian culture. This gave a daunting task to the chocolate manufacturers. If Cadbury had to expand its market it had to branch out from its limited segment and capture other segments as well. Thus expansion of the market meant christening the adult segment and all social classes with the chocolate consuming culture. The challenge for Cadbury was thus to change the local cultural habit in a country that had traditionally not eaten chocolate.

Cadbury's attempt at driving this transition came in the middle of '90s with its advertising campaign aiming to change the concept of chocolate from 'just for kids' to 'kids in all of us'. 'The real taste of life' campaign which was instrumental in redefining the concept of chocolate in India soon gave way to the 'Kya swad hai zindagi ka' campaign to make it more lingually relevant to the masses. Local culture, however, did come to the aid of the brand in the best possible way when the promotional campaigns associated the brand with festival linked celebrations. The 'Kuch meetha ho jaye' campaign associating the brand with celebrations during various local festivals did an exemplary job in infusing and initiating the chocolate consuming habit into the local culture. It would not be wrong to describe it as the phenomenon of acculturation (bringing some elements or part of a foreign culture into the country) through the process of local culture positioning.

The success that Cadbury achieved by harnessing a flavour of the local culture for repositioning its brand can be measured in terms of its growth in sales of 30% and that in profit of 20% in the year

2008-09 that makes it a market leader with a share of 70%. Local Consumer Culture Positioning was able to catapult the brand and the entire product category into a culturally relevant product which has a frequent use from a culturally obscure product with an occasional use.

ACCULTURATION THROUGH LCCP

Acculturation is a spontaneous outcome of the diffusion of the international boundaries in the age of liberalization. With the revolution in information and communication technology, opening up of communication across borders, trade becoming smooth across borders as a consequence of trade barriers crumbling down and consumers getting exposed to foreign cultures consequent to improved transportation facilities, marketing today plays a significant role in the process of acculturation. Certain aspirational products of foreign origin may be promoted using some foreign cultural elements. Use of denims, Friday dressing, and pop culture are some such examples of acculturation facilitated by some promotional campaigns of products and services. Thus FCCP, if successful and if not met by resistance to acceptance may result in acculturation. However, acculturation (albeit an incremental or a gradual one) can be achieved in a smoother way if it is camouflaged or at least accompanied by a local cultural element. The accompanying local cultural element enhances the significance of a product with a foreign cultural connotation. The positioning strategy of a number of multinational brands, particularly food and beverage brands, in the Indian market stand a strong testimony to this fact. Brands like Pizza Hut, Domino's, McDonald's and Maggi Noodles were not only able to generate an awareness for these products which were alien to the Indian cuisine and eating habits but were able to garner a substantial brand preference and demand from the consumers by virtue of their culture laden positioning strategies. Foreign products laced with Indian cultural elements (example Pizza Hut's Tandoori Pizza, McDonald's Aaloo Mc Burger, Maggi's masala noodles, Aata Noodles, etc.) and promoted by culturally congruent advertisements (example Pizza Hut's 'Great Indian Treat' campaign) facilitated the awareness of the brands while assuaging the resistance to foreign products and making the product as well as the brand culturally congruent.

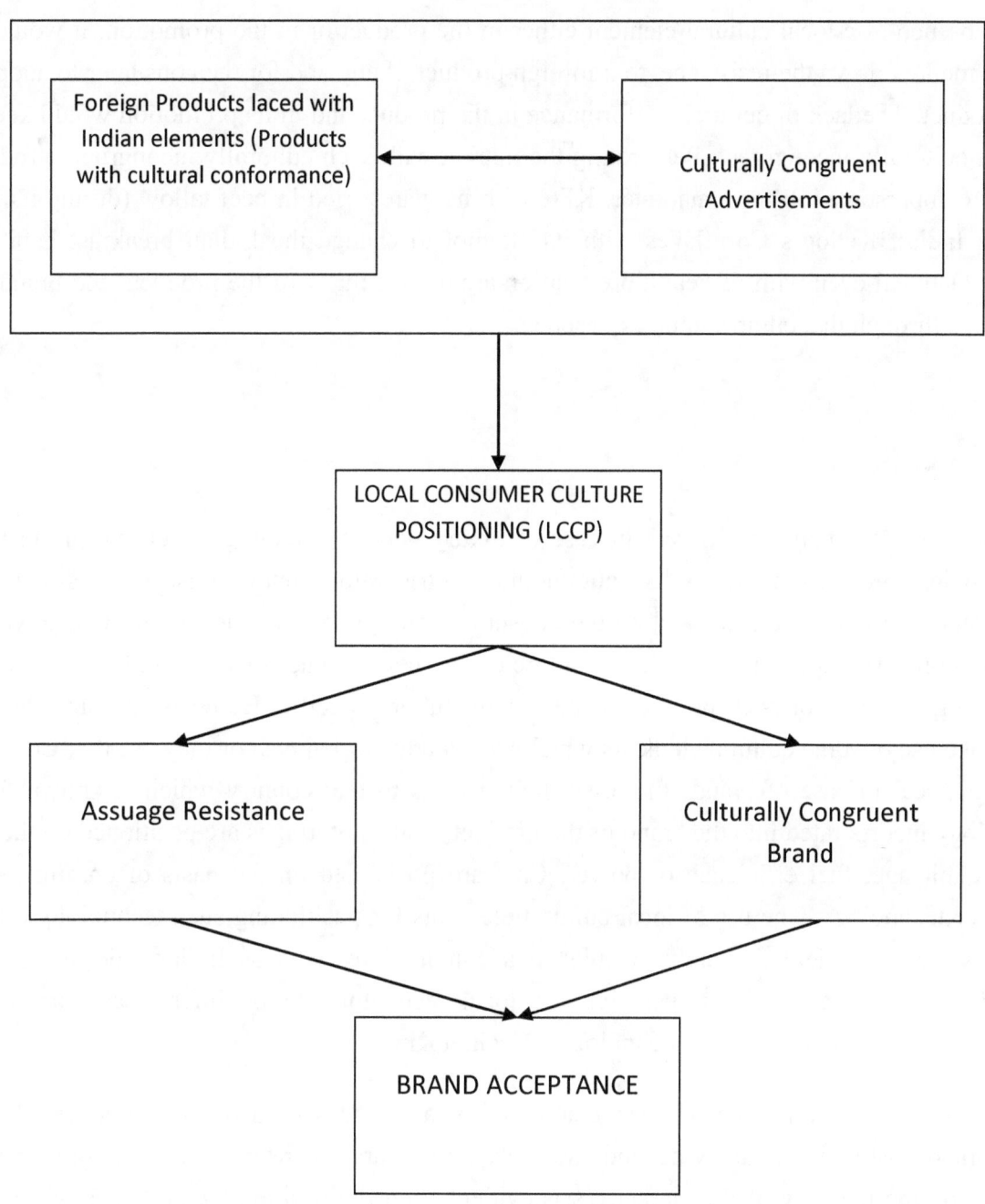

Figure 1: INCREMENTAL ACCULTURATION THROUGH LCCP

In the absence of a local cultural element either in the product or in the promotion, it would take time to mellow down the resistance, to a foreign product, if any and for the consumer to adopt to a new product. The lack of cultural conformance in the product and in its promotion would keep the product culturally incongruent. Penetrating the market with such culturally incongruent product is a fairly cumbersome job for a marketer. KFC with its wares fried in beef tallow (during its initial days in India), Kellog's Cornflakes with its attempt to change the Indian breakfast habits and Quaker Oatmeal even with its health proposition are among many of the products and brands that have gone through that cumbersome experience.

CONCLUSION

However the story may be different in case of luxury goods, technology intensive products and technological products. Products like automobiles, refrigerators, televisions, music systems and other electronic items are evaluated by the consumers on the basis of their performance which is measured on certain parameters which are more or less common across the world. Thus the brand positioning strategy for such products need not be culture specific. Brand positioning, however may make use of some cultural elements which have a universal appeal or may use the 'Country of Origin' appeal in case of brands that owe their genesis to that country which is known for the technology incorporated into the brand or the product. Thus motorbikes are positioned on the basis of their mileage, fuel efficiency or power. Cars are positioned on the basis of comfort, space, luxury or technology. The use of local cultural elements for positioning such technology oriented products may not yield favourable results in a country like India as Indians, despite strongly patronizing the local products, perceive the local technology to be inferior as compared to European, American or Japanese technology. (Neelam Kinra).

Thus the extent of competitive advantage acquired by a company by using local cultural elements in its brand positioning strategy depends not only on the target consumer and his ethnocentricity but also on the maturity of the market (as is evident from the positioning strategies of the Pizza selling brands in India. The use of LCCP in the initial years of their marketing is gradually giving way to GCCP), the sophistication and the exposure of the consumer and the product category.

****

166

REFERENCES

Alden Dana L., Steenkamp Jan- Benedict EM, & Batra Rajeev (1999); "Brand Positioning Through Advertising in Asia, North America and Europe: The role of global consumer culture"; Journal of Marketing; Vol. 63, January 1999.

Balabanis George & Diamantopoulos Adamantios (2004;, "Domestic Country Bias, Country of Origin effect and Consumer Ethnocentrisms: A Multidimensional Unfolding approach";, Journal of the Academy of Marketing Science; Vol. 32, Number 1, Winter 2004.

Gatignon Hubert, Weitz Barton, & Bansal Pradeep (1990); "Brand Introduction Strategies and Competitive Environments"; Journal of Marketing Research; Vol. 27, November 1990.

Jin Zongqui, Chansarkar Bal and Kondap N.M. (2006); " Brand origin in an emerging market: Perception of Indian Consumers"; Asia Pacific Journal of Marketing and Logistics; Vol. 18, No.4, 2006.

Kinra Neelam (2006); "The effect of country of origin on foreign brand names in the Indian Market"; Marketing Intelligence and planning; Vol. 24, Number 1, 2006.

Kippenberger (2000); "Emerging Srtategies for local Companies"; The Antidote; Vol. 5, Number 2, 2000.

Leclerc France, Schmitt Bernd H. and Dube Laurette; "Foreign branding and its effects on Product Perceptions and Attitudes"; Journal of Marketing Research; Vol. XXXI, May 1994.

Lim Kenny and Cass Aron O' (2001); "Consumer brand classifications: An assessment of culture of origin Versus Country of Origin"; Journal of Product and Brand Management; Vol. 10, Number 2, 2001.

Roth Martin S(1995); "The effects of culture and Socioeconomics on the performance of global brand image strategies"; Journal of Marketing Research; Vol. 32, No.2, May 1995.

Shocker Allan D., Srivastava Rajendra K., & Ruekert Robert W (1994); "Challenges and Opportunities facing Brand Management: An introduction to the special issue"; Journal of Marketing Research; Vol 31, May 1994.

Steenkamp Jan Benedict EM, Batra Rajeev and Alden Dana L (2003); "How Perceived Brand globalness creates brand value"; Journal of International Business Studies; Vol 34, Number 1, 2003.

Watson John J. and Wright Katrina (2000); "Consumer ethnocentrism and attitudes towards domestic and foreign products"; European Journal of Marketing; Vol. 34., 2000.

Subramanian, Bala (2002); "Culture based competitive positioning of consumer products in global markets."; Global Competitiveness; January 2002

"Cadbury sees India as cocoa growth market"; The Financial Times Limited; June 02, 2009

CHAPTER 9

IMPACT OF 'COUNTRY OF ORIGIN' ON BRAND POSITIONING AND THE INFLUENCE OF COUNTRY PERCEPTION ON BRAND PREFERENCE

ABSTRACT

Besides being influenced by other factors, the consumers' attitude towards a brand is also affected by the 'Country of Origin' of the brand. Because of this reason, a brand manager may choose to position a brand using its 'Country of Origin'. The 'Country of Origin' of a brand and 'Culture of Brand Origin' may have an influence on the brand positioning strategy. The influence, however, may not be the same across all product categories and in all countries. The paper examines the influence of 'Country of Origin' and 'Culture of Brand Origin' on the positioning strategies of FMCG brands in India. To understand the influence of 'Country of Origin' and 'Culture of Brand Origin' on the brand positioning strategies, response was sought from thirty brand managers and assistant brand managers working for different Indian and foreign MNCs, dealing in FMCG brands.

The paper also endeavours to assess the relationship between the consumers' 'quality perception' and 'reliability perception' about a given country and their preference of brands originating from that country. Responses were gathered from the users of FMCG brands using a structured questionnaire.

'Country of Origin' and 'Culture of Brand Origin' were found to have some influence on the positioning strategies of MNCs for their FMCG brands in the Indian market. Findings also indicate a strong relationship between the consumers' preference of brands from a certain country and their perception about the quality and reliability of brands from those countries.

***Keywords:** Brand Positioning, Brand Preference, FMCG, Country of Origin, Culture of Brand Origin.*

INTRODUCTION

Today, the Governments of several countries make a serious effort to create a positive perception and image of the country in the minds of the people across the world. A favourable image of the country not only boosts tourism but also has other important commercial implications. The products manufactured in the country and brands originating from the country are perceived favourably by consumers in the international market. The 'Country of Origin' association of the brand may favourably influence the purchase decision of the consumer. A positive image of the country also promotes the nation as a favourable investment destination and attracts foreign investment in its market and industry. Because of these significant commercial implications many countries across the world are being marketed like any other brand (Kotler et al, 2007).

Several countries including New Zealand, Hong Kong and India have taken such marketing initiatives. New Zealand embarked on a brand campaign by creating the 'New Zealand Way' brand represented by a fern leaf (the logo for 'New Zealand Way' brand), a descriptive short phrase on quality and the slogan 'The New Zealand Way'. A number of companies from New Zealand were licensed to use the 'New Zealand Way' brand (Keller, 2008). It can be called a government sponsored strategy to use the 'Country of Origin' association to position the product and brands from New Zealand in the international market. Similarly, Hong Kong designed the logo of a stylised dragon to be used on the products manufactured in the country and on the brands originating from Hong Kong and to represent the brand value of Hong Kong and its products (Kotler et al, 2007 & Benedict et al, 2003). India too has been endeavouring to develop a strong and favourable image for itself so as to reap commercial benefits out of it. The Government of India has set up the India Brand Equity Foundation (IBEF) to promote India as an investment destination (Benedict, et al, 2003). The present Foreign Trade Policy (ie, Foreign Trade Policy 2009-2014) has launched the 'Brand India' initiative to promote the export of goods and services from India by systematically creating a positive image for Indian products and brands. The 'Brand India' initiative proposes to organise at least six 'Brand India' shows and exhibitions across the world every year. These shows and exhibitions would showcase the products and technology being developed in India (Source: Foreign Trade Policy, Govt. of India, 2009-14). The 'Brand India' initiative is aimed at creating a positive 'Country of Origin' association for Indian brands in the minds of the consumers.

 It is a known fact that people have some general perception about different countries and countries are stereotyped for certain category of products, services or technology (Bannister et al, 1978). A brand originating from a certain country may leverage the benefit of the positive image of the country and the positive perception about it, if any by highlighting the 'Country of Origin' while positioning the brand.

The perception about a brand owing to its origin from a certain country is subject to change over time. Japan, Before World War II, was believed to be a manufacturer of poor quality products. However, as a consequence of its TQM initiative and quality revolution in Japan and as a result of the success of several automobile brands and electronic brands in the global market, Japanese technology and brands are considered to be amongst the best in the world.

LITERATURE REVIEW

Country of origin of the brand has a greater influence on the perceived quality of the brand than on the purchase intension of the consumer or on his attitude towards the brand (Verlegh et al, 1999). Dimensions of brand equity are also significantly and positively influenced by the brand's 'Country of Origin' image (Yasin Noorjaya Mohd. Et al, 2007). Research indicates that the effect of the 'Country of Origin' on consumer's brand perception differs across brands and across countries of production (Koubaa, 2008). It has been found that though, the knowledge of the country of origin of a brand influences the belief of the consumer about the brand, it does not have any direct influence on the attitude of the consumer towards the brand. However, as beliefs may be instrumental in shaping the attitude, the consumers' knowledge of the brand's origin may indirectly affect his attitude through the beliefs about the brand emanating out of this knowledge (Erickson et al, 1984). Even in case of low involvement products, the 'Country of Origin' of the brand influences the consumer's evaluation of the brand and his attitude towards low involvement products. However, in the presence of other extrinsic factors like price and brand, the brand becomes the determinant factor that influences the consumer attitude and the impact of the 'Country of Origin' significantly weakens. It has also been found that the country's positive image in any given product category does not necessarily carry over to the other product categories (Ahmed et al, 2004)

In today's era of global marketing and global integration, many brands particularly those of technology intensive products, are designed in a particular country but may be assembled in some other country. In such cases, involving brand of products like automobiles, VCRs and shoes, a combined effect of the country of design and the Country of assembly cues has a stronger impact than brand name on consumer's evaluation of quality and purchase value of the products (Ahmed & Astous, 1996). Research suggests that the image of country of brand origin and country of manufacture have significant influence on consumer's evaluation of product quality, product value and willingness to buy (Iyer & Kalita, 1997). An interesting contradiction can be seen in a research that studied the influence of the country of origin and the country of manufacture of multinational products on product evaluation and found that the Country of Manufacture has no effect on product quality evaluation when the information about the Country of Corporate ownership is available (Thakor & Layack, 2003).

Information about a product's or brand's Country of Origin influences the consumer's product evaluation even when the consumer doesn't intend to use the 'Country of Origin' as a criterion of evaluation (Liu et al, 2005). Country of Origin becomes an important element in influencing the consumer's perception about the product when any other substantial information is not available about the product (Al-Sulaiti & Baker, 1998). Experts use the 'Country of Origin' for product evaluation only when product attribute information is ambiguous. Novices use the 'Country of Origin' information in their evaluation regardless of whether the attribute information are ambiguous or unambiguous (Maheswaran, 1994).

Products from industrialised countries are perceived to be better than those from less developed countries. However, a famous brand name mellows down the perceived negative image associated with a less developed country (Cordell, 1993). Also, consumers express a preference of locally made products when price, technical features and brand names are invariant (Elliot & Cameron, 1994).

The 'Country of Origin' information about the brand is an equally salient and more enduring factor than the global characteristics of the brand in consumer product evaluation (Tse & Gorn, 1993). The phenomenon of foreign branding (the strategy of pronouncing or spelling a brand in a foreign language) triggers cultural stereotypes and influences product perceptions and attitudes (Leclerc et al, 1994). Cultural origin and heritage of a brand has a greater influence than the Country-of-Origin of the brand on consumers' perception of brands and in their classification ability of the brand. 'Culture of Brand Origin' is proposed to have replaced Country-of-Origin' as the most important origin influence regarded by consumers in their perceptions of brands (Lim & O'Cass, 2001).

In the context of the Indian market, it has been found that the Indian consumers, despite being high on ethnocentricism, perceive the foreign brands to be better in quality and superior in technology than the Indian brands (Kinra, 2006). Another study in the Indian context revealed that most of the consumers can recognise the brand origin correctly but the ability to correctly recognise the brand origin decreases when a brand has a long history of localisation (Jin et al, 2006).

Though literature indicates the impact of 'Country of Origin' on the consumers' attitude towards a brand, sufficient evidence is not present to make a conclusive comment on the impact of 'Country of Origin' and 'Culture of Brand Origin' on the positioning strategies of FMCG brands. Also, the present literature is not sufficient to understand if the Indian consumers' preference of FMCG brands from a certain country is influenced by their general perception of quality and reliability of brands from that country. The present study makes an attempt to measure the degree of impact of 'Country of Origin' and 'Culture of Brand Origin' on the positioning strategies of FMCG brands in the Indian market. The paper also studies the relationship between the consumers' 'quality perception' and 'reliability perception' of a country and their preference of brands from that country.

OBJECTIVES OF THE STUDY

The objectives of the study are:

1. To study the extent of impact of 'country of Origin' and 'Culture of Brand Origin' on positioning of FMCG brands in India.
2. To find out if the consumers' 'quality perception' of a certain country influence their preference of FMCG brands from that country.
3. To examine if the consumers' 'reliability perception' of a certain country influence their preference of FMCG brands from that country.

METHODOLOGY

The data for the study was collected using two separately designed questionnaires for the consumers and the brand managers. To measure the extent of impact of 'Country of Origin' and 'Culture of Brand Origin' on the brand positioning strategies of FMCG brands in the Indian market, a structured questionnaire was administered to the brand managers. The questionnaire was administered to thirty brand managers and assistant brand managers working for different Indian or Foreign Multinational companies operating in India and dealing in FMCG.

To understand the relationship between the consumers' 'quality perception' and 'reliability perception' of a country and their preference of FMCG bands from that country, another questionnaire was administered to 250 consumers. Consumers were selected for the study through judgemental sampling. The respondents were selected from five different states of India and included housewives, working professionals, businessmen and students (pursuing graduation and post graduation). Questions were designed to understand the consumers' perception of the quality of brands and reliability of brands from different countries and their preference of brands from these countries. Chi Square test was used to judge the relationship between the consumers' perception about quality of brands and reliability of brands from different countries and their preference of brands from these countries.

IMPACT OF COUNTRY OF ORIGIN ON BRAND POSITIONING

To understand the impact of the 'Country of Origin' of an FMCG brand on its brand positioning strategy, the brand managers surveyed were asked about the degree of influence that the 'Country of Origin' has on the positioning of the brand and whether highlighting the origin of the brand strengthens its positioning.

The response of the managers show that most of the brand managers (33.3% of respondents) are of the opinion that 'Country of Origin' of a brand has a moderate influence on the positioning strategy of the brand. The mean of the response is 2.72 and the mode is 3.00 which indicate a moderate influence (See Table 9.1).

Table 9.1: Influence of Country of Origin of the brand on Positioning

	Frequency	Percent	Valid Percent	Mean	Mode
Insignificant/ no influence (1)	6	20.0	20.0		
Weak influence (2)	7	23.3	23.3		
Moderate influence (3)	10	33.3	33.3	2.72	3.00
Significant influence (4)	3	10.0	10.0		
Strong influence (5)	4	13.3	13.3		
Total	30	100.0	100.0		

On being asked whether highlighting the 'Country of Origin' strengthens the positioning of the brand, majority of the respondents (46.7 %) indicated that it may have some impact on the strength of the positioning. 26% of the brand managers also indicated that highlighting the 'Country of

Origin' fortifies the positioning of the brand (See Table 9.2). On the whole, the brand managers were found to believe that highlighting the 'Country of Origin' of a brand has some degree of positive influence on the positioning of a brand in the consumers' mind.

Table 9.2: Highlighting the Country of Origin strengthens positioning

	Frequency	Percent	Valid Percent	Mean	Mode
Has No Impact (1)	5	16.7	16.7		
Somewhat Weakens (2)	3	10.0	10.0		
Somewhat Strengthens (3)	14	46.7	46.7	2.83	3.00
Strongly Fortifies (4)	8	26.7	26.7		
Total	30	100.0	100.0		

To study the impact of the 'Culture of Brand Origin' on the positioning strategy of the brand, the brand managers were asked up to what extent their brands reflect the culture of the country from where the brand has originated. 26.7 % of the brand managers indicated that the culture of brand origin was moderately highlighted in their brands whereas 30 % of the respondents indicated that it was highlighted up to a good extent. The mean of the response was 3.40 and the mode was 3.50 indicating a moderate to significant incorporation of 'Culture of Brand Origin' in brand positioning strategy for Fast Moving Consumer Goods (See Table 9.3).

Table 9.3: Brands reflect Culture of Origin

	Frequency	Percent	Valid Percent	Mean	Mode
Don't Reflect (1)	2	6.7	6.7		
Insignificantly (2)	5	16.7	16.7		
Moderately (3)	8	26.7	26.7	3.40	3.50
Significantly (4)	9	30.0	30.0		
Very Strongly (5)	6	20.0	20.0		
Total	30	100.0	100.0		

IMPACT OF CONSUMERS' 'QUALITY PERCEPTION' & 'RELIABILITY PERCEPTION' OF COUNTRY OF ORIGIN ON BRAND PREFERENCE

Consumers were also studied to find out if there is a significant difference in their preference for any brand based on the perception that they have about the origin of the brand. Responses were sought from the consumers' regarding their perception about quality and reliability of brands from different countries and their preference of brands originating from these countries.

Table 9.4 indicates that a majority of the respondents (66.3% of the consumers surveyed) believe that Indian brands of Fast Moving Consumer Goods are more reliable than brands from other countries.

Table 9.4

Reliability Perception Based on Country of Origin	Responses	Percent of Responses	Percent of Respondents
Indian brands are more reliable	165	43.2%	66.3%
American brands are more reliable	82	21.5%	32.9%
German brands are more reliable	45	11.8%	18.1%
French brands are more reliable	15	3.9%	6.0%
Japanese brands are more reliable	63	16.5%	25.3%
Chinese brands are more reliable	12	3.1%	4.8%
Total	382	100.0%	153.4%

Table 9.5 shows that most of the respondents (54.8%) perceive the Indian brands to be better in quality and performance followed by 38.8 % of the consumers who believe that American brands offer better quality and performance.

Table 9.5

Quality Perception Based on Country of Origin	Responses	Percent of Responses	Percent of Respondents
India brands offer better quality and performance	137	36.3%	54.8%
American brands offer better quality and performance	97	25.7%	38.8%
German brands offer better quality and performance	47	12.5%	18.8%
French brands offer better quality and performance	21	5.6%	8.4%
Japanese brands offer better quality and performance	66	17.5%	26.4%
Chinese brands offer better quality and performance	9	2.4%	3.6%
Total	377	100.0%	150.8%

The finding about the impact of the country of origin on brand preference is consistent with the findings related to the belief of the consumers about the reliability and quality of brands from different countries as exhibited in table 4 and table 5 respectively. Table 9.6 indicates that a major percentage of respondents (72.8 %) claim to have a higher preference for FMCG brands originating from India followed by 40.4 % of respondents who have a higher preference for FMCG brands originating from USA.

Table 9.6

Preference of Brands based on Country of Origin	Responses	Percent of Responses	Percent of Respondents
I have a higher preference for Indian brands	182	44.9%	72.8%
I have a higher preference for American brands	101	24.9%	40.4%
I have a higher preference for German brands	38	9.4%	15.2%
I have a higher preference for French brands	22	5.4%	8.8%
I have a higher preference for Japanese	51	12.6%	20.4%
I have a higher preference for Chinese brands	11	2.7%	4.4%
Total	405	100.0%	162.0%

To find out if there is any relationship between the consumer's 'Reliability perception based on Country of Origin' and his 'Preference of brands originating from difference countries', Chi Square test was employed (Refer Table 9.7). Table 9.7 shows that the p values for each of the variables (indicating reliability perception based on Country of Origin) are less than the significance level of 0.05. The results of the Chi Square test thus indicate that there is a significant relationship between the consumer's reliability perception about a certain country and his preference of brands from that country.

Table 9.7

		High Preference of Brands from Respective Country		d/f	Chi Square (p Value)
Reliability based on COO		Yes	No		
Indian brands are more reliable	Yes	90.9%	9.1%	1	80.371[a] (.000)
	No	37.6%	62.4%		
American brands are more reliable	Yes	85.4%	14.6%	1	102.467[a] (.000)
	No	18.5%	81.5%		
German brands are more reliable	Yes	68.9%	31.1%	1	122.724[a] (.000)
	No	3.4%	96.6%		
French brands are more reliable	Yes	80.0%	20.0%	1	100.797[a]
	No	4.3%	95.7%		(.000)
Japanese brands are more reliable	Yes	58.7%	41.3%	1	76.204[a] (.000)
	No	7.5%	92.5%		
Chinese brands are more reliable	Yes	33.3%	66.7%	1	25.086[a] (.000)
	No	2.9%	97.1%		

Similarly, Chi Square test was also used to find out if there is any relationship between the consumer's 'Quality/Performance perception based on Country of Origin' and his 'Preference of brands originating from difference countries'. Table 9.8 shows that the p values for each of the variables (indicating the quality/performance perception based on Country of Origin) are less than the significance level of 0.05.

Table 9.8

		Higher Preference of Brands from Respective Country		d/f	Chi Square (p Value)
Quality Perception based on COO		Yes	No		
Indian brands offer better quality and performance	Yes	94.2%	5.8%	1	69.841[a] (.000)
	No	46.9%	53.1%		
American brands offer better quality and performance	Yes	71.1%	28.9%	1	62.177[a] (.000)
	No	20.9%	79.1%		
German brands offer better quality and performance	Yes	59.6%	40.4%	1	88.424[a] (.000)
	No	4.9%	95.1%		
French brands offer better quality and performance	Yes	52.4%	47.6%	1	54.255[a] (.000)
	No	4.8%	95.2%		
Japanese brands offer better quality and performance	Yes	51.5%	48.5%	1	53.465[a] (.000)
	No	9.2%	90.8%		
Chinese brands offer better quality and performance	Yes	55.6%	44.4%	1	58.082[a] (.000)
	No	2.5%	97.5%		

In this case again, the results of the Chi Square test indicate that there is a significant relationship between the consumer's reliability perception about a certain country and his preference of brands from that country.

Inference: A brand manager should refrain from highlighting the 'Country of Origin' for positioning a brand until a strong quality and reliability association with the country has been established in the minds of the consumers.

FINDINGS:

The findings from the analysis of response of the brand managers regarding the influence of the 'country of Origin' and 'Culture of Brand Origin' on brand positioning strategies of FMCG brands in the Indian market are:

1. 'Country of Origin' of the brand has a moderate influence on the brand positioning strategies of FMCG brands in the Indian market.
2. A major percentage of the brand managers agree that highlighting the 'Country of Origin' of an FMCG brand in India has some degree of positive influence on the positioning of the brand in the minds of the consumers.
3. Most of the brand managers working for the multinational companies dealing in FMCG brands in India feel that their brands reflect the culture of the country from where they have originated up to a moderate or significant level. It indicates a significant influence of the 'Culture of Brand Origin' on the brand positioning strategies of FMCG brands in India.

The findings from the response of the consumers regarding perception and the consequent preference of brand form different countries as well as the relation between the consumers' perception of brands from a certain country and their preference of brands from that country is as follows:

1. A huge majority of the Indian consumers claim that they prefer to use Indian brands of fast moving consumer goods as compared to brands originating from other countries as they perceive the Indian brands to be higher in reliability and superior in quality and performance.
2. The consumers' preference of FMCG brands from a certain country is influenced by his perception about the general quality of brands from that country as well as his perception about the reliability of brands from the given country.

CONCLUSION:

From the study, it can be concluded that while there is a moderate influence of the 'Country of Origin' of an FMCG brand on its positioning strategy, the 'Culture of Brand Origin' has a significant influence on the brand positioning strategies of FMCG brands in the Indian market. Another inference that can be drawn from the study is that there is a significant relationship between the consumers' perception about the quality and reliability of brands from a certain country and their preference of FMCG brands from that country.

****

REFERENCES

Ahmed, Sadrudin, Astous, Alain d' (1996), "Country of Brand Origin and Brand Effects: A Multi-Dimensional Multi-Attribute Study", Journal of International Consumer Marketing, Vol 9, Iss. 2, pp. 93-115

Ahmed, Zafar U, Johnson, James P., Yang, Xia, Fatt, Chen Kheng, Teng, Han Sack, Boon, Lim Chee (2004), "Does country of origin matter for low-involvement products?", International Marketing Review, Vol. 21, Iss. 1, pp.102 – 120

Al-Sulaiti, Khalid I., Baker, Michael J. (1998), "Country of origin effects: a literature review", Marketing Intelligence & Planning, Vol. 16, Iss. 3, pp.150 – 199

Bannister, J.P., Saunders, J.A (1978), "UK Consumers' Attitudes towards Imports: The Measurement of National Stereotype Image", European Journal of Marketing, Volume 12, No. 8, pp. 562-570

Cordell, Victor V, (1993), "Interaction Effect of Country of Origin with Branding, Price and Perceived Performance Risk", Journal of International Consumer Marketing, Volume 5, Iss. 2, pp. 5-20.

Department of Commerce (2009), "Foreign Trade Policy August 27, 2009-March 31, 2014", Ministry of Commerce & Industry, Government of India

Elliot, Gregory R., Cameron, Ross C. (1994), "Consumer Perception of Product Quality and the Country-of-Origin Effect", Journal of International Marketing, Vol. 2, No. 2, pp. 49-62

Erickson, Gary M, Johansson, Johny K, Chao, Paul (1984), "Image Variables in Multi-Attribute Product Evaluations: Country-of-Origin Effects", Journal of Consumer Research, Vol. 11 (September), pp. 694-699

Iyer, Gopalkrishnan R., Kalita, Jukti K (1997), "The Impact of Country of Origin and Country of Manufacture Cues on Consumer Perceptions of Quality and Value", Journal of Global Marketing, Volume 11, Iss. 1, pp. 7-28

Jin, Zhongqi, Chansarkar, Bal, Kondap N.M.(2006), "Brand Origin in an Emerging Market: Perceptions of Indian Consumers", Asia Pacific Journal of Marketing and Logistics, Vol. 18, Iss. 4, pp.283 – 302

Keller, Kevin Lane (2008), Strategic Brand Management- Building, Measuring and Managing Brand Equity, 3rd ed., Pearson, New Delhi, pp. 308-309

Kinra, Neelam (2006), "The Effect Of Country-of-Origin on Foreign Brand Names in the Indian Market", Marketing Intelligence & Planning, Vol. 24, Iss. 1, pp.15 – 30

Kotler, Philip, Keller, Kevin Lane, Koshy, Abraham, & Jha, Mithileshwar (2007), Marketing Management-A South Asian Perspective, 12th ed., Pearson Prentice Hall, New Delhi, pp. 582-584

Koubaa, Yamen (2008), "Country of Origin, Brand Image Perception, and Brand Image Structure", Asia Pacific Journal of Marketing and Logistics, Vol. 20, Iss., pp.139 – 155

Leclerc, France, Schmitt, Bernd H.,Dube, Laurette (1994),; "Foreign Branding and its Effect on Product Perceptions and Attitudes", Journal of Marketing Research, Vol. 31, No. 2 (May), pp. 263-270

Lim, Kenny, O'Cass, Aron (2001), "Consumer Brand Classifications: An Assessment of Culture-of-Origin Versus Country-of-Origin", Journal of Product & Brand Management, Vol. 10, Iss. 2, pp.120 – 136

Liu, Scott S., Johnson, Keith F, Johnson, Keith F.(2005), "The Automatic Country-Of-Origin Effects On Brand Judgments", Journal of Advertising, Volume 34, Number 1 (Spring), pp. 87-97

Maheswaran, Durairaj (1994), "Country of Origin as a Stereotype: Effects of Consumer Expertise and Attribute Strength on Product Evaluations", The Journal of Consumer Research, Vol. 21, No. 2 (Sep.), pp. 354-365

Steenkamp, Jan Benedict EM, Batra, Rajeev and Alden, Dana L (2003), "How Perceived Brand globalness creates brand value", Journal of International Business Studies, Vol 34, Number 1, pp. 53-65

Thakor, Mrugank V., Lavack, Anne M. (2003), "Effect of perceived brand origin associations on consumer perceptions of quality", Journal of Product & Brand Management, Vol. 12, Iss. 6, pp. 394 – 407

Tse, David K., Gorn, Gerald J. (1993), "An Experiment on the Salience of Country-of-Origin in the Era of Global Brands", Journal of International Marketing, Vol 1, No. 1, pp. 57-76

Verlegh, Peeter W.J, Steenkamp Jan-Benedict E.M. (1999), "A Review and Meta Analysis of Country of Origin Research", Journal of Economic Psychology, Vol. 20, pp. 521-546

Yasin, Noorjaya Mohd.(2007), "Does Image of Country of Origin Matter to Brand Equity?", Journal of Product and Brand Management, Vol. 16, No. 1, pp. 38-48

IMPACT OF PERCEIVED BRAND ORIGIN (INDIAN Vs FOREIGN) ON CONSUMERS' BRAND PREFERENCE

ABSTRACT

In the pre-liberalisation era, Indian consumers were known to exhibit a distinctively higher preference for imported goods and 'foreign brands'. However, after two decades of the onset of liberalization, the market is flooded with brands with their origin in foreign countries. Indian brands too have significantly improved and many Indian brands today are considered at par with the foreign origin brands in terms of quality, technology, performance and efficacy. These brands give a tough competition to brands from the stable of foreign multinationals in the Indian market.

In this evolved scenario, though the country of origin of a brand may still remain a significant element in the brand positioning strategies for brands in certain category of products, it may not be equally relevant in influencing the preference of the consumer and his attitude towards brands in all categories.

The paper makes an attempt to examine the influence of the perceived origin of the country on the consumer's preference of brands of toiletries in the Indian market. To measure the influence of the 'Country of Origin' on the Indian consumer's perception of a brand, responses were collected from consumers from five different states of the country. Findings of the study indicate that consumers in India do not base their selection of brands of toiletries, detergents and food and beverages on the basis of their perception of the brand being 'Indian' or 'Foreign' in origin.

Keywords: *Country of Origin, Foreign Brands, Brand Perception, Brand Origin*

INTRODUCTION

Consumers have certain perceptions about different countries. Different countries conjure up different images in the consumers' mind and are stereotyped for certain category of products, services or technology (Bannister et al, 1978). For example: Germany may be perceived to be very good in automobile engineering and may be believed to be producing the best cars, Japan may be perceived to be offering the best quality precision technology and electronic goods, French products may be perceived to be sophisticated and stylish, Italy may be perceived to be better than all other countries in fashion technology and fashion accessories and USA may be perceived to be the best in high end technology products and so on. "These 'Country of Origin' perceptions are the mental associations and beliefs triggered by a country" (Kotler et al.). A brand originating from a certain country may leverage the benefit of the positive image of the country and the positive perception about it, if any by highlighting the 'Country of Origin' while positioning the brand.

'Country of Origin' is an important construct used in brand positioning and marketing of brands in the international market. The perception about the country of origin of a brand significantly influences the brand choice and preference of the consumers in several categories of products.

OBJECTIVES OF THE STUDY

The objective of the study is to examine if the consumer's perception about a brand of FMCG (toiletries, detergent and food & beverages in particular) being 'Indian' or 'Foreign' in its origin has any influence on the consumer's preference of the brand in the Indian market.

METHODOLOGY

The empirical study is based on the responses gathered from 250 consumers spread across five different states of India. The respondents included housewives, working professionals, businessmen and students (pursuing graduation and post graduation). Consumers were selected for the study through judgmental sampling. A structured questionnaire with close ended questions was administered to the respondents. Consumers were asked to indicate their perception about the origin of several brands belonging to eight different categories (Oral Care, Toilet Soap, Shampoo, Detergent, Tea/Coffee, Chocolate/Toffee, Food & Beverage and Cosmetics). The consumers were required to mark the perceived origin of the brands as Indian', 'Foreign' or 'Not Sure'. Another set of questions based on Likert scale were designed to measure the consumers' preference of the same brands chosen for the study.

ANOVA was used to identify the difference in the means of preference of brands across the category of consumers who perceived the brand to be an Indian brand and those who perceived it to be a 'Foreign' brand.

DATA ANALYSIS & DISCUSSION

To study the impact of the perceived brand origin on brand preference of various brands, ANOVA was used. The study has been conducted with several brands from different category of FMCG products. The different categories of FMCG brands included in the study are Oral Care brands, Toilet Soap brands, Shampoo brands and Cosmetics brands.

Oral Care Brands:

To check if the preference of the different oral care brands varies across categories of consumers who perceive these brands to be of Indian origin and those who perceive them to be of foreign origin, One Way ANOVA was used. The homogeneity of variance across these two categories of consumers was checked using Levene statistics (See Table 10.1). The table shows that the homogeneity of variance condition is fulfilled for all the oral care brands. Thus the difference in the means of preference of each oral care brands across these two categories of consumers can be checked using ANOVA.

Table 10.1: Test of Homogeneity of Variances (Oral Care Brands)

Preference of Brand	Levene Statistic	df1	df2	Sig.
Close Up	5.438	2	247	.005
Pepsodent	.710	2	247	.493
Colgate	.798	2	247	.452
Babool	2.175	2	247	.116

Table 10.2 shows that the p value for each of the variables (preference of each oral care brand) is more than 0.05. It indicates that the means of preference of a brand is not different for consumers

185

who believe the brand to be Indian and those who believe it to be a foreign brand. Thus, Table 10.2 shows that the preference for none of the oral care brands vary significantly across those consumers who perceive the brand to be an Indian brand and those who perceive it to be of foreign origin.

Table 10.2: ANOVA For Oral Care Brands

Brands		Sum of Squares	df	Mean Square	F	Sig.
Close Up	Between Groups	3.493	2	1.746	1.458	.235
	Within Groups	295.803	247	1.198		
Pepsodent	Between Groups	3.493	2	1.746	1.458	.235
	Within Groups	295.803	247	1.198		
Colgate	Between Groups	6.531	2	3.266	2.932	.055
	Within Groups	275.105	247	1.114		
Babool	Between Groups	5.776	2	2.888	1.949	.145
	Within Groups	365.988	247	1.482		

Inference:

In case of Oral Care brands, the consumers in the Indian market are not found to show a significant difference in their preference of brands based on their perception of the brand being Indian or foreign in its origin.

Toilet Soap Brands:

Results of Levene's test show that the p value for all the toilet soap brands except that of 'Lux' is more than 0.05 (See Table 10.3). It implies that the homogeneity of variance condition for all the brands except that for 'Lux' is fulfilled. Thus for all the brands except 'Lux', ANOVA can be applied. The difference in means of preference for 'Lux' across the two categories of consumers (Those who think it to be an Indian brand and those who believe it to be a foreign brand) can be checked using the Brown-Forsyth statistic for Robust Test for Equality of Means.

186

Table 10.3: Test of Homogeneity of Variances (Toilet Soap Brands)

Preference of Brand	Levene Statistic	df1	df2	Sig.
Lifebuoy	.030	2	247	.971
Lux	5.985	2	247	.003
Cinthol	.186	2	247	.830
Breeze	.935	2	247	.394
Dove	.571	2	247	.566
Pears	4.851	2	247	.009
Nirma Toilet Soap	.312	2	247	.732

As shown in Table 10.4, the p values for each of the variables (Toilet Soap brands) are less than 0.05, indicating that for each of the toilet soap brands there is no significant difference in the means of preference of the brand across consumers with different perception about the origin of the brand.

Table 10.4: ANOVA For Toilet Soap Brands

Brands		Sum of Squares	df	Mean	F	Sig.
Lifebuoy	Between Groups	2.368	2	1.184	.572	.565
	Within Groups	511.348	247	2.070		
Cinthol	Between Groups	3.659	2	1.830	1.060	.348
	Within Groups	426.405	247	1.726		
Breeze	Between Groups	1.832	2	.916	.702	.496
	Within Groups	322.072	247	1.304		
Dove	Between Groups	11.288	2	5.644	2.289	.104
	Within Groups	609.112	247	2.466		
Pears	Between Groups	2.840	2	1.420	.623	.537
	Within Groups	562.760	247	2.278		
Nirma	Between Groups	2.044	2	1.022	.584	.559
	Within Groups	432.472	247	1.751		

The result of the Brown-Forsythe statistic for the robust test of equality of means indicates that the means of preference of the brand 'Lux' do not vary with the perception of the consumer regarding the brand's country of origin (See Table 10.5).

Table 10.5: Robust Tests of Equality of Means for 'Lux'

	Statistic[a]	df1	df2	Sig.
Brown-Forsythe	5.578	2	163.476	.005

a. Asymptotically F distributed.

Inference:

As far as the preference of toilet soap brands in India is concerned, there is no significant difference in the preference of brands across categories of consumers who believe the brand to be Indian and those who believe it to be of a foreign origin.

Shampoo Brands:

The p value for the Levene Statistic used to test the homogeneity of variance for all the variables (preference for each of the Shampoo brands) except for that of 'Sunsilk' is more than 0.05 (See Table 10.6). Thus the means of preference for each brand (except for 'Sunsilk') across the consumers with different perception about the origin of the brand in question can be compared using ANOVA. The difference in means of preference for 'Sunsilk' across the two categories of consumers can be checked using the Welch statistic and Brown-Forsyth statistic for Robust Test for Equality of Means.

Table 10.6: Test of Homogeneity of Variances (Shampoo Brands)

Preference of Brand	Levene Statistic	df1	df2	Sig.
Sunsilk	3.274	2	247	.039
Vatika	2.849	2	247	.060
Clinic Plus	1.231	2	247	.294
Head & Shoulder	1.457	2	247	.235
Pantene	.149	2	247	.862

As shown in the result of ANOVA in Table 10.7, the p values for each of the shampoo brands is more than 0.05 indicating that the means of preference of any of these brands do not vary with the perception of the consumer regarding their origin.

Table 10.7: ANOVA For Shampoo Brands

Brands		Sum of	df	Mean	F	Sig.
Vatika	Between	5.759	2	2.879	1.537	.217
	Within Groups	462.757	247	1.874		
ClinicPlus	Between	5.075	2	2.538	1.483	.229
	Within Groups	422.589	247	1.711		
H&S	Between	.237	2	.118	.072	.930
	Within Groups	405.287	247	1.641		
Pantene	Between	2.954	2	1.477	.710	.493
	Within Groups	513.946	247	2.081		

The result of the Welch statistic and Brown-Forsythe statistic for the robust test of equality of means indicates that the means of preference of the brand 'Sunsilk' do not vary with the perception of the consumer regarding the brand's country of origin (See Table 10.8).

Table 10.8: Robust Tests of Equality of Means for 'Sunsilk'

	Statistic[a]	df1	df2	Sig.
Welch	.698	2	47.153	.503
Brown-Forsythe	.617	2	94.330	.542

a. Asymptotically F distributed.

Inference:

In case of shampoo brands, there is no significant difference in brand preference across categories of consumers who believe the brand to be Indian and those who believe it to be of a foreign origin.

Detergent Brands:

Table 10.9 shows that the homogeneity of variance condition is fulfilled for all the detergent brands as the p values for the Levene test for all these brands are more than 0.05. Thus the difference in the means of preference of each detergent brands across these two categories of consumers can be checked using ANOVA.

Table 10.9: Test of Homogeneity of Variances (Detergent Brands)

Preference of Brand	Levene Statistic	df1	df2	Sig.
Surf	.885	2	247	.414
Ariel	.148	2	247	.863
Tide	1.322	2	247	.268
Wheel	.526	2	247	.592
Sunlight	.798	2	247	.451
Nirma	2.025	2	247	.134
Rin	.859	2	247	.425

The p values for ANOVA applied to check the difference in the means of preference for each of the detergent brands across three categories of consumers (with different belief about the brand's origin) are more than 0.05 (See Table 10.10). The results of the test indicate that the preference of any of these brands do not vary with the perception of the consumer regarding their origin.

Table 10.10: ANOVA For Detergent Brands

Brands		Sum of Squares	df	Mean	F	Sig.
Surf	Between Groups	5.874	2	2.937	2.465	.087
	Within Groups	294.290	247	1.191		
Ariel	Between Groups	4.321	2	2.161	2.426	.090
	Within Groups	219.955	247	.891		
Tide	Between Groups	.230	2	.115	.075	.928
	Within Groups	378.186	247	1.531		
Wheel	Between Groups	4.410	2	2.205	1.375	.255
	Within Groups	396.090	247	1.604		
Sunlight	Between Groups	2.700	2	1.350	.983	.376
	Within Groups	339.156	247	1.373		
Nirma	Between Groups	2.938	2	1.469	.796	.452
	Within Groups	455.818	247	1.845		
Rin	Between Groups	3.435	2	1.717	.847	.430
	Within Groups	500.965	247	2.028		

Inference:

The preference of detergent brands amongst Indian consumers do not vary significantly across consumers who perceive a brand to be of foreign origin and those who perceive it to be of Indian origin.

Tea/Coffee Brands:

The p value for the Levene Statistic used to test the homogeneity of variance for all the variables (preference for each of the Tea/Coffee brands) is more than 0.05 except for that of 'Taj Mahal' (See Table 10.11). Thus the means of preference for each brand (except for 'Taj Mahal') across the consumers with different perception about the origin of the brand in question can be compared using ANOVA.

The difference in means of preference for 'Taj Mahal' across the two categories of consumers can be checked using the Welch statistic and Brown-Forsyth statistic for Robust Test for Equality of Means.

Table 10.11: Test of Homogeneity of Variances (Tea/Coffee Brands)

Preference of Brand	Levene Statistic	df1	df2	Sig.
Lipton	3.007	2	247	.051
Brooke Bond	.448	2	247	.640
Taj Mahal	7.810	2	247	.001
Tazaa	.871	2	247	.420
Agni	1.964	2	247	.142
Nestea	.339	2	247	.713
Nescafe	1.334	2	247	.265
Bru	2.548	2	247	.080

Results of ANOVA, conducted to find if the means of preference of tea/coffee brands vary for consumers who consider the brand to be an Indian brand, those who consider it to be a foreign brand and those who do not have any idea about the brand origin, are shown in Table 10.12. The table for ANOVA shows that the p value for each of the variables (preference of brand of tea/coffee) Lipton, Brooke Bond, Nestea and Bru is more than 0.05, indicating that the preferences of these brands do not vary significantly across consumers having different perceptions about the country of origin of the brand in question. As the p values for the preference of brands Taaza, Agni and Nescafe are less than the level of significance 0.05, the preferences of each of these three brands may vary with the consumer's perception about the origin of the brand.

Table 10.12: ANOVA For Tea/Coffee Brands

Brands		Sum of Squares	df	Mean	F	Sig.
Lipton	Between Groups	5.822	2	2.911	1.821	.164
	Within Groups	394.914	247	1.599		
Brooke Bond	Between Groups	.122	2	.061	.050	.951
	Within Groups	301.978	247	1.223		
Tazaa	Between Groups	11.668	2	5.834	3.255	.040
	Within Groups	442.768	247	1.793		
Agni	Between Groups	11.765	2	5.883	3.577	.029
	Within Groups	406.235	247	1.645		
Nestea	Between Groups	6.035	2	3.018	1.241	.291
	Within Groups	600.541	247	2.431		
Nescafe	Between Groups	9.331	2	4.666	7.402	.001
	Within Groups	155.693	247	.630		
Bru	Between Groups	.889	2	.444	.354	.702
	Within Groups	310.235	247	1.256		

The result of the Welch statistic and Brown-Forsythe statistic for the robust test of equality of means indicates the p values for both the tests are less than 0.05 which implies that the means of preference of the brand 'Taj Mahal' varies with the perception of the consumer regarding the brand's country of origin (See Table 10.13).

Table 10.13: Robust Tests of Equality of Means for 'Taj Mahal'

	Statistic[a]	df1	df2	Sig.
Welch	3.891	2	29.150	.032
Brown-Forsythe	5.463	2	48.942	.007

a. Asymptotically F distributed.

The Post Hoc test (Tukey HSD) conducted to find out which category of consumers show a significant difference in their preference of the brand 'Taaza' shows that there is no significant difference in the means of preference of the brand across any of the consumer categories (See Table 10.14).

Table 10.14: Tukey HSD (Post Hoc Test) for Taaza

Dependent	(I) Indicate the country of origin of Tazaa		(J) Indicate the country of origin of Tazaa		Mean Difference (I-	Std. Error	Sig.
Preference of the brand Tazaa		Indian	dimension3	Foreign	.665	.306	.078
				Not Sure	.569	.382	.298
	dimension2	Foreign	dimension3	Indian	-.665	.306	.078
				Not Sure	-.095	.472	.978
		Not Sure	dimension3	Indian	-.569	.382	.298
				Foreign	.095	.472	.978

The Post Hoc test (Tukey HSD) conducted to find out which category of consumers show a significant difference in their preference of the brand 'Agni' shows that a difference in the means of preference for the brand exists between the consumers who perceive the brand to be a foreign brand and those who are not sure about its origin. No difference in preference of the brands can be observed across consumers who perceive the brand to be either of Indian origin or of foreign origin (See Table 10.15 & Table 10.16).

Table 10.15: Tukey HSD (Post Hoc Test) for Agni

	(I) Indicate the country of origin of Agni		(J) Indicate the country of origin of Agni		Mean Difference (I-J)	Std. Error	Sig.
Preference of the brand Agni		Indian	dimension3	Foreign	-.849	.366	.055
				Not Sure	.382	.323	.465
	dimension2	Foreign	dimension3	Indian	.849	.366	.055
				Not Sure	1.231*	.473	.026
		Not Sure	dimension3	Indian	-.382	.323	.465
				Foreign	-1.231*	.473	.026

Table 10.16: Homogeneous Subsets for preference of the brand

		Indicate the country of origin of Agni	N	Subset for alpha = 0.05	
				1	2
Tukey HSD		Not Sure	17	2.00	
	dimension1	Indian	220	2.38	2.38
		Foreign	13		3.23
		Sig.		.594	.079
Waller-Duncan		Not Sure	17	2.00	
	dimension1	Indian	220	2.38	2.38
		Foreign	13		3.23

Means for groups in homogeneous subsets are displayed.

The Post Hoc test (Tukey HSD) conducted to find out which category of consumers show a significant difference in their preference of the brand 'Nescafe' shows that a difference in the means of preference of the brand 'Nescafe' exists between the consumers who perceive the brand to be Indian and those who are not sure about its origin. Difference in the preference for the brand also exists between the consumers who perceive the brand to be a foreign brand and those who are not sure about its origin. However, no difference in preference of the brands can be observed across consumers who perceive the brand to be of Indian origin and those who perceive it to be of foreign origin (See Table 10.17 & Table 10.18).

Table 10.17 Tukey HSD (Post Hoc Test) for Nescafe

	(I) Indicate the country of origin of Nescafe		(J) Indicate the country of origin of Nescafe	Mean Difference (I-J)	Std. Error	Sig.
Preference of the brand Nescafe	Indian	dimension3	Foreign	.078	.106	.743
			Not Sure	1.067*	.278	.000
	dimension2 Foreign	dimension3	Indian	-.078	.106	.743
			Not Sure	.989*	.272	.001
	Not Sure	dimension3	Indian	-1.067*	.278	.000
			Foreign	-.989*	.272	.001

195

Table 10.18: Homogeneous Subsets for preference of the brand

	Indicate the country of origin of Nescafe		N	Subset for alpha = 0.05	
				1	2
Tukey HSD		Not Sure	9	3.67	
	dimension 1	Foreign	151		4.66
		Indian	90		4.73
		Sig.		1.000	.940
Waller-Duncan	dimension 1	Not Sure	9	3.67	
		Foreign	151		4.66
		Indian	90		4.73

Means for groups in homogeneous subsets are displayed.

Table 10.19: Tukey HSD (Post Hoc Test) for Taj Mahal

	(I) Indicate the country of origin of Taj Mahal		(J) Indicate the country of origin of Taj Mahal	Mean Difference (I-J)	Std. Error	Sig.
Preference of the brand Taj Mahal	Indian	dimension3	Foreign	.789*	.218	.001
			Not Sure	-.111	.298	.927
dimension2	Foreign	dimension3	Indian	-.789*	.218	.001
			Not Sure	-.900*	.352	.030
	Not Sure	dimension3	Indian	.111	.298	.927
			Foreign	.900*	.352	.030

The Post Hoc test (Tukey HSD) conducted to find out which category of consumers show a significant difference in their preference of the brand 'Taj Mahal' shows that a difference in the means of preference of the brand exists between the consumers who perceive the brand to be Indian and those who perceive it to be of foreign origin (See Table 10.19).

As exhibited in Table 10.20, the mean preference for the brand 'Taj Mahal' is significantly lower in consumers who perceive the brand to be a foreign brand as compared to those who perceive it to be an Indian brand.

Table 10.20: Homogeneous Subsets for preference of the brand ' Taj Mahal'

	Indicate the country of origin of Taj Mahal	N	Subset for alpha = 0.05	
			1	2
Tukey HSD	Foreign	30	3.37	
dimension 1	Indian	205		4.16
	Not Sure	15		4.27
	Sig.		1.000	.925
Waller-Duncan	Foreign	30	3.37	
dimension 1	Indian	205		4.16
	Not Sure	15		4.27

Means for groups in homogeneous subsets are displayed.

Inference:

In general, the preference of Tea or Coffee brands amongst the consumers in India do not vary significantly between consumers who think of a brand as an Indian brand and those who think of it to be a foreign brand. However the brand 'Taj Mahal' was found to be an exception where the brand exhibits a higher preference amongst those consumers who believe the brand to have an Indian origin as compared to those who believed it to be a foreign brand.

Chocolate/Toffee Brands:

Results of Levene's test used to test the homogeneity of variance for all the variables (preference for each of the Chocolate/Toffee brands) show that the p values for all the chocolate/toffee brands except that of 'Cadbury Dairy Milk' and 'Five Star' are more than 0.05 (See Table 10.21). It implies that the homogeneity of variance condition for all the brands except that for 'Cadbury Dairy Milk' and 'Five Star' is fulfilled. Thus for all the chocolate and toffee brands except for these two brands, ANOVA can be applied. The difference in means of preference for 'Cadbury Dairy Milk' as well as for 'Five Star' across the three categories of consumers (Those who think it to be an Indian brand, those who believe it to be a foreign brand and those who are not sure about its origin) can be checked using the Brown-Forsyth statistic for Robust Test for Equality of Means.

Table 10.21: Test of Homogeneity of Variances (Chocolate/Toffee Brands)

Preference of Brand	Levene Statistic	df1	df2	Sig.
Cadbury Dairy Milk	12.910	2	247	.000
Cadbury Bournville	.863	2	247	.423
Cadbury Eclairs	.303	2	247	.739
Bar One	1.716	2	247	.182
Five Star	3.176	2	247	.043
Kit Kat	.021	2	247	.980
Munch	.519	2	247	.596
Alpenliebe	.449	2	247	.639
Poppins	2.833	2	247	.061
Hajmola	.995	2	247	.371

As shown in the result of ANOVA in Table 10.22, the p values for each of the chocolate and toffee brands is more than 0.05 indicating that the means of preference of any of these brands do not vary with the perception of the consumer regarding their origin.

Table 10.22: ANOVA For Chocolate/Toffee Brands

Brands		Sum of Squares	df	Mean	F	Sig.
Cadbury Bournville	Between Groups	4.282	2	2.141	1.219	.297
	Within Groups	433.862	247	1.757		
Cadbury Eclairs	Between Groups	2.650	2	1.325	.904	.406
	Within Groups	361.926	247	1.465		
Bar One	Between Groups	4.995	2	2.497	1.660	.192
	Within Groups	371.649	247	1.505		
Kit Kat	Between Groups	5.887	2	2.943	1.496	.226
	Within Groups	486.113	247	1.968		
Munch	Between Groups	.043	2	.022	.011	.989
	Within Groups	490.761	247	1.987		
Alpenliebe	Between Groups	1.726	2	.863	.384	.681
	Within Groups	554.610	247	2.245		
Poppins	Between Groups	5.235	2	2.617	1.190	.306
	Within Groups	543.469	247	2.200		
Hajmola	Between Groups	2.828	2	1.414	.573	.565
	Within Groups	609.748	247	2.469		

The Robust test of Equality of Means has been used to compare the means of preference of Cadbury Dairy Milk across category of consumers and that of Five star across consumer categories based on the consumer's perception about the origin of the brand. The Welch statistic and Brown-Fosyth statistic for Dairy Milk are less than 0.05 indicating that the means of preference of 'Cadbury Dairy Milk' is different across different consumer groups based on their belief about the origin of the brand. On the other hand the Welch statistic and Brown-Fosyth statistic for Five Star are more than 0.05 indicating that the means of preference of 'Five Star' do not vary across different consumer groups based on their belief about the origin of the brand (See Table 10.23).

Table 10.23: Robust Tests of Equality of Means for 'Dairy Milk' & 'Five Star'

		Statistic[a]	df1	df2	Sig.
Dairy Milk	Welch	4.092	2	16.338	.036
	Brown-Forsythe	3.760	2	20.556	.041
Five Star	Welch	2.473	2	51.285	.094
	Brown-Forsythe	1.985	2	110.700	.142

a. Asymptotically F distributed.

Table 10.24: Homogeneous Subsets for preference of 'Cadbury

	Indicate the country of origin of Cadbury Dairy Milk		N	Subset for 1
Tukey HSD	dimension 1	Not	7	4.43
		Foreign	151	4.48
		Indian	92	4.75
		Sig.		.420
Waller-Duncan	dimension 1	Not	7	4.43
		Foreign	151	4.48
		Indian	92	4.75

Means for groups in homogeneous subsets are displayed.

The homogeneous subsets for the 'Preference of Cadbury Dairy Milk' formed from the Post Hoc tests (Tukey HSD and Waller-Duncan) indicate that the mean preferences for the brand across category of consumers who think the brand to be an Indian brand, those who think of it as a foreign brand and those who are not sure of its origin are not significantly different (See Table 10.24)

Inference:

In case of Chocolate and Toffee brands, the consumers in the Indian market are not found to show a significant difference in their preference of brands based on their perception of the brand being Indian or foreign in its origin.

Cosmetics Brands:

Levene's test conducted to check the homogeneity of variance of the variables 'Preference of the cosmetic brands' give p values more than 0.05 except in case of the brand 'Vaseline' where the p value is less than 0.05 (See Table 10.25). As the prerequisite of homogeneity of variance is fulfilled in all cases except that of 'Vaseline', ANOVA can be applied to check whether the mean preference for each of these brands vary with the perception of consumers about the origin of the concerned brand. To check the same for the brand 'Vaseline' the Welch statistic and Brown-Forsythe statistic for the robust test for equality of means have been applied.

Table 10.25: Test of Homogeneity of Variances (Cosmetics Brands)

Preference of Brand	Levene Statistic	df1	df2	Sig.
Ponds	.622	2	247	.538
Fem	.123	2	247	.884
Garnier	1.680	2	247	.188
L'oreal	2.199	2	247	.113
Vaseline	3.305	2	247	.038
Boroline	1.352	2	247	.261
Boroplus	.663	2	247	.516

As shown in the result of ANOVA in Table 10.26, the p values for each of the cosmetics brands except for that of Boroline are more than 0.05 indicating that the means of preference of any of these brands do not vary with the perception of the consumer regarding their origin. However the p value for the preference of Boroline being less than 0.05, indicate that the mean preference of Boroline is different in different categories of consumers.

Table 10.26: ANOVA For Cosmetics Brands

Brands		Sum of	df	Mean	F	Sig.
Ponds	Between	2.455	2	1.227	1.004	.368
	Within Groups	301.821	247	1.222		
Fem	Between	.764	2	.382	.225	.799
	Within Groups	419.112	247	1.697		
Garnier	Between	1.209	2	.605	.332	.718
	Within Groups	449.687	247	1.821		
L'oreal	Between	1.714	2	.857	.445	.641
	Within Groups	475.630	247	1.926		
Boroline	Between	13.411	2	6.706	3.444	.033
	Within Groups	480.913	247	1.947		
Boroplus	Between	.791	2	.396	.177	.838
	Within Groups	553.145	247	2.239		

However when the Post Hoc test was conducted to check amongst which groups of consumers the preference of Boroline significantly varies, it was found that the significant difference in the preference for the brand is in case of consumers who perceive the brand to be Indian and those who don't have any clear idea about the origin about the brand. No difference in mean preference for the brand exists in case of consumers who perceive the brand to be Indian and those who perceive it to be a foreign brand (See Table 10.27).

Table 10.27: Tukey HSD (Post Hoc Test) for Boroline

	(I) Indicate the country of origin of Boroline		(J) Indicate the country of origin of Boroline	Mean Difference (I-J)	Std. Error	Sig.
Preference of the brand Boroline	Indian	dimension3	Foreign	.509	.312	.235
			Not Sure	.812	.373	.077
dimension2	Foreign	dimension3	Indian	-.509	.312	.235
			Not Sure	.303	.467	.793
	Not Sure	dimension3	Indian	-.812	.373	.077
			Foreign	-.303	.467	.793

202

The robust test for equality of means conducted for the brand 'Vaseline' also shows that the mean preference of 'Vaseline' does not vary amongst consumers with different perceptions about the country of origin of 'Vaseline' (See Table 10.28).

Table 10.28: Robust Tests of Equality of Means for 'Vaseline'

	Statistic[a]	df1	df2	Sig.
Welch	3.081	2	43.108	.056
Brown-Forsythe	2.782	2	54.970	.071

a. Asymptotically F distributed.

Inference:

The Indian consumers, while purchasing cosmetics, do not exhibit any significant difference in their preference of brands based on their perception of the brands being Indian or foreign in their origin.

Food & Beverage Brands:

Table 10.29 shows that the homogeneity of variance condition is fulfilled for all the Food & Beverage brands except AMUL as the p values for the Levene test for all the brands other than AMUL are more than 0.05. Thus the difference in the means of preference of each of these brands across the different categories of consumers can be checked using ANOVA. The difference in the means of preference of 'AMUL' across the different categories of consumers can be checked using the Welch statistic and Brown-Forsythe statistic for robust test of equality of means.

Table 10.29 Test Of Homogeneity Of Variances (Food & Beverage Brands)

Preference Of Brand	Levene	Df1	Df2	Sig.
Maggi	.335	2	247	.716
Everyday	.773	2	247	.463
Tropicana	.437	2	247	.647
Real Juice	.187	2	247	.830
Minute Maid	.659	2	247	.518
Frooti	1.413	2	247	.245
Maaza	.603	2	247	.548
Amul	3.624	2	247	.028

The results of ANOVA shown in Table 10.30 indicate that except that for brand 'Minute Maid', the p value for each of the other brands is more than the level of significance 0.05. Thus except that for Minute Maid, the mean preference for none of the food and beverage brands vary significantly amongst consumers who perceive the brand as an Indian brand, those who perceive it as a foreign brand and those who don't have any idea about the origin of the brand.

Table 10.30: ANOVA For Food & Beverage Brands

Brands		Sum of Squares	df	Mean Square	F	Sig.
Maggi	Between Groups	.328	2	.164	.163	.849
	Within Groups	248.072	247	1.004		
Everyday	Between Groups	10.459	2	5.230	2.653	.072
	Within Groups	486.917	247	1.971		
Tropicana	Between Groups	6.117	2	3.059	1.561	.212
	Within Groups	483.839	247	1.959		
Real Juice	Between Groups	1.707	2	.854	.397	.673
	Within Groups	530.649	247	2.148		
Minute Maid	Between Groups	27.906	2	13.953	7.205	.001
	Within Groups	478.350	247	1.937		
Frooti	Between Groups	5.818	2	2.909	1.970	.142
	Within Groups	364.698	247	1.477		
Maaza	Between Groups	1.266	2	.633	.407	.666
	Within Groups	383.634	247	1.553		

The result for the robust test of equality of means conducted to check the difference in the means of preference of 'AMUL' across the different categories of consumers, also show that the mean preference of the brand 'AMUL' is not significantly different across consumers with different perceptions about the origin of the brand 'AMUL' (See Table 10.31).

Table 10.31: Robust Tests of Equality of Means for 'AMUL'

	Statistic[a]	df1	df2	Sig.
Welch	1.135	2	16.378	.345
Brown-Forsythe	1.313	2	23.519	.288

a. Asymptotically F distributed.

Table 10.32: Tukey HSD (Post Hoc Test) for Minute Maid

	(I) Indicate the country of origin of Minute Maid	(J) Indicate the country of origin of Minute Maid	Mean Difference (I-J)	Std. Error	Sig.
Preference of Minute Maid	Indian dimension3	Foreign	.728*	.196	.001
		Not Sure	.246	.344	.755
dimension2	Foreign dimension3	Indian	-.728*	.196	.001
		Not Sure	-.483	.324	.297
	Not Sure dimension3	Indian	-.246	.344	.755
		Foreign	.483	.324	.297

To understand the way in which the mean preference of the brand 'Minute Maid' vary with the perception about the origin of the brand, Post Hoc Test was conducted. The test reveals that mean preference for the brand 'Minute Maid' is different for consumers who think that the brand is of Indian origin and those who think it is of foreign origin (See Table 10.32).

The homogeneous subsets for the 'Preference of Minute Maid' formed from the Post Hoc tests (Tukey HSD and Waller-Duncan) indicate that the mean preference of the brand is lower in consumers who believe the brand to be of foreign origin as compared to those who believe it to be of Indian origin (See Table 10.33).

Table 10.33: Homogeneous Subsets for preference of ' Minute Maid'

	Indicate the country of origin of Minute Maid	N	Subset for alpha = 0.05	
			1	2
Tukey HSD	Foreign	154	2.56	
dimension 1	Not Sure	21	3.05	3.05
	Indian	75		3.29
	Sig.		.233	.683
Waller-Duncan	Foreign	154	2.56	
dimension 1	Not Sure	21	3.05	
	Indian	75	3.29	

Means for groups in homogeneous subsets are displayed.

Inference:

In case of food & beverage brands in general, there is no significant difference in brand preference across categories of consumers who believe the brand to be Indian and those who believe it to be of a foreign origin. However, Minute Maid was found to be an exception where the consumers who thought the brand to be an Indian brand had a significantly higher preference for it in comparison to those consumers who believed it to be a foreign brand.

FINDINGS

In none of the category of FMCG brands taken up for the study, consumers exhibit any significant difference in their preference of the brands based on their perception about the origin of the brand. Of the 56 brands (from 8 different categories of FMCG) studied the only exceptions were the brands 'Taj Mahal' and 'Minute Maid'. In both these cases consumers who perceived the brands to be of Indian origin had a significantly higher preference for them. The finding implies that the 'Country of Origin' perception of the mass market brands do not have any traceable influence on the consumer's preference of the selected brands in the Indian market.

IMPLICATION OF THE STUDY

While positioning brands of toiletries, detergents or packaged food and beverages targeted at the mass market in India, the mere use of the 'Country of Origin' as the main brand positioning construct would not ensure an enhanced preference for the brands in the Indian market.

****

REFERENCES

Ahmed Sadrudin, Astous Alain d' (1996), "Country of Brand Origin and Brand Effects: A Multi-Dimensional Multi-Attribute Study", *Journal of International Consumer Marketing*, Vol 9, Issue 2, pp.93-115,

Ahmed Zafar U, Johnson James P., Yang Xia, Fatt Chen Kheng, Teng Han Sack, Boon Lim Chee (2004), "Does country of origin matter for low-involvement products?", *International Marketing Review*, Vol. 21 Iss: 1, pp.102 – 120

Al-Sulaiti Khalid I., Baker Michael J. (1998), "Country of origin effects: a literature review", *Marketing Intelligence & Planning*, Vol. 16 Iss: 3, pp.150 – 199

Bannister, J.P., Saunders, J.A (1978), "UK Consumers' Attitudes towards Imports: The Measurement of National Stereotype Image", *European Journal of Marketing*, Volume 12, Number 8, 1978 , pp. 562-570

Cordell Victor V, (1993), "Interaction Effect of Country of Origin with Branding, Price and Perceived Performance Risk", *Journal of International Consumer Marketing*, Volume 5, Issue 2, 1993, pp. 5-20.

Elliot Gregory R., Cameron Ross C. (1994), "Consumer Perception of Product Quality and the Country-of-Origin Effect", *Journal of International Marketing*, Vol. 2, No. 2, 1994, pp. 49-62.

Erickson Gary M, Johansson Johny K, Chao Paul (1984), "Image Variables in Multi-Attribute Product Evaluations: Country-of-Origin Effects", *Journal of Consumer Research*, Vol. 11, September 1984, pp. 694-699

Iyer Gopalkrishnan R., Kalita Jukti K (1997), "The Impact of Country of Origin and Country of Manufacture Cues on Consumer Perceptions of Quality and Value", *Journal of Global Marketing*, Volume 11, Issue 1, 1997, pp. 7-28.

Jin Zhongqi, Chansarkar Bal, Kondap N.M.(2006), "Brand Origin in an Emerging Market: Perceptions of Indian Consumers", *Asia Pacific Journal of Marketing and Logistics*, Vol. 18 Iss: 4, 2006, pp.283 – 302

Kinra Neelam (2006), "The Effect Of Country-of-Origin on Foreign Brand Names in the Indian Market", *Marketing Intelligence & Planning*, Vol. 24 Iss: 1, 2006, pp.15 – 30.

Koubaa Yamen (2008), "Country of Origin, Brand Image Perception, and Brand Image Structure", *Asia Pacific Journal of Marketing and Logistics*, Vol. 20 Iss: 2, pp.139 – 155, 2008

Leclerc France, Schmitt Bernd H.,Dube Laurette (1994) , "Foreign Branding and its Effect on Product Perceptions and Attitudes", *Journal of Marketing Research*, Vol. XXXI (May 1994), pp. 263-270

Lim Kenny, O'Cass Aron (2001), "Consumer Brand Classifications: An Assessment of Culture-of-Origin Versus Country-of-Origin", *Journal of Product & Brand Management*, Vol. 10 Iss: 2, pp.120 – 136.

Liu, Scott S. Liu, Johnson, Keith F., Johnson, Keith F.(2005), "The Automatic Country-Of-Origin Effects On Brand Judgments", Journal of Advertising, Volume 34, Number 1 / Spring 2005, pp. 87-97

Maheswaran Durairaj (1994), "Country of Origin as a Stereotype: Effects of Consumer Expertise and Attribute Strength on Product Evaluations", The Journal of Consumer Research, Vol. 21, No. 2(Sep., 1994), pp. 354-365

Thakor Mrugank V., Lavack Anne M. (2003), "Effect of perceived brand origin associations on consumer perceptions of quality", Journal of Product & Brand Management, Vol. 12 Iss: 6, pp.394 – 407.

Tse David K., Gorn Gerald J. (1993), "An Experiment on the Salience of Country-of-Origin in the Era of Global Brands" Journal of International Marketing, Vol 1, No. 1,1993, pp. 57-76

Verlegh Peeter W.J, Steenkamp Jan-Benedict E.M. (1999), "A Review and Meta Analysis of Country of Origin Research", Journal of Economic Psychology (20), 1999, pp:521-546

Yasin Noorjaya Mohd.(2007), "Does Image of Country of Origin Matter to Brand Equity?", Journal of Product and Brand Management 16/1, 2007, pp. 38-48

CHAPTER 11

EVALUATION OF THE IMPACT OF COO AND COBO ON BRAND POSITIONING STRATEGIES OF MNCs DEALING IN FMCG IN INDIA

ABSTRACT

Positioning may not be as simple a construct as it appears. It may be influenced by several dimensions of the market, company philosophy and consumer behaviour which intertwine together to produce a specific result. Two such factors which are often found to be reflected in certain category of products and in certain brands are the 'Country of Origin' (COO) and 'Culture of Brand Origin' (COBO). Different markets may have different perceptions about brands originating from different countries and hence may respond in different ways to the explicit display of Culture of Brand Origin and the claim of Country of Origin of a brand.

India, with its consumer diversity and paradoxical characteristics of affinity to tradition and modern outlook, is an interesting as well as challenging market for many a marketer. Understanding the consumers' preference for global brands as compared to local products and brands in this market is a matter of genuine curiosity. Of similar curiosity is the issue related to deciphering the approach of brand managers towards the use of 'COO' and 'COBO' constructs in positioning their FMCG brands in India. The study aims at evaluating the impact of 'Country of Origin' and 'Culture of Brand Origin' on the positioning of FMCG brand offered by multinational companies in India. An attempt has also been made through this study to figure out if global FMCG brands experience higher purchase likelihood amongst Indian consumers as compared to local brands.

To conduct the study response has been collected from brand managers working for MNCs dealing with FMCG brands in India and from consumers across five states from India. The findings of the study reveal that the culture of the country from where the brand originates is not so strongly reflected in the FMCG brands sold in the Indian market. It was also found that Indian consumers have a significantly high purchase preference for global as compared to that of local brands.

Keywords: *Brand Positioning, FMCG, FMCG Brands, Economic Characteristics, Psychographic Characteristics*

INTRODUCTION:

The fate of a brand in a market is decided by how it is positioned in the minds of the consumer. A positioning that is unique, pre-emptive and is of value to the consumer empowers the brand, endows it with a competitive edge and gives it a sustainable competitive advantage. However, positioning may not be as simple a construct as it appears. It may be influenced by several dimensions of the market, company philosophy and consumer behaviour which intertwine together to produce a specific result. Two such factors which are often found to be reflected in certain category of products and in certain brands are the 'Country of Origin' (COO) and 'Culture of Brand Origin' (COBO).

In certain cases, incorporating the 'COO' construct or the 'COBO' construct into the brand positioning strategy for positioning a brand may be a good idea but it may not be so for all markets and for all product categories. Different markets may have different perceptions about brands originating from different countries and hence may respond in different ways to the explicit display of Culture of Brand Origin and the claim of Country of Origin of a brand.

India, with its consumer diversity and paradoxical characteristics of affinity to tradition and modern outlook, is an interesting as well as challenging market for many a marketer. Understanding the consumers' preference for global brands as compared to local products and brands in this market is a matter of genuine curiosity. Of similar curiosity is the issue related to deciphering the approach of brand managers towards the use of 'COO' and 'COBO' constructs in positioning their FMCG brands in India.

LITERATURE REVIEW:

Brand positioning is not merely a one-step phenomenon or a single distinct concept. It involves a series of decisions (Maggard, 1976) taken in the context of the environment, competition, consumer and the company's and the brand's objective. The phenomenon of brand positioning is therefore referred to as brand positioning strategy.

The main points of reference for positioning a brand are the consumer, in whose mind the brand has to be placed, and the competitor, in whose comparison it has to be positioned (Keller, 2008; Kotler et al, 2009).

An important job of the brand manager is to communicate the brand identity to the consumer and establish a desired and favourable image for the brand in the consumer's mind (Park et al, 1986).

Before positioning a brand it is important that the market is divided into relevant segments, the characteristics of the chosen segment is understood well and a suitable brand positioning strategy is drawn accordingly. A market may be segmented on the basis of geographic characteristics, demographic characteristics, psychographic characteristics and behavioural characteristics (Kotler, 1996). A brand may need to be positioned differently in these different market segments. Whether or not to differently position a brand in different markets may also be an important decision in the positioning strategy for a brand.

With globalisation creeping in and with the consumers becoming much more exposed to cultures from across the world, a new dimension has been added to brand positioning. Globalisation has ushered in an era of cultural positioning (Alden et al, 1999). A decision regarding the use of cultural element for brand positioning is a part of the brand positioning strategy.

Consumers have certain perceptions about different countries. The attitude of the consumer towards certain products may be substantially changed if the country of origin of the product is revealed (Bannister et al, 1978). A distinctively favourable perception for a country may be used to create a favourable and desired image for the brand in the consumer's mind. Thus a decision to associate a brand with its country of origin and to leverage the image of the country for positioning the brand also forms an important part of the brand positioning strategy.

OBJECTIVES OF THE STUDY:

The objectives of the study are:

1. To study the Impact Of 'Country Of Origin' And 'Culture Of Brand Origin' On Brand Positioning Of FMCG Brands
2. To check whether the culture of the country from where the brand originates has its imprints on the positioning of the brand.
3. To figure out if global brands experience higher purchase likelihood as compared to local brands.

RESEARCH METHODOLOGY:

The study has been carried out to evaluate the impact of 'Country of Origin' of a brand and 'Culture of Brand Origin' on brand positioning strategies of multinational companies dealing in fast moving consumer goods in India. The product categories for which the study has been conducted are: Food & Beverage, Confectionary, Soaps & Detergents, Cosmetics and Home Care products and Over-the-Counter products (OTC).

The universe of the study consists of the managers with the responsibility of handling FMCG brands from multinational companies operating in India and consumers of Fast Moving Consumer Goods in India. The two types of sampling elements required for the study were managers at multinational companies dealing in FMCG brands and users of FMCG brands in the age group of 18 to 75 years in India. The sampling units were identified as individual consumers of FMCG brands who also formed the sampling element and multinational companies of Indian and foreign origin dealing in FMCG brands in India from which the other sampling elements (managers dealing in FMCG brands) were to be drawn. For the objectives (i) and (ii), response was obtained from brand managers working for MNCs and dealing with FMCG brands. For the objective (iii), response was obtained from the consumers of FMCG brands. The response obtained from the consumers for objective (iii), was also cross checked by asking the brand managers about the preference of the consumers for global brands and foreign brands.

To collect the data from the managers of multinational companies dealing in FMCG brands, a list of multinational companies dealing in FMCG brands in India was prepared. Fifty multinational companies dealing in FMCG brands were found to operate in the Indian market. A request letter to participate in the survey along with the questionnaire designed for the survey was either mailed or given in person to forty such managers from these companies who had the responsibility of handling the FMCG brands offered by their companies. After several reminders to these managers, 31 responses were obtained. 30 of these responses were found to be usable.

Convenience sampling was used to collect the data from the consumers using pretested structured questionnaires. 400 questionnaires were administered to consumers of FMCG brands spread across five states of India namely Uttar Pradesh, Uttarakhand, Delhi, West Bengal and Karnataka. 292 questionnaires were received out of which 250 were found to be usable for the research.

Primary data was collected from consumers and brand managers using two different structured questionnaires. The questionnaire administered to the brand managers as well as to the consumers consisted of close ended, non-disguised questions. The response of the brand managers were recorded using 5 point Likert scales (*Insignificant or No Influence, Weak Influence, Moderate Influence, Significant Influence, Strong Influence*). The response of consumers were recorded using a 4 point verbal balanced scale (*Strongly Agree, Somewhat Agree, Somewhat Disagree, Strongly Disagree*)

ANALYSIS & DISCUSSION:

Impact of 'Country of Origin' and 'Culture of Brand Origin' on Brand Positioning of FMCG Brands

To understand the impact of the 'Country of Origin' of an FMCG brand on its brand positioning strategy, the brand managers surveyed were asked about the degree of influence that the 'Country of Origin' has on the positioning of the brand and whether highlighting the origin of the brand strengthens its positioning.

The response of the managers show that most of the brand managers (33.3% of respondents) are of the opinion that 'Country of Origin' of a brand has a moderate influence on the positioning strategy of the brand. The mean of the response is 2.72 and the mode is 3.00 which indicate a moderate influence (See Table 11.1).

Table 11.1: Influence of Country of Origin of the brand on Positioning

	Frequency	Percent	Valid Percent	Mean	Mode
Insignificant/ no influence (1)	6	20.0	20.0		
Weak influence (2)	7	23.3	23.3		
Moderate influence (3)	10	33.3	33.3	2.72	3.00
Significant influence (4)	3	10.0	10.0		
Strong influence (5)	4	13.3	13.3		
Total	30	100.0	100.0		

To study the impact of the 'Culture of Brand Origin' on the positioning strategy of the brand, the brand managers were asked up to what extent their brands reflect the culture of the country from where the brand has originated. 26.7 % of the brand managers indicated that the culture of brand origin was moderately highlighted in their brands whereas 30 % of the respondents indicated that it was highlighted up to a good extent. The mean of the response was 3.40 and the mode was 3.50 indicating a moderate to more than moderate level of incorporation of 'Culture of Brand Origin' in brand positioning strategy for Fast Moving Consumer Goods (See Table 11.2).

Table 11.2: Brands reflect Culture of Origin

	Frequency	Percent	Valid Percent	Mean	Mode
Don't Reflect (1)	2	6.7	6.7		
Insignificantly (2)	5	16.7	16.7		
Moderately (3)	8	26.7	26.7	3.40	3.50
Significantly (4)	9	30.0	30.0		
Very Strongly (5)	6	20.0	20.0		
Total	30	100.0	100.0		

Hypothesis 1: The culture of the country from where the brand originates has its imprints on the positioning of the brand.

Null Hypothesis 1 (H1$_0$): The culture of the country from where the brand originates does not have its imprints on the positioning of the brand.

Alternate Hypothesis 1 (H1$_a$): The culture of the country from where the brand originates has its imprints on the positioning of the brand.

Chi Square test was conducted to test the null hypothesis which states that "The culture of the country from where the brand originates does not have its imprints on the positioning of the brand".

As the calculated value of chi square for the variables 'Culture of Brand Origin Reflected in the Brand' is 5.00 which less than the table value of chi square (9.488) at degree of freedom 4 and level of significance 0.05, and as the p value for the variables is 0.287 (ie, more than 0.05), the null hypothesis 3 ($H3_0$) is not rejected (See Table 11.3). It implies that the 'Culture of Brand Origin' (COBO) is not significantly represented or reflected by the FMCG brands from the stable of multinational companies in the Indian market.

Table 11.3: Chi Square Test to Judge if the Brands Reflect the Culture of the Country from Where they Originate

Factors / Influence on Positioning (Percentage)	Insignificant or no Influence	Weak Influence	Moderate Influence	Significant Influence	Strong Influence	d/f	Chi Square (p Value)
Brands Reflect Culture of Brand Origin	6.7	16.7	26.7	30.0	20.0	4	5.000 (0.287)

Thus the null hypothesis ($H1_0$: The culture of the country from where the brand originates does not have its imprints on the positioning of the brand) is not rejected.

Hypothesis 2: Global brands experience higher purchase likelihood as compared to local brands.

Null Hypothesis 2 ($H2_0$): Global brands do not experience higher purchase likelihood as compared to local brands.

Alternate Hypothesis (H2$_\alpha$): Global brands experience higher purchase likelihood as compared to local brands.

To figure out if the Indian consumers have a higher preference for the purchase of global brands, the respondents (consumers) were asked if they prefer to buy brands that have a global presence and whether they prefer such Indian brands which have become global. The level of agreement of the respondents to the statements 'I prefer to buy brands that have a global presence' and 'I prefer to buy those Indian brands that have also expanded into other countries vis-à-vis those Indian brands which are only locally available' was collected using a 4 point balanced scale (The scale parameters were 'Strongly Disagree', 'Somewhat Disagree', 'Somewhat Agree' and 'Strongly Agree'). To test the null hypothesis which states that "Global brands do not experience higher purchase likelihood as compared to local brands", Chi Square test was applied. Chi Square test was applied to the two hypotheses which were stated as follows:

Null Hypothesis 2a (H2a$_\theta$): Consumers do not prefer to buy brands that have a Global presence.

Alternate Hypothesis 2a (H2a$_\alpha$): Consumers prefer to buy brands that have a Global presence.

And

Null Hypothesis 2b (H2b$_\theta$): Consumers do not have a higher preference for Indian brands that have expanded into other countries.

Alternate Hypothesis 2b (H2b$_\alpha$): Consumers have a higher preference for Indian brands that have expanded into other countries.

As the calculated value of chi square for the variables 'Preference to buy brands that have a global presence' and 'Preference to buy Indian brands that have expanded into other countries' are 115.216 and 138.832 both of which are greater than the table value of chi square (7.815) at degree of freedom 3 and level of significance 0.05 and as the p values for the variables 'Preference to buy brands that have a global presence' and 'Preference to buy Indian brands that have expanded into other countries' are less than 0.05, the null hypothesis H2a$_\theta$ and H2b$_\alpha$ are rejected (See Table 11.4). It implies that consumers have a significantly high purchase preference for global brands in comparison to their purchase preference for local brands.

Table 11.4: Chi Square Test to Judge the Consumers' Purchase Likelihood of Global Brands

	Strongly Disagree	Somewhat Disagree	Somewhat Agree	Strongly Agree	d/f	Chi Square (p
I prefer to buy brands that have a global presence	4.8%	11.6%	42.0%	41.6%	3	115.216 (0.000)
Prefer to buy Indian brands that have expanded into other countries	2.0%	12.0%	47.6%	38.4%	3	138.832 (0.000)

Thus the null hypothesis (H2$_0$: Global brands do not experience higher purchase likelihood as compared to local brands) is rejected whereas the alternate hypothesis (H2$_a$: Global brands experience higher purchase likelihood as compared to local brands) is not rejected.

The opinion of the brand managers was also sought regarding a possibly higher purchase likelihood of global FMCG brands in the Indian market. Chi Square test has been used to check the null hypothesis that "Global brands do not experience higher brand preference". As the p value for the chi square test is less than 0.05, it indicates that the statement "Global brands do not experience higher brand preference" is rejected (See Table 11.5). It implies that the brand managers believe that global brands experience a higher brand preference. Their opinion is in conformance with the findings from the response of the consumers.

Table 11.5: Chi Square Test to Judge the Brands Managers Opinion Regarding the Purchase Likelihood of Global and Foreign Brands

Factors / Influence on Positioning (Percentage)	Strongly Disagree	Somewhat Disagree	Somewhat Agree	Strongly Agree	d/f	Chi Square (p
Global brands and Foreign brands have a higher brand preference	10.0	16.7	50.0	23.3	3	11.067 (0.011)

FINDINGS:

The study found that the culture of the country from where the brand originates is not so strongly reflected in the FMCG brands sold in the Indian market. The 'Country of Origin' of an FMCG brand was found to have a moderate influence on the positioning strategy of the brand.

As far as the preference of the Indian consumers towards global brands is concerned, it was found that consumers have a significantly high purchase preference for global brands in comparison to their purchase preference for local brands of fast moving consumer goods. This finding was further corroborated by another finding derived from the response of the brand managers who were found to believe that global brands experience a higher brand preference amongst the Indian consumers.

****

REFERENCES

Maggard, John P. (1976), "Positioning Revisited", *Journal of Marketing*, Vol. 40, No. 1 (Jan), pp. 63-66

Kotler Philip (1996), *Marketing Management-Analysis, Planning, Implementation, and Control*, 8th ed. (New Delhi: Prentice Hall of India), pp. 264-313

Alden, Dana L., Steenkamp, Jan-Benedict, E.M., Batra Rajeev (1999), "Brand Positioning Through Advertising in Asia, North America and Europe: The Role of Global Consumer Culture", *Journal of Marketing*, Vol. 63, No. 1 (Jan), pp. 75-87

Park, C. Whan, Jaworski, Bernard J. and MacInnis, Deborak J. (1986), "Strategic Brand Concept-Image Management", *The Journal of Marketing*, Vol. 50, No. 4 (Oct.), pp. 135-145

Van den Putte, Bas (2002), "An Integrative Framework for Effective Communication", in Bartels, G & W. Nellissen (ed.s), *Marketing for Sustainability: Towards Transactional Policy Making*, (Amsterdam: IOS Press), pp. 83-95

Van den Putte, Bas (2009), "What Matters the Most in Advertising Campaigns? The Relative Effect of Media Expenditure and Message Content Strategy", *International Journal of Advertising*, Vol. 28, No. 3, pp. 669-690

Keller, Kevin Lane (2008), Strategic Brand Management: Building, Measuring and Managing Brand Equity, 3rd ed. (New Delhi: Pearson Education Inc.), pp.120-139

Keller, Kevin Lane, Strenthal, Brian and Tybout Alice (2002), "Three Questions You Need to Ask About Your Brand", Harvard Business Review, September 2002, pp. 81-86

Kotler, Philip, Keller Kevin Lane, Koshy Abraham and Jha Mithileshwar (2009), Marketing Management-A South Asian Perspective, 13th ed. (New Delhi: Pearson Prentice Hall), pp. 282-289

Bannister, J.P., Saunders, J.A (1978); "UK Consumers' Attitudes towards Imports: The Measurement of National Stereotype Image"; *European Journal of Marketing*; Volume 12, Number 8; 1978 ; pp. 562-570

CHAPTER 12

IMPACT OF SOME PSYCHOGRAPHIC & ECONOMIC CHARACTERISTICS OF THE INDIAN CONSUMER ON BRAND POSITIONING STRATEGIES OF MNCs DEALING IN FMCG

ABSTRACT

For a Multinational company, operating in the Indian FMCG market, brand positioning may involve several critical decisions like whether or not to adapt brand and its features to the local culture, what values to inculcate into the brand, what values to emphasise while positioning it, whether to emphasise the country of origin of the brand or not, the extent of attention to be given to the values, beliefs and faith of the target consumer and whether to differentiate a brand on the basis of the income pattern, income levels and saving habits of the targeted consumers of the brand.

This paper studies the degree of influence of consumer values and beliefs and the impact of the economic characteristics of the targeted Indian consumer on the positioning strategies of multinational companies selling FMCG brands in the Indian market. For the study, response was sought from the brand managers with the responsibility of handling FMCG brands from multinational companies operating in India.

The study concluded that the values, beliefs and faith of the Indian consumer have a significant influence on the brand positioning strategies drawn by the MNCs dealing in FMCG brands in the Indian market. Economic characteristics of the target market segment particularly the income pattern and the disposable income of the consumers were also found to have a significant impact on the brand positioning strategies of the products.

Keywords: *Brand Positioning, FMCG, FMCG Brands, Economic Characteristics, Psychographic Characteristics*

INTRODUCTION:

The FMCG sector is one of the sectors that have undergone a dramatic change in the post liberalization era owing to the entry of an array of Multinational Companies which are using all the possible tactics to lure the Indian consumer. The fate of their brands in a market is decided by how they are positioned in the minds of the consumer. A positioning that is unique, pre-emptive and is of value to the consumer empowers the brand, endows the brand with a competitive edge and gives it a sustainable competitive advantage.

The foremost desire of every brand manager is to create a distinctive identity and a pre-emptive position for his/her brand in the consumer's mind space. Finding a position that is meaningful for the consumer and assures him of a distinctive benefit offered by no other competitor ensures survival and sustainability for the brand.

Like every nation, India also has a unique set of values, beliefs and customs which further vary from one region to another within the country itself. These values and beliefs have a strong influence on the perception and attitude of the people and their predisposition towards any object, product or brand. If a brand is able to reflect these values and conform to the beliefs of the people, it is likely to experience a favourable impact on its brand acceptability and brand preference. So the challenge of a company lies in identifying the need of the people, their values, beliefs, preferences, buying habits, saving habits, likings and disliking and in finding their expectations from a product or a brand so as to inculcate the desired values into the brand. A knowledge of customer preference and an understanding of the customer's perception and attitude helps in positioning the brand in a suitable manner and in establishing some favourable, strong and unique associations that may result in strong brand equity.

For a Multinational company, operating in the Indian FMCG market, brand positioning may involve several critical decisions like whether or not to adapt brand and its features to the local culture, what values to inculcate into the brand, what values to emphasise while positioning it, whether to emphasise the country of origin of the brand or not, the extent of attention to be given to the values, beliefs and faith of the target consumer and whether to differentiate a brand on the basis of the income pattern, income levels and saving habits of the targeted consumers of the brand.

LITERATURE REVIEW

Brand positioning is not merely a one-step phenomenon or a single distinct concept. It involves a series of decisions (Maggard, 1976) taken in the context of the environment, competition, consumer and the company's and the brand's objective. The phenomenon of brand positioning is therefore referred to as brand positioning strategy.

An important job of the brand manager is to communicate the brand identity to the consumer and establish a desired and favourable image for the brand in the consumer's mind (Park et al, 1986). Before positioning a brand it is important that the market is divided into relevant segments, the characteristics of the chosen segment is understood well and a suitable brand positioning strategy is drawn accordingly. A market may be segmented on the basis of geographic characteristics, demographic characteristics, psychographic characteristics and behavioural characteristics (Kotler, 1996). A brand may need to be positioned differently in these different market segments. Whether or not to differently position a brand in different markets may also be an important decision in the positioning strategy for a brand.

The main points of reference for positioning a brand are the consumer, in whose mind the brand has to be placed, and the competitor, in whose comparison it has to be positioned (Keller, 2008; Kotler et al, 2009). Therefore the factors related to the consumer, his characteristics, his psychology and his behaviour and the factors related to competition may have some bearing on the brand positioning strategies adopted for positioning a brand. Moreover, as brand positioning is about establishing a valued differentiation for the brand in the consumer's perceptual space (Kotler, 1996), the brand attributes, the product characteristics and the distinguishing characteristics of the company may have an influence on the brand positioning strategy used by a company to position a brand (Keller et al, 2002). From the above discussion it follows that to understand the brand positioning strategy adopted by a company for positioning its brand, it is important to understand which factors have an impact on the positioning strategy and to assess the degree of influence of the product related factors, company related factors, competition related factors, consumer related factors and consumer behaviour related factors.

The paper attempts to study the degree of influence of consumer values and beliefs and the impact of the economic characteristics of the targeted Indian consumer on the positioning strategies of multinational companies selling FMCG brands in the Indian market.

OBJECTIVES OF THE STUDY:

The objectives of the study are:

1. To evaluate the influence of the values and beliefs of the Indian consumer on brand positioning strategies of FMCG brands from MNCs
2. To study the impact of the economic characteristics of the target market segment on the brand positioning strategies of FMCG brands from the stable of multinational companies in India.

RESEARCH METHODOLOGY:

The study has been carried out to understand the impact of some psychographic characteristics and economic characteristics of the targeted Indian consumer on brand positioning strategies of multinational companies dealing in fast moving consumer goods in India. The product categories for which the study has been conducted are: Food & Beverage, Confectionary, Soaps & Detergents, Cosmetics and Home Care products and Over-the-Counter products (OTC).

The universe of the study consists of the managers with the responsibility of handling FMCG brands from multinational companies operating in India and consumers of Fast Moving Consumer Goods in India. The sampling elements required for the study were managers at multinational companies dealing in FMCG brands. The sampling units were identified as multinational companies of Indian and foreign origin dealing in FMCG brands in India from which the sampling elements (managers dealing in FMCG brands) were to be drawn.

To collect the data from the managers of multinational companies dealing in FMCG brands, a list of multinational companies dealing in FMCG brands in India was prepared. Fifty multinational companies dealing in FMCG brands were found to operate in the Indian market. A request letter to participate in the survey along with the questionnaire designed for the survey was either mailed or given in person to forty such managers from these companies who had the responsibility of handling the FMCG brands offered by their companies. After several reminders to these managers, 31 responses were obtained. 30 of these responses were found to be usable.

Primary data was collected from brand managers using a structured questionnaire. The questionnaire administered to the brand managers consisted of close ended non-disguised questions. The response of the brand managers were recorded using 5 point Likert scales

(*Insignificant or No Influence, Weak Influence, Moderate Influence, Significant Influence, Strong Influence*).

ANALYSIS & DISCUSSION:

Influence of the Values and Beliefs of the Indian Consumer on Brand Positioning Strategies

The brand managers were asked to indicate the impact of the 'Value System of the Consumer', 'Culture of the Consumer' and 'Faith and Belief of the Consumer' on the brand positioning strategies designed by them. They were asked to rate the degree of influence on a 5 point verbal rating scale. Results from the study indicate that the 'Value System of the Consumer', 'Culture of the Consumer' and 'Faith and Belief of the Consumer' have a significantly strong influence on the brand positioning strategies of multinational companies dealing in Fast Moving Consumer Goods in India. The mean values for the influences of 'Value System of the Consumer', 'Culture of the Consumer' and 'Faith and Belief' of the consumer are 3.90, 3.97 and 3.63 respectively indicating a significant influence of these factors on the brand positioning strategies for FMCG brands. The modal values, which represent the response of the majority of the respondents, for these factors are 5.0, 5.0 and 4.0 respectively. When interpreted, it indicates a strong influence of the factors 'Consumer's Value System' and 'Culture of the Consumer' and a significant influence of the factor 'Consumer's Faith and Belief' (See Table 12.1).

Table 12.1

	Influence of the value system of the consumer on positioning	Influence of the culture of the consumer on positioning	Influence of the faith and belief of the consumer on positioning
Mean	3.90	3.97	3.63
Mode	5	5	4

Table 12.2 also shows that more than 66 percent of the respondents indicate that each of the factors 'Consumer's Value System', 'Culture of Consumer' and 'Consumer's Faith and Belief' have a

significant to strong influence on the brand positioning strategies adopted by them for positioning FMCG brands in the Indian market.

Table 12.2: Influence of Consumer Values & Beliefs on Brand Positioning

Values & Beliefs / Degree of Preference (in percentage)	Insignificant or no Influence	Weak Influence	Moderate Influence	Significant Influence	Strong Influence
The value system of the consumer	0.0	16.7	16.7	26.7	40.0
Culture and tradition of the consumer	3.3	6.7	23.3	23.3	43.3
Faith and belief of the consumer	6.7	16.7	10.0	40.0	26.7

Hypothesis 1: The brand positioning strategies adopted by the MNCs in India are influenced by the values and beliefs of the Indian consumer.

Null Hypothesis1 (H1$_0$): The brand positioning strategies adopted by the MNCs in India are not influenced by the values and beliefs of the Indian consumer.

Alternate Hypothesis1 (H1$_a$): The brand positioning strategies adopted by the MNCs in India are influenced by the values and beliefs of the Indian consumer.

Chi Square test was conducted to test the null hypothesis which states that "The brand positioning strategies adopted by the MNCs in India are not influenced by the values and beliefs of the Indian consumer".

As the calculated values of chi square for the variables 'Influence of consumer's value system on brand positioning', 'influence of the culture of the consumer on brand positioning' and 'influence of the faith and belief of the consumer on brand positioning' at degree of freedom 4 and level of significance 0.05 are 13.000, 15.333 and 11.000 respectively, each of which is more than the table value of chi square (9.488) at degree of freedom 4 and level of significance 0.05, and as the p value for each of these variables is less than 0.05, it indicates that there is a significant influence of these factors on the brand positioning strategies (Refer Table 12.3). It implies that the brand positioning strategies adopted by MNCs dealing in FMCG in India are significantly influenced by the value system of the consumer, the culture of the consumer and the faith and belief of the consumer.

Table 12.3: Chi Square Test to Judge the Influence of Indian Values & Beliefs on Brand Positioning

Factors / Influence on Positioning	Insignificant or no Influence	Weak Influence	Moderate Influence	Significant Influence	Strong Influence	d/f	Chi Square (p Value)
The value system of the consumer	0.0	16.7	16.7	26.7	40.0	4	13.000 (0.011)
Culture and tradition of the consumer	3.3	6.7	23.3	23.3	43.3	4	15.333 (0.004)
Faith and belief of the consumer	6.7	16.7	10.0	40.0	26.7	4	11.000 (0.027)

Thus the null hypothesis ($H1_0$: The brand positioning strategies adopted by the MNCs in India are not influenced by the values and beliefs of the Indian consumer) is rejected whereas the alternate hypothesis ($H1_\alpha$: The brand positioning strategies adopted by the MNCs in India are influenced by the values and beliefs of the Indian consumer) is not rejected.

Impact of Economic Characteristics of the Target Market Segment on the Brand Positioning Strategies for FMCG Brands

The brand managers were asked to indicate the impact of the 'Earning Pattern of the Consumer', 'Disposable Income of the Consumer' and 'Influence of saving habit of the consumer' on their brand positioning strategies. They were asked to rate the degree of influence on a 5 point verbal rating scale. The mean value for the influences of 'Earning Pattern of the Consumer' as well as that for 'Disposable Income of the Consumer' is 4.10. The modal value for each of these two factors is 5.10. It signifies a significant influence of these two factors on brand positioning strategies. However the mean value for the variable 'Influence of saving habit of the consumer' is 3.10 and the modal value is 2.0. It implies not so strong influence of the factor 'Saving Habit of the Consumer' on brand positioning strategies of FMCG brands in the Indian market (See Table 12.4).

Table 12.4

	Influence of the earning pattern of the consumer on positioning	Influence of the disposable income of the consumer on positioning	Influence of the saving habit of the consumer on positioning
Mean	4.10	4.10	3.10
Mode	5	5	2

The frequency table also exhibits that 70 percent of the respondents surveyed indicate that the earning pattern of the target consumer has a significant to strong influence on the brand positioning strategies formulated for FMCG brands. Also, more than 73 percent of the respondents indicate that the disposable income of the target consumer has a significant to strong influence on the strategies meant for positioning FMCG brands in the Indian market (See Table 12.5).

Table 12.5: Degree of Influence of Economic Characteristics of Target Market Segment on Brand Positioning

Economic Characteristics / Degree of Influence	Insignificant or no Influence	Weak Influence	Moderate Influence	Significant Influence	Strong Influence
Earning patterns of the target consumer	0.0	3.3	26.7	26.7	43.3
Disposable income of the target	3.3	0.0	23.3	30.0	43.3
Saving habits of the target consumer	10.0	33.3	10.0	30.0	16.7

Hypothesis 2: Economic characteristics of the target market segment have an impact on the brand positioning strategies of the products.

Null Hypothesis 2 (H2$_0$): Economic characteristics of the target market segment do not have an impact on the brand positioning strategies of the products.

Alternate Hypothesis 2 (H2$_a$): Economic characteristics of the target market segment have an impact on the brand positioning strategies of the products.

Chi Square test was applied to test the null hypothesis which states that "Economic characteristics of the target market segment do not have an impact on the brand positioning strategies of the products". The sub hypotheses were stated as follows:

Null Hypothesis 2a (H2a$_0$): Earning Pattern of the Consumer does not have a significant impact on the brand positioning strategies

Alternate Hypothesis 2a (H2a$_a$): Earning Pattern of the Consumer has a significant impact on the brand positioning strategies

Null Hypothesis 2b (H2b$_0$): Disposable Income of the Consumer does not have a significant impact on the brand positioning strategies

Alternate Hypothesis 2b (H2b$_a$): Disposable Income of the Consumer has a significant impact on the brand positioning strategies

Null Hypothesis 2c (H2c$_0$): Saving Habit of the Consumer does not have a significant impact on the brand positioning strategies

Alternate Hypothesis 2c (H2c$_a$): Saving Habit of the Consumer has a significant impact on the brand positioning strategies

As the calculated chi square values for the variables 'Influence of the earning pattern of the consumer on brand positioning' and 'influence of the disposable income of the consumer on brand positioning' at degree of freedom 4 and level of significance 0.05 are 19.667 and 20.000 respectively, which are greater than the table value of chi square (9.488) at degree of freedom 4 and level of significance 0.05 and as the p values for these variables are 0.001 and 0.000, both of which are less than 0.05, the null hypothesis H2a$_0$ and the null hypothesis H2b$_0$ are rejected. However the calculated chi square values for the variable 'influence of the consumer's saving habit' at degree of freedom 4 and level of significance 0.05 is 7.333, which is less than the table value of chi square (9.488) at degree of freedom 4 and level of significance 0.05. Also the p value for the variable 'influence of the consumer's saving habit' is greater than 0.05. Thus the null hypothesis $H2c_{\varnothing}$ is not rejected (See Table 12.6).

It implies that the factors earning pattern of the consumer and the disposable income of the consumer have a significant influence on the brand positioning strategies adopted by MNCs dealing in FMCG in India but the brand positioning strategies of these companies are not significantly influenced by the consumer's saving habit. On the whole it may be concluded that the economic characteristics of the target market have an influence on the brand positioning strategies adopted by the MNCs in positioning FMCG brands in India.

Table 12.6: Chi Square Test to Judge the Impact of the Economic Characteristics of the Target Market Segment on Brand Positioning Strategies

Factors / Influence on Positioning	Insignificant or no Influence	Weak Influence	Moderate Influence	Significant Influence	Strong Influence	d/f	Chi Square (p
Earning Pattern of the consumer	0.0	3.3	26.7	26.7	43.3	4	19.667 (0.001)
Disposable Income of the consumer	3.3	0.0	23.3	30.0	43.3	4	20.000 (0.000)
Saving Habit of the consumer	10.0	33.3	10.0	30.0	16.7	4	7.333 (0.119)

Thus the null hypothesis ($H2_o$: The economic characteristics of the target market segment do not have an impact on the brand positioning strategies of the products) is rejected.

FINDINGS:

The study found that the factors like 'The Value System of the Consumer', 'The Culture and Tradition of the Consumer', 'The Faith and Belief of the Consumer', 'Earning Pattern of Consumer' and 'Disposable Income of the Consumer' significantly influence the brand positioning strategies of MNCs selling FMCG brands in India. Thus, it was concluded that the brand positioning strategies adopted by the MNCs in India are influenced by the values and beliefs of the Indian consumer.

The study also concluded that the economic characteristics of the target market segment have an impact on the brand positioning strategies of the products. However within the economic characteristics, 'Saving Pattern of the Consumer' was not found to have a significantly strong influence on the brand positioning strategies of the multinational companies.

****

REFERENCES

Maggard, John P. (1976), "Positioning Revisited", *Journal of Marketing*, Vol. 40, No. 1 (Jan), pp. 63-66

Kotler Philip (1996), *Marketing Management-Analysis, Planning, Implementation, and Control*, 8th ed. (New Delhi: Prentice Hall of India), pp. 264-313

Alden, Dana L., Steenkamp, Jan-Benedict, E.M., Batra Rajeev (1999), "Brand Positioning Through Advertising in Asia, North America and Europe: The Role of Global Consumer Culture", *Journal of Marketing*, Vol. 63, No. 1 (Jan), pp. 75-87

Park, C. Whan, Jaworski, Bernard J. and MacInnis, Deborak J. (1986), "Strategic Brand Concept-Image Management", *The Journal of Marketing*, Vol. 50, No. 4 (Oct.), pp. 135-145

Keller, Kevin Lane (2008), Strategic Brand Management: Building, Measuring and Managing Brand Equity, 3rd ed. (New Delhi: Pearson Education Inc.), pp.120-139

Keller, Kevin Lane, Strenthal, Brian and Tybout Alice (2002), "Three Questions You Need to Ask About Your Brand", Harvard Business Review, September 2002, pp. 81-86

Kotler, Philip, Keller Kevin Lane, Koshy Abraham and Jha Mithileshwar (2009), Marketing Management-A South Asian Perspective, 13th ed. (New Delhi: Pearson Prentice Hall), pp. 282-289

Bannister, J.P., Saunders, J.A (1978); "UK Consumers' Attitudes towards Imports: The Measurement of National Stereotype Image"; *European Journal of Marketing*; Volume 12, Number 8; 1978 ; pp. 562-570

CHAPTER 13

EVALUATION OF BRAND POSITIONING STRATEGIES OF MNCs DEALING IN FMCG

The main points of reference for positioning a brand are the consumer, in whose mind the brand has to be placed, and the competitor, in whose comparison it has to be positioned (Keller, 2008; Kotler et al, 2009). Therefore the factors related to the consumer, his characteristics, his psychology and his behaviour and the factors related to competition may have some bearing on the brand positioning strategies adopted for positioning a brand. Moreover, as brand positioning is about establishing a valued differentiation for the brand in the consumer's perceptual space (Kotler, 1996), the brand attributes, the product characteristics and the distinguishing characteristics of the company may have an influence on the brand positioning strategy used by a company to position a brand (Keller et al, 2002). From the above discussion it follows that to understand the brand positioning strategy adopted by a company for positioning its brand, it is important to understand which factors have an impact on the positioning strategy and to assess the degree of influence of the product related factors, company related factors, competition related factors, consumer related factors and consumer behaviour related factors.

An important job of the brand manager is to communicate the brand identity to the consumer and establish a desired and favourable image for the brand in the consumer's mind (Park et al, 1986). Communication of brand identity requires the use of the various elements of the message strategy like functional elements, cultural elements, emotional elements and hedonistic elements (Van den Putte, 2002, 2009). Different elements of the message strategy need to be evaluated for the suitability for this purpose and the most suitable element need to be identified by the brand manager and effectively employed for positioning a brand. A brand positioning strategy therefore involves the decision regarding the use of the elements of message strategy to communicate the brand identity.

A market may be segmented on the basis of geographic characteristics, demographic characteristics, psychographic characteristics and behavioural characteristics (Kotler, 1996). A brand may need to be positioned differently in these different market segments. Whether or not to differently position a brand in different markets may also be an important decision in the positioning strategy for a brand.

AN EMPIRICAL STUDY OF THE BRAND POSITIONING STRATEGIES ADOPTED BY MNCs DEALING IN FMCG IN INDIA

To assess the brand positioning strategies of multinational companies dealing in Fast Moving Consumer Goods in India responses were sought from brand managers, assistant brand managers and marketing managers regarding the influence of the various factors on brand positioning strategies, the factors that form the preliminary basis for designing/formulating the brand positioning strategies, the elements of the message strategy used to communicate the differentiation and positioning of the brand to the consumer, the impact of the country of origin and the culture of brand origin on the brand positioning strategies and the difference in the strategies adopted for different economic, psychographic and geographic segments of the market.

FACTORS THAT AFFECT BRAND POSITIONING STRATEGIES OF MNCs DEALING IN FMCG IN INDIA

Selected managers dealing in brands of Fast Moving Consumer Goods in India were asked to indicate the extent of influence of the various types of factors on brand positioning strategies for Fast Moving Consumer Goods in the Indian market. The response from the brand managers regarding the influence of these factors is discussed under the headings:

A) Influence of Product Related Factor on Brand Positioning
B) Influence of Competition Related Factor on Brand Positioning
C) Influence of Company Related Factor on Brand Positioning
D) Influence of Consumer Related Factor on Brand Positioning
E) Influence of Consumer Behaviour Related Factor on Brand Positioning

A) Influence Of Product Related Factor On Brand Positioning

In product related factors, the category of the product and some unique and distinctive brand attribute/characteristics of the product are the most influencing factors affecting the brand positioning strategies of FMCG brands in the Indian market. As indicated in Table 13.1, brand managers indicate the highest average influence of the factors 'Unique Characteristics of Product'

(Mean: 4.37 & Mode: 5.0) and 'Product Category' (Mean: 4.03 & Mode: 5.0) on the brands positioning strategies for FMCG brands.

Table 13..1

	Influence of Product category on positioning	Influence of Product Technology on Positioning	Influence of the unique characteristic of the product on positioning	Influence of Country of Origin of the brand on Positioning	Influence of Geographical presence of the brand on positioning
Mean	4.03	3.37	4.37	2.73	3.77
Mode	5	3	5	3	4

Table 13.2 shows that 46.7 percent of respondents and 43.3 percent of respondents have rated 'Unique Characteristics of the Product' to be having a 'Strong Influence' and 'Significant Influence' respectively on brand positioning. 43.3 percent and 30.0 percent of respondents have indicated a 'Strong Influence' and 'Significant Influence' respectively of the 'Product Category' on brand positioning. Thus in the product related factors, 'Unique Characteristics of the Product' emerges as the most influential factor in affecting the brand positioning strategy for a brand followed by the 'Product Category'.

Table 13..2: Degree of Influence of Product Related Factors on Brand Positioning

Product Related Factors / Degree of Preference (in percentage)	Insignificant or no Influence	Weak Influence	Moderate Influence	Significant Influence	Strong Influence
Product category	0.0	13.3	13.3	30.0	43.3
Technology of Product	3.3	10.0	46.7	26.7	13.3

Table 13..2: Degree of Influence of Product Related Factors on Brand Positioning

Product Related Factors / Degree of Preference (in percentage)	Insignificant or no Influence	Weak Influence	Moderate Influence	Significant Influence	Strong Influence
Unique characteristics of the product	0.0	0.0	10.0	43.3	46.7
'Country of origin' of the Brand	20.0	23.3	33.3	10.0	13.3
Geographical presence of the brand	10.0	30.0	33.3	26.7	10.0

B) Influence Of Competition Related Factor On Brand Positioning

In competition related factors, the brand preference and loyalty enjoyed by competing brands are believed to have a significantly strong influence (Mean: 4.28 & Mode: 5.0) followed by the number of competitors in the market (Mean: 4.13 & Mode: 5.0) (Refer Table 13.3)

Table 13.3

	Influence of number of competitors on positioning	Influence of the Market Share of the Competitors	Size of Competing Firms	Influence of brand preference & loyalty that competing brands command	Influence of Positioning Strategies of Competitors
Mean	4.13	4.03	3.33	4.28	4.03
Mode	5	4	4	5	4

Table 13.4 indicates that out of several competition related factors, 'Brand Preference and Loyalty of Competing Brands' is believed to have a strong influence by 53.3 percent of respondents and a significant influence by 20.0 percent of the respondents. The table also shows that 43.3 percent of the respondents believe that the factor 'Number of Competitors in the Market' has a strong influence while 30.0 percent of the respondents believe that it has a significant influence on brand positioning.

Table 13.4: Degree of Influence of Competition Related Factors on Brand Positioning

Competition Related Factors / Degree of Preference (in percentage)	Insignificant or no Influence	Weak Influence	Moderate Influence	Significant Influence	Strong Influence
No. of competitors in the market	0.0	3.3	23.3	30.0	43.3
Market share of the competitors	0.0	6.7	13.3	46.7	30.0
Size of the competing firms	10.0	10.0	20.0	56.7	3.3
Brand preference & loyalty that competing brands command	0.0	3.3	20.0	20.0	53.3
Positioning strategies of competitors	3.3	3.3	16.7	40.0	36.7

C) Influence Of Company Related Factor On Brand Positioning

In the category of company related factors, 'Marketing Philosophy of the Company' is the factor that has a profound influence on the brand positioning of FMCG brands in India. As indicated in Table 13.5, the respondents have indicated a higher average influence (Mean: 4.27 & Mode 5.0) of this factor on brand positioning.

Table 13.5

	Influence of the Value N Culture of the company on Positioning	Influence of the the history n tradition of company on Positioning	Influence of the marketing philosophy of the company on Positioning	Influence of the geographical coverage of the company on positioning	Influence of the duration of presence of the company in a market on its positioning
Mean	3.60	3.27	4.27	3.63	3.90
Mode	3[a]	3	5	3	4

a. Multiple modes exist. The smallest value is shown

Table 13.6 also shows that a majority of the brand managers surveyed (46.7%) are of the opinion that the factor 'Marketing Philosophy of the Company' has a strong influence on the brand positioning strategies for Fast Moving Consumer Goods in the Indian market.

Table 13.6: Degree of Influence of Company Related Factors on Brand Positioning

Company Related Factors / Degree of Preference (in percentage)	Insignificant or no Influence	Weak Influence	Moderate Influence	Significant Influence	Strong Influence
Value and culture of the company	0.0	10.0	36.7	36.7	16.7
History and tradition of the company	3.3	20.0	36.7	26.7	13.3
The marketing philosophy of the company	0.0	3.3	13.3	36.7	46.7
Geographical coverage of the company	3.3	10.0	33.3	26.7	26.7
The duration of presence of the company in a given	0.0	13.3	6.7	56.7	23.3

D) Influence Of Consumer Related Factor On Brand Positioning

In the opinion sought from the brand managers regarding the influence of consumer related factors, the factors 'Culture and Tradition of the Consumer' and 'Value System of the Consumer' exhibit a higher average value (Mean: 3.90 & Mode: 5.0 in case of the former and Mean: 3.97 & Mode: 5.0 in case of the latter) indicating a higher influence of these factors on brand positioning of FMCG brands in India (Refer Table 13.7).

Table 13.7

	Influence of the value system of the consumer on positioning	Influence of the culture of the consumer on positioning	Influence of the faith and belief of the consumer on positioning	Influence of the religion of the consumer on positioning	Influence of the geographic location n origin of the consumer on positioning
Mean	3.90	3.97	3.63	2.30	3.43
Mode	5	5	4	1	4

Table 13.8 shows that a majority of the respondents (43.3%) are of the opinion that 'Culture and Tradition of the Consumer' strongly influence the brand positioning of FMCG brands followed by 40 percent of the respondents who are of the opinion that 'The Value System of the Consumer' strongly influences the brand positioning of FMCG brands in the Indian market.

Table 13.8: Degree of Influence of Consumer Related Factors on Brand Positioning

Consumer Related Factors / Degree of Preference (in percentage)	Insignificant or no Influence	Weak Influence	Moderate Influence	Significant Influence	Strong Influence
The value system of the consumer	0.0	16.7	16.7	26.7	40.0
Culture and tradition of the consumer	3.3	6.7	23.3	23.3	43.3
Faith and belief of the consumer	6.7	16.7	10.0	40.0	26.7
Religion of the consumer	46.7	10.0	16.7	20.0	6.7
Geographic location and origin of the consumer	3.3	20.0	23.3	36.7	16.7

E) Influence Of Consumer Behaviour Related Factor On Brand Positioning

The factors 'consumption Pattern & Habit of Consumer' and 'Purchase Habit of Consumer' were reported to have a higher degree of influence on brand positioning with their mean values being 4.27 and 4.13 respectively and their modal values being 4 and 5 respectively (Refer Table 13.9).

Table 13.9

	Influence of the purchase habit of the consumer on positioning	Influence of the consumption pattern & habit of the consumer on positioning	Influence of the media habit of the consumer on positioning
Mean	4.13	4.27	3.63
Mode	5	4	3[a]

a. Multiple modes exist. The smallest value is shown

As far as 'Pattern of Consumption and Consumption Habit of the Consumer' is concerned, 40 percent of the managers surveyed have indicated a strong influence of the factor on brand positioning and 46.7 percent of the managers have indicated a significant influence of this factor on brand positioning. As far as 'Purchase Habit of the Target Consumer' is concerned, 40 percent of the respondents have indicated a strong influence of this factor on brand positioning and 33.3 percent of the respondents have indicated a significant influence of the factor on brand positioning of FMCG brands in the Indian market (Refer Table 13.10).

Table 13.10: Degree of Influence of Consumer Behaviour Related Factors on Brand Positioning

Consumer Behaviour Related Factors / Degree of Preference (in percentage)	Insignificant or no Influence	Weak Influence	Moderate Influence	Significant Influence	Strong Influence
Purchase habits of the target consumer	0.0	0.0	26.7	33.3	40.0
Pattern of consumption & consumption habits of the consumer	0.0	0.0	13.3	46.7	40.0
Media habits of the consumer	3.3	13.3	30.0	23.3	30.0

FACTORS PRIMARILY TAKEN INTO ACCOUNT WHILE DESIGNING THE POSITIONING STRATEGIES

A majority of the brand managers surveyed for the study (36.7%) reported that the factor considered most important and primarily taken into account by them while formulating the brand positioning strategies for the brands that they deal in is the 'Rural, Urban or Suburban background of the target consumer' (See Table 13.11).

Table 13.11: Most important factor considered while designing positioning strategy

	Rural/Urban/Suburban background of consumer	Education of consumer	Culture and belief of consumer	Disposable Income of the consumer	Lifestyle of the consumer	Total
Frequency	11	1	6	4	8	30
Percent	36.7	3.3	20.0	13.3	26.7	100.0

The factor that emerges as the second most important factor to be considered while designing the brand positioning strategies for the FMCG brands by the managers surveyed is the 'Lifestyle of the Consumer'. 26.7 percent of the respondents marked it as the second most important factor (See Table 13.12).

Table 13.12: Second most important factor considered while designing positioning strategy

	Rural/Urban/Suburban background	Occupation	Family Life Cycle	Culture and belief	Traditional Practices	Gross Income	Disposable Income	Lifestyle
Frequency	4	3	1	2	4	6	1	8
Percent	13.3	10.0	3.3	6.7	13.3	20.0	3.3	26.7

The factor that is treated as least important to be considered for formulating the brand positioning strategy for an FMCG brand is 'Religion of the Consumer'. A huge majority of the brand managers (70%) consider it absolutely irrelevant for designing the brand positioning strategies (See Table 13.13).

Table 13.13: Factor Treated Least Important to be Considered While Designing Positioning Strategy

	Family Life Cycle	Family Size	Cherished Traditional Practices	Religion of the consumer	Gross Income of the consumer	12
Frequency	1	1	1	21	1	5
Percent	3.3	3.3	3.3	70.0	3.3	16.7

ELEMENT OF MESSAGE STRATEGY USED FOR POSITIONING FMCG BRANDS IN INDIA

Hypothesis 2: Products targeted towards the mass market are positioned more commonly by using the cultural and functional elements of brand positioning.

Sub Hypothesis:

H2a: Products targeted towards the mass market are positioned more commonly by using the functional elements of brand positioning.

H2b: Products targeted towards the mass market are positioned more commonly by using the cultural elements of brand positioning.

An analysis of the frequency table showing the brand managers' preference of the message elements for positioning brands of FMCG in the Indian market, reveals that most of the brand managers (46.7%) of multinational companies dealing in FMCG brands in the Indian market prefer to use the sensory/experiential element followed by the emotional element as well as the functional element (as indicated in 43.3% of the cases) while positioning their FMCG brands (Refer Table13.14).

Table 13.14: Brand Managers' Preference of Message Elements for Positioning FMCG Brands

Association	Responses (N)	Percent	Percent of Cases
physical elements	12	20.3%	40.0%
functional elements	13	22.0%	43.3%
cultural elements	7	11.9%	23.3%
emotional elements	13	22.0%	43.3%
sensory/experiential elements	14	23.7%	46.7%
Total	59	100.0%	196.7%

Chi Square test has been used to find out which element of the advertising message strategy is commonly used to position a brand of consumer packaged goods by the MNCs operating in India. As the p value for the item 'preference of physical elements' (0.273) at degree of freedom 1 is more than 0.05, the statement that "Brand Managers prefer to use physical elements while positioning" is not rejected.

As the p value for the item 'preference of functional elements' (0.465) at degree of freedom 1 is more than 0.05, the statement that "Brand Managers prefer to use functional elements while positioning" is not rejected.

As the p value for the item 'preference of emotional elements' (0.465) at degree of freedom 1 is more than 0.05, the statement that "Brand Managers prefer to use emotional elements while positioning" is not rejected.

As the p value for the item 'preference of experiential/hedonistic elements' (0.715) at degree of freedom 1 is more than 0.05, the statement that "Brand Managers prefer to use experiential/hedonistic elements while positioning" is not rejected.

However as the p value for the item 'preference of cultural elements' (0.003) at degree of freedom 1 is lesser than 0.05, the statement that "Brand Managers prefer to use cultural elements while positioning" is rejected (Refer Table 13.15).

Table 13.15: Chi Square Test

	YES	NO	d/f	Chi Square (p value)
Preference of Physical Elements in positioning	12	18	1	1.200 (.273)
Preference of Functional Elements in positioning	13	17	1	0.533 (0.465)
Preference of Cultural Elements in positioning	7	23	1	8.533 (.003)
Preference of Emotional Elements in positioning	13	17	1	.533 (.465)
Preference of Sensory/ Experiential Element in positioning	14	16	1	.133 (.715)

Thus the null hypothesis (H2a: Products targeted towards the mass market are positioned more commonly by using the functional elements of brand positioning.) is not rejected.

The null hypothesis (H2b: Products targeted towards the mass market are positioned more commonly by using the cultural elements of brand positioning.) is rejected.

TO EXPLORE IF THE FMCG MNCS BRING ABOUT SOME ALTERATIONS IN THEIR POSITIONING STRATEGIES TO TARGET DIFFERENT DEMOGRAPHIC AND PSYCHOGRAPHIC SEGMENT IN THE INDIAN MARKET

An overwhelming majority of the brand managers (83.8 percent) surveyed for the study reported that an alteration in the brand positioning strategies is brought about for positioning FMCG brands in different demographic and psychographic segments in the Indian market. 89.5 percent of managers working for FMCG companies of foreign origin and 72.7 percent of managers working for Indian multinationals dealing in FMCG in the Indian market were of the opinion that the brand positioning criteria for FMCG brands change with a change in the demographic and psychographic segment (See Table 13.16).

Table 13.16: Different Positioning Criteria in Different Economic Segments

	Different positioning criteria	
Origin of Company	No	Yes
Indian	27.3%	72.7%
Foreign	10.5%	89.5%
Total	16.7%	83.3%

The frequency table shows that more than 63 percent of the respondents were of the opinion that the brand positioning strategy is changed with the change in the gross income of the consumer and more than 73 percent of the brand managers were of the opinion that the brand positioning strategy changes with the change in the purchasing power of the consumer. 70 percent of the managers reported that their companies have different brand positioning strategies for targeting consumers with different levels of disposable income. It was reported by 70 percent of the managers surveyed that the companies change their positioning strategies while targeting consumers from different occupations. More than 76 percent of the brand managers indicated that the FMCG companies use different brand positioning strategies for targeting consumers with different lifestyle (Refer Table 13.17).

Table 13.17: Positioning Strategy According to Demographic & Psychographic Characteristics

	Origin	Not Applicable	Strongly Disagree	Somewhat Disagree	Somewhat Agree	Strongly Agree
The positioning strategy is changed with the change in the	Indian	27.3%		18.2%	36.4%	18.2%
	Foreign	10.5%		21.1%	31.6%	36.8%
	Overall	16.7%		20.0%	33.3%	30.0%
The positioning strategy is changed with the change in the	Indian	27.3%		9.1%	36.4%	27.3%
	Foreign	10.5%		10.5%	21.1%	57.9%
	Overall	16.7%		10.0%	26.7%	46.7%
The positioning	Indian	27.3%	.0%	9.1%	27.3%	36.4%

strategy is changed with the change in the	Foreign	10.5%	5.3%	10.5%	21.1%	52.6%
	Overall	16.7%	3.3%	10.0%	23.3%	46.7%
The positioning strategy is changed with the change in the	Indian	27.3%		9.1%	45.5%	18.2%
	Foreign	10.5%		15.8%	52.6%	21.1%
	Overall	16.7%		13.3%	50.0%	20.0%
The positioning strategy is changed with the change in the	Indian	27.3%	.0%	.0%	9.1%	63.6%
	Foreign	10.5%	5.3%	5.3%	15.8%	63.2%
	Overall	16.7%	3.3%	3.3%	13.3%	63.3%

TO EXPLORE IF THE FMCG MNCS BRING ABOUT SOME ALTERATIONS IN THEIR POSITIONING STRATEGIES TO TARGET DIFFERENT GEOGRAPHIC SEGMENT IN THE INDIAN MARKET

The study showed that 83.3 percent of the brand managers working for foreign multinationals that deal in FMCG brands in the Indian market use different brand positioning strategies and positioning criteria for selling a brand in different geographic segments in India. In contrast only 45.5 percent of brand managers working for Indian MNCs that sell FMCG brands in the Indian market use different positioning criteria for positioning a brand in different geographic segments within the country. In all 69 percent of the respondents stated that their companies position a brand differently in different geographic segments (See Table 13.18).

Table 13.18: Different Positioning Criteria in Different Geographic Segments

	Different positioning criteria	
Origin of	No	Yes
Indian	54.5%	45.5%
Foreign	16.7%	83.3%
Total	31.0%	69.0%

The frequency table shows that in more than 66 percent of cases the brand managers stated that the companies use a different brand positioning criteria for positioning a brand of Fast Moving Consumer Good in urban, rural and suburban markets. More than 53 percent of the respondents also reported that when a brand is targeted to different states or geographical regions within the country, different positioning strategies are formulated for the brand in different regions. However, in much fewer cases (43.3 %) it was reported that the positioning criteria or strategy for a given brand is changed according to the climatic conditions of the different market segments where the brand is sold (Refer Table 13.19).

Table 13.19: Positioning Strategy According to Geographic Characteristics of the Target Market

	Origin	Not Applicable	Strongly Disagree	Somewhat Disagree	Somewhat Agree	Strongly Agree
The positioning strategy changes according to the urban/ rural background of the target consumer	Indian	54.5%	0%	.0%	18.2%	27.3%
	Foreign	15.8%	0%	5.3%	26.3%	52.6%
	Overall	30.0%	0%	3.3%	23.3%	43.3%
The positioning strategy changes with the change in the geographical regions or states within the nation	Indian	54.5%	.0%	.0%	18.2%	27.3%
	Foreign	15.8%	5.3%	21.1%	31.6%	26.3%
	Overall	30.0%	3.3%	13.3%	26.7%	26.7%
The positioning strategy changes with the difference in the climatic conditions of the target segments	Indian	54.5%	.0%	.0%	36.4%	9.1%
	Foreign	15.8%	21.1%	21.1%	26.3%	15.8%
	Overall	30.0%	13.3%	13.3%	30.0%	13.3%

CONCLUSION

The study found that the factors that significantly influence the brand positioning strategies of MNCs selling FMCG brands in India are 'Unique Characteristics of the Product', 'Product

Category', 'Brand preference and loyalty enjoyed by competing brands', 'Number of competitors in the market', 'Marketing Philosophy of the Company', 'Culture and Tradition of the Consumer', 'The Value System of the Consumer', 'Consumption Pattern & Habit of Consumer' and 'Purchase Habit of Consumer'. The factor considered most important and primarily taken into account by the brand managers while formulating the brand positioning strategies for the brands that they deal in is the 'Rural, Urban or Suburban background of the target consumer'

It was found that the brand positioning strategies adopted by the MNCs in India are influenced by the values and beliefs of the Indian consumer. It was also found that the Products targeted towards the mass market are positioned more commonly by using the hedonistic element, emotional element and functional elements of brand positioning. Cultural element is not commonly used for the brand positioning of Products targeted towards the mass market.

The study further concluded that the multinational companies selling FMCG brands prefer to use different positioning criteria and strategies for different demographic segments, psychographic segments and geographic segments in the Indian market.

****

REFERENCES

Maggard, John P. (1976), "Positioning Revisited", *Journal of Marketing*, Vol. 40, No. 1 (Jan), pp. 63-66

Kotler Philip (1996), *Marketing Management-Analysis, Planning, Implementation, and Control*, 8th ed. (New Delhi: Prentice Hall of India), pp. 264-313

Alden, Dana L., Steenkamp, Jan-Benedict, E.M., Batra Rajeev (1999), "Brand Positioning Through Advertising in Asia, North America and Europe: The Role of Global Consumer Culture", *Journal of Marketing*, Vol. 63, No. 1 (Jan), pp. 75-87

Park, C. Whan, Jaworski, Bernard J. and MacInnis, Deborak J. (1986), "Strategic Brand Concept-Image Management", *The Journal of Marketing*, Vol. 50, No. 4 (Oct.), pp. 135-145

Van den Putte, Bas (2002), "An Integrative Framework for Effective Communication", in Bartels, G & W. Nellissen (ed.s), *Marketing for Sustainability: Towards Transactional Policy Making*, (Amsterdam: IOS Press), pp. 83-95

Van den Putte, Bas (2009), "What Matters the Most in Advertising Campaigns? The Relative Effect of Media Expenditure and Message Content Strategy", *International Journal of Advertising*, Vol. 28, No. 3, pp. 669-690

Keller, Kevin Lane (2008), Strategic Brand Management: Building, Measuring and Managing Brand Equity, 3rd ed. (New Delhi: Pearson Education Inc.), pp.120-139

Keller, Kevin Lane, Strenthal, Brian and Tybout Alice (2002), "Three Questions You Need to Ask About Your Brand", Harvard Business Review, September 2002, pp. 81-86

Kotler, Philip, Keller Kevin Lane, Koshy Abraham and Jha Mithileshwar (2009), Marketing Management-A South Asian Perspective, 13th ed. (New Delhi: Pearson Prentice Hall), pp. 282-289

Bannister, J.P., Saunders, J.A (1978); "UK Consumers' Attitudes towards Imports: The Measurement of National Stereotype Image"; *European Journal of Marketing*; Volume 12, Number 8; 1978 ; pp. 562-570

CHAPTER 14

CASE STUDIES OF THE BRAND POSITIONING STRATEGIES OF SELECTED MNCs DEALING IN FMCG

The chapter takes a closer look at the brand positioning strategies that are being used by some selected, well known multinational companies operating in the Indian market. The three companies that have been selected for the study are Godrej Consumer Products Ltd., Dabur India Ltd. and Marico Ltd.

The three companies selected for the study are Godrej Consumer Products Ltd., Dabur India Ltd. and Marico Ltd. are Indian multinationals having a significant presence in the International market and a formidable market share in the domestic market.

For conducting each of these three case studies, the type of brand positioning being used by these companies have been identified by analysing the content of the advertisements copies for brands from these companies. The positioning strategies being adopted by these companies have been understood by interacting with the managers from these companies and seeking response from them on some structured questions related to the brand positioning strategies.

THE CASE OF GODREJ CONSUMER PRODUCTS LTD. (GCPL)

Godrej Consumer Products Ltd. is a part of the Godrej Group of Companies. GCPL was incorporated in the year 2001 after being demerged from the erstwhile Godrej Soaps Ltd. which later on came to be known as Godrej Industries Ltd. GCPL is a leading player in the Indian FMCG sector. It is the second largest player in India in the toilet soap segment (Source: GCPL Letter of Offer for Equity Shareholders of the Company; March 14, 2008) and is a market leader in Hair Colour and Household Insecticide categories (Source: CRISIL Company Report, February 2011). According to the CRISIL Report 2011, GCPL is the second largest player in toiletries in India with a market share of 10.3% and leads the Hair Care category with a market share of 33.9% and the Household Insecticide category with a market share of 33.1%. The company is also a leader in the liquid detergent category with a market share of 75.8%.

From 2005 onwards GCPL has expanded inorganically in the international market by undertaking several acquisitions in the Asian, African and Latin American markets. It has acquired Keyline brands in the U.K., Rapidol and the Kinky Group in South Africa, Tura in Nigeria, Megasari Makmur in Indonesia, Issue Group and Argencos in Latin America, Godrej Sara Lee in India and Cosmetica Nacional in Chile. The Company owns international brands and trademarks in Europe, Australia, Africa, Middle East, Latin America and Canada. It exports to 31 countries some of which are Bangladesh, Thailand, Singapore, Mauritius, Afghanistan, UAE, Iraq, SAARC Countries, Egypt, Jordan, Sudan, South Africa and the Caribbean. Table 14.1 shows a list of the companies acquired and the brands acquired thereof by Godrej Consumer Products Ltd. in the international market.

GCPL has taken the inorganic route to enter and expand into the international market. Instead of growing organically, it has expanded in the international market through acquisition of companies and brands in different countries. The company has spent around Rs. 2000/- Crores to acquire companies, brands and distribution networks across several continents (Iyer, 2010). Today, around a quarter of GCPL's business comes from the international market.

Table 14.1: International Acquisitions by GCPL

Company Acquired	Country/Market	Brands Acquired	Year
Keyline Brands	UK	Cuticura, Erasmic, Adorn, Nulon, Apri	2005
Rapidol	South Africa	Inecto (ethnic hair colour brand), Soflene (hair and skin colour brand)	2006
Tura	Nigeria	Tura	2010
Megasari Mukmur	Indonesia	Hit, Stella, Mitu	2010
Issue Group	Latin America (Argentina,		2010
Argencos	Latin America	Roby, 919	2010
Cosmetica Nacional	Chile	Pamela Grant, Illict, U2	2012

As mentioned by Executive Vice President (International Operations) at Godrej, Jimmy Anklesaria during the interaction with him, GCPL is expanding in the international market using the '3 by 3 matrix' strategy which refers to the company's focus on three product categories (Home Care also including insecticides, Personal Wash and Hair Care) in three markets (Asia, Africa and Latin America all of which are emerging markets).

GCPL's Brand Positioning Strategy in India:

Like in the international market, in the domestic market also GCPL sells different brand of products in the three product categories: Home Care, Personal Wash and Hair Care. The Godrej group, established in 1897, is more than hundred years old and is one of the oldest corporate houses in the country. The company and the brand 'Godrej' command respect amongst the Indian consumer. The Indian consumers perceive Godrej products to be reliable and of good quality. The brand 'Godrej' has a strong brand equity in the Indian market. GCPL makes a conscious effort to leverage this strong brand equity while positioning its brands in the Indian market. The brand positioning strategy is thus based on the principle of leveraging the 'Godrej' brand equity. The letter of offer for the equity share holders of GCPL therefore states "One of our key strengths is being part of the Godrej group of companies and the strong brand equity generated by the 'Godrej' brand name. We believe that the Godrej brand commands a recall amongst the consumers in India due to its image and goodwill established over the years. We intend to leverage the brand equity that we enjoy as a result of our relationship with the Godrej group of companies".

However, in addition to leveraging the strong brand equity of 'Godrej' while positioning its brands in the psyche of the Indian consumer, the company also wanted to ensure that it remains contemporarily relevant to the Indian consumer, particularly in the light of the fact that by the year 2010 half of the Indian population would be under 25 years. The company, under the leadership of Adi Godrej, Chairman, Godrej Group, realised that the name 'Godrej' despite enjoying a strong reputation of trust and reliability was in danger of being perceived as an old company particularly by the young consumer. To ward off this danger and to remain relevant in modern times, the company repositioned the brand 'Godrej' to reflect its commitment to innovation and better living. The immediate changes brought about as a result of this exercise was a colourful brand insignia- the brand name embellished with vibrant stripes of colours and the introduction of the brand slogan and concept "Brighter Living". Godrej is aggressively involved in giving a facelift to a 115 year old company and brand. This sentiment was also reflected in the words of Adi Godrej in one of his interviews to Business Standard in which, while mentioning about the succession plan at Godrej, he says "I am much older than the typical Indian consumer today. There are youngsters in the group who understand them much better than I".

A look at the brands of GCPL indicates that as a branding strategy, the company uses the family brand name along with the individual brand name. The different brands sold under the three categories by GCPL in the Indian market are shown in table 14.2.

Table 14.2: Brands of GCPL in India

HOME CARE	PERSONAL WASH	HAIR CARE
Good Knight	Cinthol	Godrej Expert
Hit	Godrej No.1	Renew
Jet	Godrej Fairglow	Colour Soft
Ezee	Godrej Vigil	Nupur
Godrej Dish Wash	Godrej Protekt	Kesh Kala
Genteel	Godrej Shikakai	Godrej Kali Mehandi
	Godrej Swastik	Anoop Hair Oil
	Godrej Shaving Cream	

As mentioned earlier, GCPL operates in three product categories in the Indian market which are: Home Care, Personal Wash and Hair Care. The products from GCPL in the home care segment include household insecticides, dish wash and liquid detergent. Important brands from GCPL in this category are Good Knight, Hit, Ezee and Genteel.

The product forms under the Good Knight brand of mosquito repellent include coils, cream based mosquito repellent and vapouriser. Good Knight mosquito repellent coil is targeted at the lower middle class Indian family. It is positioned as a low smoke coil with a higher efficacy. The type of positioning is benefit positioning. The value proposition of the product is low smoke and higher effectiveness. The element of message strategy used to communicate the positioning is functional element. While highlighting the value proposition of the product, the advertisement for the product claims "Dhuan kam lekin asar aisa ki ek bhi macchar na mile. Dhuan nahi, asar dikhega" which means that the coil emits less smoke but is so effective that no a single mosquito can be spotted.

The company uses celebrity appeal to promote 'Good Knight Natural Mosquito Repellent Cream'. The product was earlier endorsed by the film star Rani Mukherjee and is now endorsed by another film star Vidya Balan. The advertisements for the brand highlight the natural ingredients in the product: Tulsi, Lavender and Milk Cream and focuses on the benefit of 'no allergy' and 'no rashes' derived from the brand. The message element used to convey the positioning of the brand is the functional element. A combination of attribute positioning and benefit positioning is used for the brand by the company. The product 'Good Knight Advanced Active Plus' is also endorsed by Vidya Balan. The type of brand positioning in this case is a combination of attribute positioning and benefit positioning. The voice over in the advertisement for the brand mentions "Do modes ke sath. Normal mode dabao jab macchar ho kam aur active mode jab macchar ho zyada" which means that the product comes with two modes; Press normal mode in case of less mosquitoes and press the active mode when mosquitoes are more in number. Functional element of message strategy is used to communicate the positioning of the brand.

Another brand of household insecticide sold by GCPL at the national level in the domestic market is 'Hit' which is available in two variants: Red Hit for killing cockroaches and Black Hit for killing mosquitoes. The type of positioning used for positioning the brand 'Hit' is benefit positioning. The message communicated through the advertisement copies is that 'Hit' kills mosquitoes and protects from malaria. The element of the message strategy employed for positioning the brand is functional element. Similarly Red 'Hit' that is positioned as a spray that brings out hidden cockroaches and kills them also uses benefit positioning. Here also the functional element of the message strategy is used for communicating the positioning of the brand.

In the homecare category of GCPL, the brand 'Ezee' has more than 70% of the liquid detergent market share in India. The brand is promoted as a product that specialises in washing woollens. The advertisement copies for the brand call it as 'Woolens ka specialist" i.e., a specialist for woollens. The type of positioning is use/application positioning.

The products from GCPL in the personal wash category include toilet soaps, fairness soap and hand sanitizer. The brands of soaps offered by GCPL in the Indian market are Cinthol, Fairglow and Godrej No. 1 which is available in several variants. Godrej No. 1 is the largest selling brand from GCPL in the Indian market. It is the first brand from GCPL to cross the Rs. 500 crore mark in sale. Godrej No. 1 is the third largest selling brand of toilet soap after Lifebuoy and Lux, both from Hindustan Unilever Ltd. The brand is targeted at the rural as well as the urban market. The non glossy simple pack of the product as well as its relatively lower price differentiates the brand from its competitors. The brand of soap was re-launched in 1997 to compete against the low priced brands in the market like Breeze and Nirma which were gradually eating away into the market share of Cinthol, the flagship brand of Godrej. Today the brand uses price positioning and attribute positioning as its positioning strategy. The different variants of Godrej No.1 are positioned as made up of natural ingredients that keep the skin soft and beautiful. The elements of the message strategy used to communicate the value proposition to the consumer are the physical and functional elements. The different variants of the soap are Godrej No. 1 Almond & Milk, Godrej No.1 with Natural Oils, Godrej No. 1 Papaya & Lotus, Godrej No. 1 Strawberry & Walnut and Godrej No. 1 Saffron & Milk.

Godrej Fairglow is targeted at the beauty conscious and fairness seeking young female consumer. It is positioned as a fairness soap for fair and glowing skin. The type of positioning is benefit positioning and the element of message strategy used to communicate the positioning is functional element.

The brand 'Cinthol' from GCPL is positioned by the company as a brand that instils 24 hour confidence to enable an active lifestyle. The type of positioning is benefit positioning. The advertisement for the brand uses celebrity appeal. The brand 'Cinthol' is endorsed by Hritik Roshan who has an image of an active, fit and confident filmstar. The element of message strategy used for positioning the brand is Hedonistic element.

A new offering from GCPL is the brand of hand sanitizer 'Godrej Protekt'. It is targeted at the health and hygiene conscious consumer. 'Godrej Protekt' is positioned as an instant hand sanitizer with the ability to kill 99.99 percent germs in 15 seconds. The type of positioning is application positioning and benefit positioning.

The hair care products offered by GCPL to the Indian market are Godrej Expert Powder Hair Dye, Godrej Renew Hair Colour, Godrej Colour Soft Hair Colour, Godrej Nupur Mehandi and Godrej Shikakai. The company is the market leader in hair colourants. In the hair colour category it has different brands available at different price points.

Godrej Expert Powder Hair Dye is targeted at the mass market and the middle class Indian consumer. It is positioned as a hair colour that gives a uniform colour and natural looks. The value proposition of Godrej Expert Powder Hair Dye is 'Colour so natural, it is difficult to make out'. Here also it is benefit positioning that is being used. Another brand of hair colour from Godrej is Godrej Renew. It is a cream based hair colour targeted at the young and upwardly mobile middle income Indian consumer. Godrej Renew is promoted as a hair colour cream enriched with the goodness of Aloe Vera and Hibiscus. Hedonistic element is the element of message strategy used for positioning the brand. The slogan for the brand is "New Godrej Renew Hair Colour Cream. Renew your Hair; Renew your Life".

The premium brand of hair colour from GCPL targeted at the upper middle class and the fashion conscious consumer is 'Godrej Colour Soft'. It is positioned as an "Ultra Gentle Hair Colour". The value proposition of the brand is that it conceals grey strands of hair and is gentle on the hair. Benefit positioning is being used by the company to position this brand. Functional element of message strategy is used to communicate the brand benefit.

'Godrej Nupur Mehandi' is a mehandi blend that offers natural hair treatment using natural extracts such as Amla, Brahmi and Bhringraj. It is positioned as a product that is 100 percent natural made up of nine herbal extracts that give colour, conditioning and shine to the hair. The brand positioning is a mix of attribute positioning and benefit positioning.

Factors Affecting the Brand Positioning Strategies at GCPL

According to Jimmy Anklesaria, Executive Vice President (International Business), GCPL, the brand positioning strategy at GCPL is most strongly influenced by the cultural factors of the target market which include the culture of the consumer and the consumer's value system. Other factors which have a strong influence on the positioning strategies for GCPL brands are the purchase habits of the consumers, product characteristics and the brand positioning strategies of competitors.

The factor considered most important by the company and primarily taken into account while formulating the positioning of the brands from GCPL is the culture and belief of the consumer. Factors like Rural/Urban/Suburban background of the consumer and lifestyle and income of the consumer are also taken into account by the company while designing its brand positioning strategies.

While talking of the elements of message strategy, Jimmy Anklesaria pointed out that the preferred element of the message strategy used to communicate the value proposition and the positioning of the brand from the company are Sensory elements, Physical elements and Functional elements. Mr. Anklesaria mentioned that GCPL brands in India reflect the Indian culture up to a certain extent. In his opinion brands that reflect and conform to the culture and belief of the consumer experience a relatively higher degree of acceptance amongst the consumers. When asked about

GCPL's approach on repositioning a brand, Jimmy Anklesaria mentioned that frequent repositioning is not good but may be used to revive a falling brand and to rejuvenate it.

THE CASE OF DABUR INDIA LTD.

Dabur India Ltd. is the fourth largesr FMCG Company in India with a turnover of over Rs. 5300/- crore (Source: Outlook Business, July 24,2010). The international business of Dabur is Rs. 678 crore and contributes to a fifth of the revenues of Dabur India. Unlike Godrej, Dabur has expanded into the international market through the organic route. Dabur started its international operations in1983 by exporting hair oil and honey to the middle east. In the year 1989 it established a manufacturing unit in Dubai and set up a subsidiary there. Today Dabur has manufacturing units located in Dubai, Nepal, Bangladesh, Egypt, Nigeria and the UAE. The company also has its regional offices in the U.K., USA and several other countries. Dabur markets its products in more than sixty countries across the world.

Unlike GCPL which is a polycentric multinational, Dabur is an ethnocentrically oriented company. While products and brands of GCPL vary with the country in which it operates, the brands sold by Dabur across the world are the same as sold by it in the domestic market. The strength of the company lies in its expertise of manufacturing Ayurvedic formulations. It has a strong legacy of developing, manufacturing and marketing Ayurvedic formulations and natural products. It is these products and brand, the origin of which is in India, which the company sells in the international market. Thus Dabur operates in a number of countries across the world where it sells brands and products originally developed for the Indian market and having their roots in Ayruveda and Nature. However minor modifications are made in these formulations according to the specific requirements of the consumers in different markets. Therefore technically speaking, Dabur is an ethnocentrically oriented International Company.

Dabur's Brand Positioning Strategy in India:

As the strength of Dabur lies in its Ayurvedic legacy, Ayurveda and Nature forms the basis of its brand positioning strategy. Except its products sold under the brand name 'Fem' which the company acquired in 2008, all the products of Dabur Ltd. are nature based products.

Dabur is a 125 year old company that has enjoyed the trust of the Indian consumer over the years because of its quality products and strong goodwill in the market. It always had an identity of an herbal product company. In the beginning of the new millennium when the growth rate of the Indian FMCG sector had slowed down, Dabur made a conscious effort to revamp its brand architecture and transform itself into a pure FMCG company that would differentiate itself by virtue of its expertise in manufacturing natural and ayurvedic/herbal products. Dabur envisaged to become a true and modern FMCG company that would be identified as a herbal brand and started making a systematic and concerted effort in this direction from the year 2002. It was through a study conducted by Accenture during this venture that Dabur realised that despite being a respected brand and having a strong brand equity, the brand 'Dabur' connects better with consumers over 35 years of age. The realisation directed the company to reposition the ageing brand and endow it with the spirit of youth and vibrancy. The brand logo of an old and overbearing Banyan tree was replaced by a youthful, vibrant looking, animated image of a Banyan tree. The leaves of the tree suggest growth and energy and the trunk represents three people exulting with joy. The broad trunk symbolises stability and the twin colour of the tree (saffron trunk and green leaves) indicate stability, vigour and freshness. Even the font used in the brand name was changed to give a young and contemporary look to it. "Celebrate Life" became the new brand concept and the brand slogan. As a part of this repositioning venture special marketing attention was focused on 'Dabur', 'Vatika', 'Anmol', 'Real' and 'Hajmola' brands (Shahjahan, 2011).

Dabur has different brands across four distinct business portfolios: Personal Care, Health Care, Home Care and Foods (See Table 14.3).

Table 14.3: Brands of Dabur India Ltd.

PERSONAL CARE BRANDS		
HAIR CARE BRANDS	**ORAL CARE BRANDS**	**SKIN CARE BRANDS**
Dabur Amla Hair Oil	Dabur Babool Toothpaste	Fem Range
Dabur Vatika Hair Oil	Dabur Meswak	Gulabari Range
Dabur Vatika Shampoo	Dabur Lal Toothpaste	Dabur Uveda Range
HEALTH CARE BRANDS		
HEALTH SUPPLEMENTS	**DIGESTIVES**	**OTC-HEALTH CARE**
Dabur Chyawanprash	Dabur Pudin Hara	Dabur Honitus
Dabur Honey	Dabur Hajmola	Dabur Lal Tail
HOME CARE BRANDS		
Odonil	Odomos	Odopic
Sani Fresh		
FOOD BRANDS		
Dabur Real	Dabur Real Active	Homemade

In its Personal Care portfolio, Dabur India Ltd. has hair care products, oral care products and skin care products. Hair Care offerings from Dabur in the Indian market are Dabur Amla Hair Oil, Dabur Vatika Hair Oil and Dabur Vatika Shampoo. One of the hair care brands from Dabur, Dabur Aonla is one of the largest selling hair oil brand in the country with 35 million dedicated consumers (Source: Dabur Annual Report, 2010-2011). 'Dabur Amla' positions itself against the other Amla oils in the market and claims to be the original Amla oil: 'Asli Amla Dabur Amla' ('Original Amla is Dabur Amla'). Competitor positioning strategy is used by Dabur to position its brand 'Dabur Amla' hair oil.

Another widely promoted brand of hair oil from Dabur is 'Dabur Vatika' hair oil. Dabur Vatika is considered a master brand by the company. Even in the Middle East, Dabur Vatika is the fastest growing hair care brand (Source: Dabur Annual Report, 2010-2011). In its positioning, Dabur Vatika highlights the natural ingredients present in the oil (Pure coconut oil, henna, soya, amla and lemon) and the resultant benefit of stopping hair fall, making hair stronger and giving better dandruff control. Thus it is a combination of attribute positioning and benefit positioning. The brand is endorsed by Priety Zinta.

In line with the natural and Ayurvedic Legacy of Dabur, the different brands of shampoo from Dabur are also positioned using the 'Natural ingredient, Natural Product' platform. Using the same positioning platform, Dabur Vaktika root strengthening shampoo highlights the natural ingredients -almonds and coconut milk in the product. The advertisement copy to promote the brand categorically mentions the absence of any harmful chemical in the product. The value proposition of the brand is its root strengthening virtue derived from its natural ingredients- almonds and coconut milk. Thus the positioning is a combination of benefit positioning and attribute positioning. Similarly Dabur Vatika black shine uses a combination of attribute positioning and benefit positioning when it highlights the natural ingredients in the product (Black Olive and Amla, sans any harmful chemical) and the resultant ability to make hair naturally black and shiny. Physical element of positioning used in the marketing communication tool, advertisement to be more precise, conveys the brand identity by overtly highlighting and exhibiting the ingredients of the product.

Just like the other variants of Dabur Vatika shampoo, Dabur Vatika Henna conditioning shampoo also highlights the natural ingredients of the product (Green almonds and Henna conditioning) and the benefit of silky hair derived from the use of the product. The value proposition of the brands is naturally silky hair derived from a natural product. The positioning strategy in this case is also a combination of attribute positioning and benefit positioning.

Dabur is perceived as a company that manufactures Ayurvedic, herbal and natural products. As discussed earlier in this chapter, the strength of the company and the brand lies in its legacy of providing natural products and products derived from the traditional knowledge of Ayurveda. Strictly in line with the perceived image of Dabur, it positions two of its toothpaste brands: Dabur Babool and Dabur Meswak. The product formulations and the brand names are rooted in Ayurveda and traditional Unani medicine respectively. Dabur Meswak in its positioning highlights the natural ingredients of the product (the extract of Meswak plant), the bactericidal and germicidal properties of which strengthen the teeth and give fresh breath and protect the teeth from cavity, plaque and tartar. The positioning strategy consists of a mix of attribute positioning (the product made up of pure extracts of Meswak plant) and benefit positioning (Fresh breath, strong teeth, prevention of cavity, plaque and tartar). The advertisement uses celebrity appeal wherein Bipasha Basu, the brand ambassador for Dabur Meswak, advocates the use of the brand. The promotional campaign makes use of humour appeal in its advertisement copy.

Dabur Babool is positioned as a product that gives strong teeth and a lively day. The advertising campaign for the brand is characterized by a series of advertisement copies used over a period of time, each of which is very lively. The very first ad copy showed a young man becoming very active and filled with liveliness and energy after brushing his teeth with Babool. The jingle for the ad copy went as "Subah Babool ki to din tumhara" which means "If you start your morning with Babool, the day is yours". The advertisement copy effectively communicated the benefit positioning of "A lively day with Babool". A subsequent advertisement copy used humour appeal while showing a young white man solving the water scarcity problem of a village by breaking open a fountain of water by biting on an underground/concealed water pipe using his teeth and earning the title 'Fountain Guru'. The benefit positioning of 'Strong teeth' with Babool is conveyed in a humorous way. Another advertisement copy uses the film star Vivek Oberoi in it. This ad copy is also lively and full of energy and dwells on the benefit positioning (strong teeth and lively day) of the brand. Dabur Babool has used the hedonistic element throughout its advertising campaign to promote and position the brand.

Fem Herbal bleach cream, though targeting the instant fairness market, does not have a direct competition from any of the well known brands of fairness creams like Fair & Lovely, Fairever or Fair One as these creams promise fairness after weeks of use whereas Fem is about instant fairness. Fem Herbal bleach is specifically targeted to the Indian women who have facial hair. This is not a global phenomenon but a problem typical to the Indian subcontinent. For such women, one way to hide their facial hair is to use a bleach lotion. Since this is not a worldwide problem none of the foreign MNCs have ventured into this product segment and Dabur has some sort of monopoly in this segment. However, there are some lesser known regional players is this market segment.

Women who use a bleach lotion are often concerned about the harmful effect of the product on their skin. To alleviate these fears Dabur has modified the Fem bleach cream and launched Fem Herbal bleach cream with 16 herbs. So the product is now positioned on the basis of the benefit it offers, i.e. instant fairness in a natural way that is safe for the skin and the advertisement for the product claims "15 minutes to fairness naturally". The brand positioning strategy in use is benefit positioning. (Bhandari, 2009).

Dabur Gulabari, a skin care product from Dabur is targeted at the young female consumer. It is positioned as a natural product (made up of extracts of rose petals) that keeps the skin hydrated and soft and keeps the skin glowing. The different products under the Gulabari brand name are Gulabari Rose Water (pure extracts of rose petals- 'gulab jal'), Gulabari Spray and Gulabari Cold Cream (made of natural rose extracts). The positioning is a combination of attribute and benefit positioning. In line with Dabur's brand concept 'Celebrate Life', the message element used for positioning the brand is hedonistic element.

In the health care brands Dabur Honey has been strategically positioned as a food brand which has transformed the brand into a market leader with more than 75 percent of the market share. The company uses celebrity appeal to promote the brand. The brand is endorsed by Amitabh Bacchan. To convey the 'healthy food' value propostion, film star Shilpa Shetty who is considered as a youth icon as well as a fitness icon has been roped in for the advertisement of the brand. The punch-line for the brand is 'Dabur Honey- Healthy hai, Tasty hai'. The type of positioning is product category positioning and benefit positioning. The element of message strategy used to communicate the positioning of the brand is hedonistic element.

Dabur was the first company to launch a branded Chyawanprash in the Indian market in the year 1949. Today it has 67 percent of the market share. As per a research conducted by Indian Council of Market Research, the brand 'Dabur Chyawanprash' was voted as a power brand by the consumers (Source: Dabur Annual Report, 2010-2011). The brand, endorsed by the cricketer Mahendra Singh Dhoni, uses celebrity appeal in its advertisements. It is promoted on health grounds as a product that enhances immunity, fights diseases and keeps one fit and strong in all seasons. The element of message strategy used to communicate the message is hedonistic element. Hedonistic element of the message strategy is conspicuously used in the advertisement copies that depict fun, frolic, mischief, enjoyment and a feel good feeling. Here also the advertisement for the brand as well as the brand positioning reflects the brand concept 'Celebrate Life'. To further extend this brand concept, the product 'Dabur Chyawanprash' has been launched in various palatable variants for children as well as adults. These variants are 'Dabur Chyawanprash Mango' and 'Dabur Chyawanprash Orange' for kids and 'Dabur Chyawanprash Sugar Free' particularly for diabetics.

Another category in the healthcare portfolio of Dabur India is 'Digestives'. The two brands in this segment are 'Dabur Pudin Hara' and 'Dabur Hajmola'. 'Dabur Pudin Hara' is positioned as an instant solution to gastric problems. A pinch of celebrity appeal is used in the promotion of this brand that is endorsed by the film star Raveena Tandon and Sanjay Suri. The type of positioning is use positioning as well as benefit positioning. The message element used for positioning the brand is functional element.

The other digestive brand in Dabur's kitty is 'Dabur Hajmola'. According to the Annual Report of the company for the year 2010-2011, about 2.6 crore Dabur Hajmola tablets are consumed in India everyday. 'Dabur Hajmola' has also emerged as one of the strongest brands from Dabur in Pakistan. The brand is positioned as a tasty and essential digestive to be consumed after every meal. The advertisement copies for the brand emphasise the joys of eating and making the indulgence enjoyable with a Hajmola after the meal. The element of message strategy is hedonistic and functional element. The type of positioning is benefit positioning.

Two main brands from Dabur India Ltd. in the OTC-Health Care category are Dabur Honitus (Cough Syrup and Cough Lozenges) and Dabur Lal Tail. Dabur Honitus is positioned as an effective and harmless Ayurvedic solution to cough. In the positioning for the brand, the ayurvedic composition and attribute of the product is highlighted. The product is positioned as being free from the harmful effects that other cough syrups have. Therefore the type of positioning is attribute positioning as well as benefit positioning. Functional and Physical elements of the message strategy are used to position the brand.

Dabur Lal Tail has a user positioning and is positioned as a massage oil for strengthening the musculoskeletal system of the baby. Unlike that in other category of products, celebrity appeal is not used by Dabur to promote the OTC-Healthcare brands.

In the homecare category, 'Odonil' is a well known brand from Dabur. Odonil blocks are positioned as small space fragrancers with natural floral fragrances to be used in bathrooms, cupboards, etc. Odonil air freshner spray is positioned as a natural room freshner with the ability to elevate the mood. The type of positioning is use positioning.

In the food category, the juice brand Dabur Real Active from the stable of Dabur is positioned on health proposition. The film star Bipasha Basu, who carries an image of a brand conscious celebrity, has been roped in by Dabur to endorse the Dabur Real Active brand. The brand positioning strategy is a blend of attribute positioning ("made up of fresh fruits and vegetables Real Active is a healthy snack") and benefit positioning ("No added sugar. 50% lesser calories"). The advertisement copy for the brand loudly declares "Fresh fruits aur vegetables se bane. Real Active is a healthy snack" (which means "Made up of fresh fruits and vegetables, Dabur Active is a healthy snack") and further adds that the product contains "No added sugar. 50 % less calories". Functional element of positioning is employed to communicate the brand identity which is: Real and healthy fruit and vegetable juice with no added sugar.

Factors Influencing the Brand Positioning Strategies of Dabur India Ltd.

According to Rana Bannerjee, Category Head Oral Care at Dabur India Ltd, the brand positioning strategies of Dabur India Ltd. are strongly influenced by several factors like rural/urban background of the consumer, the value system of the consumer and the marketing philosophy of the company. Some other factors that have an equally strong influence on the brand positioning strategies of Dabur are the characteristics of the company, positioning strategies of the competitors and the consumers' consumption pattern, consumers' preference of competing brands and the loyalty enjoyed by those brands.

Rana Bannerjee pointed out that the factor primarily and consciously taken into account while designing the brand positioning strategies is the background of the consumer (urban/rural/suburban). This factor becomes increasingly more important for the oral care and packaged food brands. The second most important factor that is taken into account while formulating the brand positioning strategy is the culture and belief of the consumer followed by the nature of occupation of the consumer.

At Dabur, celebrity appeal is frequently used to promote the brands and position them in the minds of the consumers. Film stars and sportsmen who have a mass appeal and who have the ability to influence the psyche of the young consumer are roped in to endorse the Dabur brands. Rana Bannerjee believes that celebrity appeal as well as the special experience appeal, (hedonistic appeal) which also echoes in the brand concept 'Celebrate Life', is most effective in affecting brand recall.

Physical element of message strategy (to highlight product attributes) and functional element of message strategy (to highlight product usage) are most preferred by the company for establishing the positioning of the brands. The brands from Dabur have their roots in Ayurveda, and Ayurveda and natural products form the basic positioning platform for Dabur. In light of this fact, Rana Bannerjee also pointed out that Dabur brands are very strongly associated with the culture of India and strongly reflect the Indian culture. According to him brands that reflect the consumers' culture experience a higher degree of consumer acceptance. He is not of the opinion that global brands in India have a higher preference as compared to domestic brands like Dabur. As could be understood from his response, Dabur is open to reposition its brands to match and to keep pace with changing preferences of the consumers. As mentioned by Bannerjee, repositioning if done properly rejuvenates a brand but frequent repositioning should be avoided at any cost.

THE CASE OF MARICO LTD.

Marico Ltd. is an Indian FMCG company that has taken its business to the international market and operates in several countries across the world. Prior to being established as Marico Industries Ltd. in the year 1990, the company existed as merely a consumer product division of Bombay Oil Industries Ltd. Today, the homegrown FMCG giant operates in more than twenty five countries and had a turnover of Rs. 3,128 Crore in the year 2011 (Source: Marico Annual Report, 2010-2011). The company operates in the beauty and wellness space. In the domestic market as well as in the international market, the company has its brands that compete in the hair care, skin care and food categories. It has expended in the international market using both the organic and inorganic routes.

The company started its international operations in 1991-92 by exporting its flagship brand of coconut oil 'Parachute' to the Middle East. It set up its first manufacturing plant outside the country in Bangladesh in the year 2002. Its first overseas acquisition was also made in Bangladesh in the same year when the company acquired two soap brands in the country, Camelia and Aromatic. From the year 2006, Marico has rapidly entered into several markets including Egypt, South Africa, Malaysia, Singapore and Vietnam. Besides taking its own brands into the international market, the company has acquired a number of brands in the foreign markets it has entered. Table 14.4 gives a glimpse of the international operations of Marico, its organic presence and acquisitions made by Marico in the international market.

Table 14.4: International Operations of Marico Ltd.

COUNTRY	ORGANIC PRESENCE	BRANDS ACQUIRED	YEAR OF ENTRY
Middle East (Entire GCC, Yemen, Sudan, Levant Region)	Parachute Hair Oil, Parachute Hair Creams		1991-92
Bangladesh	Parachute Hair Oil	Camelia, Aromatic	2002
Egypt	Parachute	Fiancee Haircare Brand, Hair Code Haircare Brand	2006
South Africa		Enaleni Pharmaceuticals Ltd. (Having Ethnic Haircare brands Caivil and Chic), Hercules (OTC Brand)	2007
Malaysia	Parachute, Nihar	Code 10 (Hair Styling Brand)	2010
Singapore		Derma RX, Asia Pacific Pte	2010
Vietnam		International Poduct Corporation (Has brands like X-Men, L'ovite, Thuan Phat)	2011

Positioning Strategy of Marico Ltd. in India:

Marico Ltd. operates in the beauty and wellness space and is guided by its motto "Be More. Everyday" in the domestic as well as in the international market. This motto of "Be More. Everyday" forms the basic brand positioning credo for the company in all its markets and constitutes the brand concept of the company. In the Indian market Marico offers products in the categories of Hair Care, Skin Care, Home Care and Foods. Some well known brand and products from Marico in the Indian market are Parachute Advansed Hair Oil, Parachute Advensed range of products, Saffola Edible Oil, Saffola Oats, Saffola Salt, Saffola Arise brand of rice, Nihar Hair Oil, Shanti Amla Hair Oil, Hair & Care, Mediker and Revive.

'Parachute' is the flagship brand of Marico. It is the largest selling brand of hair oil in the country. 'Parchute' has a market leadership in the coconut oil segment with a market share of 45.8 percent during 2010-2011. The overall market share of Marico in this segment along with its brands 'Parachute', 'Nihar' and 'Oil of Malabar' is 52.6 percent as of March 2011 (Source: Marico Annual Report 2010-2011). The brand identity of the flagship brand 'Parachute Advansed' is care and nurturance. Branded coconut oil in the country is best represented by the brand 'Parachute' with its trademark blue coloured container depicted on which is a coconut tree. Today the brand is positioned as an essential supplement for shampoo for maintaining shiny and gorgeous hair and for preventing dryness. The positioning strategy is that of benefit positioning. Functional element of positioning is used to convey the brand identity.

To leverage the brand equity of the brand 'Parchute', Marico has gone for line extension whereby it has launched several variants of hair oil under the brand name 'Parachute Advansed'. The different variants are 'Parachute Jasmine Non Sticky Hair Oil', 'Parchute Advansed Ayurvedic Hair Oil', 'Parachute Advansed Ayurvedic Hot Oil' and 'Parachute Advansed Cooling Oil'. The brand has also been extended to the skin care category. The company has launched a body lotion called 'Parachute Advansed Body Lotion'. It is positioned as a body lotion that makes the skin soft and makes you feel young. Love appeal is used in the advertisement of the brand. The element of message strategy used for positioning the product is emotional element. The positioning strategy is benefit positioning.

'Nihar Naturals' hair oil from Marico is positioned as a hair oil made of coconut and natural extracts that nourishes the hair and instils confidence. Hedonistic element of message strategy is used for positioning the brand. The other product under the 'Nihar' brand name, 'Nihar Almond Hair Oil' is positioned as a hair oil made up of almond extracts that nourishes the hair. The value proposition of the brand 'Nihar' and of this product is nourishment for the hair. Benefit positioning is the type of positioning used for positioning the brand.

Shanti Amla Hair Oil and Shanti Badam Amla Hair Oil from the stable of Marico are targeted at the young and aspiring female consumer from the middle income class in the rural and semi urban market. The value proposition of the brand is strong and nourished hair. The type of positioning in this case is also benefit positioning.

Hair and Care from Marico is an important player in the light hair oil category. It tries to occupy the benefit position of "Up to 50 percent less hair fall and style with nourishment". The voice over in the advertisement copy for the brand says "Hair & Care ke herbal proteins balon ka jharna kare 50 percent tak kam aur de poshan bhara style" ("The herbal protein of Hair & Care reduces hairfall up to 50 percent and give you style enriched with nutrition").

In the homecare category, a known product from Marico is Revive. The brand is positioned as a liquid starch that is gentle on the fabric, protective for the colour of the cloth and keeps clothes looking new and bright. The type of positioning is benefit positioning. Functional element of message strategy is used in the advertisement to communicate the benefit of the brand to the consumer.

One of the strongest positioning in the edible oil market is that of Saffola. Marico has positioned Saffola as an edible oil that reduces bad cholesterol and keeps the heart healthy. Through its advertisements the company appeals to the consumers to start using Saffola as it reduces cholesterol and keeps the heart young. The type of positioning is benefit positioning (reduces cholesterol and keeps the heart young). In order to strengthen its association with the cause of keeping the heart healthy, the company set up the Saffola Healthy Heart Foundation in the year 1991. The foundation is actively involved in conducting cardiac camps and free cholesterol checkups. These cardiac camps build awareness about the risks that the modern lifestyle poses to the heart and help people lower those risks. For the family of those recuperating from cardiac ailments, Saffola organizes 'Healthy Hearts' seminars to tell them how to take care of the patients (Kar, 2010). Thus Saffola has identified the cause of 'Healthy Heart' and tries to associate itself with it strongly. Saffola is into cause marketing and cause branding.

The company further leverages the brand equity of Saffola by extending it into other functional foods like salt, rice and flour additives. While Saffola oil talks of checking bad cholesterol so as to prevent heart ailments, its salt, rice and flour additives claim to keep under control diseases and problems that increase the probability of the occurrence of heart diseases and diseases such as hypertension, diabetes and lethargy.

In an interview to Business Standard, Sameer Satpathy, Head of Marketing (Consumer Products) at Marico, while talking about the brand Saffola mentioned "In our interaction with consumers, we realised that we needed more than cooking oil to have a larger impact". Extending the brand 'Saffola' to salt, oats and rice brought the brand out of the kitchen to the dining table. This intensified the contact of the brand with the consumer and enhanced the health equity of the brand

'Saffola'. 'Saffola Arise', the brand of Basmati Rice from Marico is targeted at the health conscious urban consumer in India. Saffola Arise is positioned as a healthy rice that keeps one active and fit. It is pitched as a health food that the company claims as having 20 percent less carbohydrate and calories than any other rice. Marico also claims that the product has low glycemia index because of which it releases glucose steadily throughout the day. Functional element of message strategy is used to communicate the benefit positioning of the brand to the consumer.

Factors Influencing the Brand Positioning Strategies at Marico Ltd.

According to Alok Kohli, Brand Manager at Marico Ltd., the characteristics of the target consumer as well as the characteristics of the competing brands have a strong bearing on the brand positioning strategies adopted by Marico for its brands in the Indian market. The brand positioning strategies of Marico Ltd. are significantly influenced by the brand positioning strategies of the competitors as well as the consumers' loyalty and preference enjoyed by the competing brands in those markets where Marico operates. The positioning of the Marico brands are also influenced by the culture and tradition of the consumer and his value system. The other consumer related characteristics that influence the positioning strategy of Marico Ltd. is the purchase habit as well as the consumption pattern of the target consumer.

As mentioned by Alok Kohli, the factors that are primarily taken into account by the brand managers at Marico while formulating the brand positioning strategies are the cultural factors (which include the culture and belief of the consumer and the traditional customs and practices in the target market) and the lifestyle of the target consumer. He was of the opinion that if brands are able to conform to the culture of the consumer, they are easily accepted by the consumer and experience a higher preference amongst the consumers.

Alok Kohli also pointed out that the most preferred elements of the message strategy for positioning brands at Marico are the functional element and the sensory/hedonistic element. It was revealed during the interaction with Mr. Kohli that while targeting different geographies and different states in India, the company uses different positioning criteria. The interaction also brought the fact that while targeting different economic segments, Marico takes into account the lifestyle of the consumer in those economic segments and formulates the positioning of the brands accordingly.

Mr. Kohli categorically pointed out that the same factors may not be equally relevant for all the companies. The significance of these factors may vary with the characteristics of the company. For example the factors relevant for the global biggies like Coca Cola, Pepsico, Unilever and P&G may not be so relevant for homegrown multinationals like Godrej, Dabur and Marico. Similarly an entirely different set of factors may be of utmost importance for local level and regional FMCG companies like Ghari, Nirma, etc. He was also of the opinion that factors taken into account while positioning a brand and the elements of message strategy preferred by a brand manager for communicating the positioning are significantly different for products in the lifestyle category than those for the products in the daily use category in the FMCG sector.

****

REFERENCES

Bhandari, Bhupesh (2009), "Dabur Finds its Missing Link", *The Strategist* (July 28), p. 1

Iyer, Byravee (2009), "Soap Opera", *The Strategist* (August 25), p. 1

Iyer, Byravee (2010), "Overseas Call", *The Strategist* (April 19), p. 1

Kar, Sayantani (2010), "A Healthy Headstart", *The Strategist* (March 30), p. 1

Kar, Sayantini (2012), "On a New Trajectoty", *The Strategist* (February 27), p. 1

Pinto, Roy (2010), "New Age Godrej", *Business India* (July 11), pp: 46-55

Shahjahan, S. (2011), *Applied Case Studies in Marketing*, Primus Books, New Delhi, p: 109

Shashidhar, Ajita (2010), "Good to Global", *Outlook Business* (July 24), pp:42-53

Marico Annual Report 2010-2011

Dabur Annual Report 2010-2011

CHAPTER 15

SUMMARY OF IMPORTANT FINDINGS

The chapter presents the major findings of the book and lists some research based suggestions for the multinational companies and their brand managers dealing in FMCG brands in the Indian market. It also discusses the limitations of the study and the future scope of research in the studied area.

FINDINGS FROM THE STUDY

The findings from the study have been discussed under the following headings:

A) Brand Building and Positioning a Brand in The Indian FMCG Market
B) A Description of the Brand Positioning Strategies of companies in the FMCG sector in India
C) Factors Affecting Consumers' Preference of FMCG Brand in India
D) Use of The Elements of The Message Content Strategy in Positioning FMCG Brands by MNCs in India
E) Positioning a Brand Through the Use of the Cultural Element of The Message Content Strategy
F) Alteration of Brand Positioning Strategies for Different Geographic Demographic and Psychographic Segment
G) Preference of Local Brands Vs Global Brands
H) Impact and Significance of the 'Country Of Origin' in Brand Positioning of FMCG Brands by MNCs in India
I) Factors Affecting Brand Positioning Strategies of MNCs Dealing in FMCG in India
J) Brand Positioning Strategies Adopted by Selected Indian MNCs Dealing in FMCG in India

BRAND BUILDING AND POSITIONING A BRAND IN THE INDIAN FMCG MARKET

Brand building is a dynamic process through which a brand evolves over a period of time. The evolution of a brand takes place through different stages. In the first stage the brand expresses the identity of the producer. In the second stage of its evolution the brand establishes its functional superiority (Perceived by customers as differentiation). Stage third is the one in which the brand establishes an emotional touch with the consumers. A brand is said to have reached the stage 4 of its evolution when it generates the power of self expression. The brand achieves the pinnacle of its glory when it reaches the stage 5 where it becomes a cult.

(a) Brand Positioning

Brand Positioning doesn't simply mean finding or creating a suitable place in the mind of the target customer but doing so with a watchful eye on the competitor (Ries & Trout, 1981) and simultaneously making points of parity with the competitor and establishing relevant and sustainable points of difference. Thus a brand Positioning exercise starts with understanding the target market segment, and is followed by understanding the competitor and establishing points of parity and points of difference. Thus the points of reference used for positioning a brand are the consumers' mind and the competing brands.

(b) Positioning Brands of Fast Moving Consumer Goods by Multinational Companies in the Indian Market

The dimensions and nuances of brand positioning for an MNC in India are different from those in the western markets. Multinationals need to chalk out different value propositions for consumers in the emerging markets like India. Their marketing programmes need to be specifically adapted to the needs of the emerging market consumers. In order to effectively position a foreign brand of fast moving consumer goods in the Indian market, a company should use the marketing mix with which the host country consumer is familiar with.

A DESCRIPTION OF THE BRAND POSITIONING STRATEGIES OF COMPANIES IN THE FMCG SECTOR IN INDIA

The different types of brand positioning strategies are Attribute Positioning, Benefit Positioning, Use/ Application Positioning, User Positioning, Quality/ Price Positioning, Product category Positioning and Competitor Positioning. Besides positioning their brands in the conventional markets in India an emerging challenge for companies operating in the Indian market is to effectively position their brands in the bottom of pyramid market and in the rural markets. Inclusive marketing, Product and Packaging modifications and Pricing modifications are the three important tools that are being used by the companies today to position their brands in the rural market.

Content analysis of advertisement copies was undertaken to understand the types of positioning being used by the FMCG companies in the Indian market.

(a) Brand Positioning Strategies of FMCG Companies in India

The type of brand positioning strategies being used by the FMCG companies for positioning some of their brands in the Indian market is summarized in the table 15.1 below:

Table 15.1: POSITIONING STRATEGIES FOR SOME FMCG BRANDS IN INDIA

BRAND	HIGHLIGHT/EXPLANATION	ELEMENT
ORAL CARE BRANDS		
Dabur Babool	Positioned as a product that gives strong teeth and a lively day. The type of positioning is Benefit positioning.	Hedonistic & Functional
Colgate Active Salt	Positioned as a salt laced toothpaste to fight germs and strengthen gums. A combination of attribute positioning and benefit positioning.	Physical & Emotional
Colgate	The brand is positioned on the basis of its ability to to effectively fight tooth decay. Type of positioning is benefit positioning.	Functional

Colgate Total	The value proposition of the brand is to fight twelve tooth related ailments.	Functional
Close Up	The brand offers the benefit of enhanced and talks about a 'feel good' feeling because of fresh breath. The type of positioning is benefit positioning.	Hedonistic
TOILET SOAP		
Lifebuoy Care	The brand is positioned as one that provides all day protection from germs. The type of positioning is benefit positioning.	Functional
Lifebuoy Handwash	Presented as the 'fastest handwash' ie, fights germs fastest.	Functional
Liril	Positioned as an original freshness soap. Benefit positioning.	Hedonistic
Pears	Brand identity of the product is a caring soap for the soft, young skin. The positioning strategy is benefit positioning	Emotional
Dettol	Benefit positioning is used whereby the brand is positioned as a product that ensures good health for the entire family.	Functional
Dove	Positioned as being different from soap, a bathing bar with one quarter moisturizer. Category Positioning.	Functional
Lux	The brand always associates itself with film stars and the fantasy of looking beautiful.	Hedonistic
DETERGENT		

Tide	The brand talks about the whiteness benefit and associate itself with whiteness.	Functional
Ariel	The value proposition is being gentle on clothes and protecting them while cleaning. Benefit Positioning.	Functional
Surf Excel	Positioned on the basis of its stain removing capability. Benefit Positioning.	Functional
Sunlight	The ads promise the benefit of protecting and maintaining the bright colours of the clothes. Benefit Positioning.	Functional
SHAMPOO		
Sunsilk	The brand promises the benefit of gorgeous, shiny hair and thick and long hair. 'Sunsilk black shine with UV protector' offers protection from the harmful effects of ultra violet rays.	Functional
Clinic Plus	The ads communicate and focus on the benefit of long hair.	Functional
Clear	Highlights the dandruff fighting efficiency. Benefit Positioning.	Functional
Pantene	Promises the benefit of healthy and strong hair.	Functional
Head & Shoulder Anti Hairfall	Positioned as a brand that "Removes hairfall by 95%".	Functional

Garnier Fructis Long & Strong	The brand is positioned as one that strengthens the hair. Benefit Positioning.	Functional
Garnier Shampoo+ Oil 2 in 1	Positioned on the basis of its contents and benefits derived from the contents. "A bend of shampoo and oil for nourished healthy hair". Attribute Positioning & Benefit Positioning.	Physical & Functional
HAIR OIL		
Prachute	Positioned as an essential supplement to shampoo for maintaining shiny and gorgeous hair. Benefit Positioning	Functional
Hair & Care	The brand claims that "The herbal protein of Hair & Care reduces hairfall upto 50 percent and give you style enriched with nutrition". Benefit Positioning & Attribute Positioning.	Hedonistic
TEA		
Red Label	Positioned on the basis of the physical and sensory virtues of the tea like colour, flavour and aroma. Attribute Positioning.	Physical & Sensory
Brookebond Sehatmand	An association is established with health. Benefit Positioning	Functional
Tata Tea	The brand associates itself with the social cause of anti corruption. Social Cause Positioning.	Emotional
SOFT DRINKS		
Pepsi	Positioned as a drink for the young. User Positioning.	Hedonistic

Coca Cola	The brand doesn't promise any functional or emotional benefit but promises fun and happiness.	Hedonistic
Limca	Positioned as a refreshing drink that brings good times.	Hedonistic
Slice	Promises Pure mango pleasure. Combination of benefit positioning and attribute positioning (taste of mango).	Hedonistic
PACKAGED FRUIT JUICE		
Dabur Real Active	Positioned on health proposition. Combination of attribute positioning (made of fresh fruits and vegetables) & benefit positioning (No added sugar. 50% less calories).	Functional
Coca Cola Minute Maid Pulpy Orange	Differentiated on the basis of its ingredients (fruit pulp). Attribute Positioning.	Physical
Tropicana 100%	Positioned as a complete and real fruit juice for a nutritious and wholesome breakfast. Combination of attribute positioning & benefit positioning.	Functional
FOOD & BEVERAGES		
Complan	Value proposition is the benefit of taller height for children. Benefit Positioning.	Functional Element
Horlicks	Claims to make children 'Taller, Stronger, Sharper'. Benefit Positioning.	Functional
NOODLES		

Maggi	Value proposition is health and taste. Benefit positioning.	Functional
Kellog's Chocos	Value proposition is health and nutrition for children. Benefit positioning.	Functional
Kellog's K	Promises the benefit of reduced weight. Benefit positioning.	Functional
Quaker Oats	Promises the benefit of healthy heart and reduced cholesterol. Benefit positioning.	Functional
CHOCOLATES		
Cadbury	Positioned as a substitute of 'mithai' to be consumed before embarking on something pious and to be consumed as dessert. Cultural Positioning	Cultural & Emotional
Cadbury Dairy Milk Silk	Offers a smooth, creamy taste and promises a captivating experienced.	Hedonistic
Cadbury Five Star	Promises a captivating experience.	Hedonistic
Cadbury Perk	Positioned as a fun snack with the benefit of glucose. Benefit positioning.	Hedonistic & Functional
Nestle Munch	Positioned as a fun snack.	Hedonistic
COSMETICS		

Vaseline Petroleum Jelly	Positioned as a product that gives a healthy, shiny and glowing skin. Benefit Positioning.	Functional
Vaseline Men	Offers anti spots and whitening benefit for men. Benefit positioning & User positioning.	Functional
Lakme Fruit Blast face wash	Positioned as a face wash made up of natural ingredients and containing different real fruits extracts. Attribute positioning.	Physical & Functional
Ponds Cold Cream	Value proposition is soft skin. Benefit positioning.	Hedonistic
Ponds Age Miracle	Positioned as a product that delays the signs of ageing in women above 30. Benefit positioning & User positioning.	Functional
Olay Total Effects 7 in 1 Anti Ageing Cream	Differentiated from the other anti aging creams on the basis of its ability to fight the seven signs of ageing and presents the product as a solution or as a means of alleviating these signs. Benefit Positioning.	Functional Element
Garnier Age Lift	Offers the triple benefit of smoothening wrinkles, removing dark spots & bringing glow to the skin. Benefit Positioning.	Functional Element

FACTORS AFFECTING CONSUMERS' PREFERENCE OF FMCG BRAND IN INDIA

The consumers' preference of brands may be influenced by several factors. The factors influencing the consumers' preference of brands need to be taken into account for effectively positioning brands in the perceptual space of the consumers.

(a) Influence of Product Related Factors on Consumers' Brand Preference

The most influential characteristics of a brand influencing the brand preference of consumers purchasing FMCG brands in the Indian market is the technology used in the brand and the resulting perceived superior quality of the brand. The study found that the brand preferences of the female consumers are more strongly influenced by the brand quality and the global nature of the brands. Technology used in the product and the quality of the product is a factor considered most essential in the evaluation of an FMCG brand by consumers of both the sexes.

There is no significant difference in the influence of product related factors on the brand preference of consumers from different occupational groups. It was also found that as compared to consumers in other age groups, senior citizens and elderly people belonging to the age group 56-75 years are more ethnocentric in their preference and prefer to use brands of brands of Fast Moving Consumer Goods made in India.

(b) Influence of Consumer Related Factors on Consumers' Brand Preference

In the study of consumer related factors it has been found that the consumers have a greater preference for those brands that conform to their lifestyle and to their value system. The lifestyle and value system of the consumer strongly determine their brand preference and constitute important factors that should be taken into account while positioning brands of fast moving consumer goods in the Indian market.

Gender was not found to have any significant impact on the degree of influence of consumer related factors (like consumer's value system, culture and tradition, faith and belief, religion, lifestyle and purchase habit) on the brand preference of consumers. Students as well as education professionals are more influenced by brands that reflect and conform to their faith and belief.

Purchase habit of the consumer also seems to have an impact on consumers' brand preference. Certain category of consumers particularly the education professionals and housewives seek economy in their purchase and their preference of brands is influenced by the 'economy' factor. Brands that are positioned on 'economy' platform are more preferred by these consumers. As compared to other category of consumers, housewives and students are more strongly influenced by 'Lifestyle' in their choice of brands. So brands targeted at housewives and students can be positioned on the basis of lifestyle.

Relative Importance of Social, Cultural and Economic Factors in Consumers' Evaluation of FMCG Brands

The economic factor emerges as the most important factor in the consumers' evaluation of a Fast Moving Consumer Good brand and can therefore be considered as the most important factor in designing the brand positioning strategies of MNCs followed by the Social factor. Though the cultural factor can in no way be called as an unimportant factor, it is less important when compared with the economic factors. Cultural factors form the least important parameters for the professionals from the education sector in their evaluation of FMCG brands.

USE OF THE ELEMENTS OF THE MESSAGE CONTENT STRATEGY IN POSITIONING FMCG BRANDS BY MNCs IN INDIA

Brand Managers believe that a combination of functional and emotional element of the advertising message strategy is most effective in affecting the response from the consumer and is thus important for positioning the brand.

None of the message elements when present as a constituent of different advertising appeals has a distinctively stronger influence on brand recall. However, the brand managers feel that the use of hedonistic element as part of the special experience association facilitates brand recall. Emotional element (reflected through celebrity association) is believed to be the second most effective element in facilitating brand recall. Thus brand managers tend to believe that hedonistic element is most effective in influencing brand recall followed by the emotional element.

From these findings it can be concluded that emotional element, hedonistic element and a combination of emotional and functional elements are thought to be most important by the brand managers in influencing the positioning of a brand.

Somewhat in conformance with the belief of the brand managers regarding the importance and influence of the communication elements on brand positioning, the most preferred message element for positioning an FMCG brand by the brand managers in the Indian market is the hedonistic element followed by the emotional element and the functional element.

As indicated from the response of the consumers surveyed, consumers are most influenced by the use of functional element. This is in conformance with the perception of the brand managers regarding the effectiveness of the communication elements.

Proving the belief (regarding the impact of message elements on brand recall) of the brand managers fairly correct, emotional element of message (projected in the form of celebrity association) is found to be most influential in facilitating brand recall followed by the functional communication element (in the form of performance association). Hedonistic element that is regarded by brand managers to be very significant in influencing brand recall is not so potent in reality. The response of the consumers clearly indicates that emotional element of communication is most effective in influencing and facilitating brand recall followed by the functional element.

From the response of the consumers it can be concluded that the message elements that have the most significant impact on the consumers' perception of the brand and his ensuing response to it are the emotional element and the functional element.

POSITIONING A BRAND THROUGH THE USE OF THE CULTURAL ELEMENT OF THE MESSAGE CONTENT STRATEGY

(a) Culture as an Element of Brand Positioning

Different elements of culture have been successfully used for positioning several brands in the Indian market. Brands are commonly positioned using elements of the local culture or foreign culture. In certain cases global cultural elements may also be used for brand positioning. These types of brand positioning are known a Local Consumer Culture Positioning (LCCP), Foreign Consumer Culture Positioning (FCCP) and Global Consumer Culture Positioning (GCCP).

(b) Competitive Advantage through Cultural Positioning

Though elements of culture are increasingly being used to position several brands, the study found that FMCG brands that use local consumer culture positioning do not have any significant competitive advantage as compared to those brands that use foreign consumer culture positioning or those that use global consumer culture positioning. Neither does the use of foreign consumer culture positioning ensure any greater competitive advantage to FMCG brands as compared to the use of local consumer culture positioning or that of global consumer culture positioning. This finding was in contradiction to the belief of the brand managers. The brand managers from multinational companies dealing in FMCG brands in the Indian market were found to believe that the use of Local Consumer Culture Positioning endows the brand with a significant competitive advantage and enhances the acceptance of the brand amongst the consumers.

ALTERATION OF BRAND POSITIONING STRATEGIES FOR DIFFERENT GEOGRAPHIC, DEMOGRAPHIC AND PSYCHOGRAPHIC SEGMENTS

The study found that a large percentage of multinational companies selling FMCG brands in India use different positioning criteria for positioning their brands in different geographic segments in the country. A substantial percentage of the companies used different positioning criteria for positioning their brands in the rural market and in the urban market. Quite a few of these companies changed their positioning strategies according to the states or geographical regions in which they sold their brands.

The practice of having different brand positioning strategies for different geographic segments was found to be more prevalent in case of multinational companies of foreign origin than those from India.

An overwhelming percentage of brand managers from multinational companies dealing in FMCG brands in India were found to report that their companies change the positioning criteria used for positioning the FMCG brands according to the demographic and psychographic segments in which the brands are sold. The practice has been found to be prevalent in a very high percentage of the foreign multinationals and a significantly high percentage of Indian multinationals. The main demographic and psychographic criteria according to which the positioning strategies of these multinationals are changed are the lifestyle of the consumer followed by the purchasing power of the consumer. The positioning strategies for several FMCG products and brands may also be altered according to the disposable income of the consumer and the occupation of the consumer.

PREFERENCE OF LOCAL BRANDS Vs GLOBAL BRANDS

From the study it has been found that the Indian consumers exhibit a significantly higher preference for global brands or those Indian brands which have extended into several countries across the world. An analysis of the opinion of the brand managers surveyed also reveals that the brand managers from multinational companies dealing in FMCG brands in India believe that global brands experience a higher brand preference. Thus the opinion of the brand managers is in congruence with the findings from the response of the consumers.

HYPOTHESIS 1: THE BRAND POSITIONING STRATEGIES ADOPTED BY THE MNCs IN INDIA ARE INFLUENCED BY THE VALUES AND BELIEFS OF THE INDIAN CONSUMER

Null Hypothesis1 ($H1_{\emptyset}$): The brand positioning strategies adopted by the MNCs in India are not influenced by the values and beliefs of the Indian consumer.

Alternate Hypothesis1 ($H1_{\alpha}$): The brand positioning strategies adopted by the MNCs in India are influenced by the values and beliefs of the Indian consumer.

Chi Square test was conducted to test the null hypothesis which states that "The brand positioning strategies adopted by the MNCs in India are not influenced by the values and beliefs of the Indian consumer". As the calculated values of chi square for the variables 'Influence of consumer's value system on brand positioning', 'influence of the culture of the consumer on brand positioning' and 'influence of the faith and belief of the consumer on brand positioning' at degree of freedom 4 and level of significance 0.05 are 13.000, 15.333 and 11.000 respectively, each of which is more than the table value of chi square (9.488) at degree of freedom 4 and level of significance 0.05, and as the p value for each of these variables is less than 0.05, it indicates that there is a significant influence of these factors on the brand positioning strategies (Refer Table 7.16). It implies that the brand positioning strategies adopted by MNCs dealing in FMCG in India are significantly influenced by the value system of the consumer, the culture of the consumer and the faith and belief of the consumer.

Thus the null hypothesis ($H1_{\emptyset}$: The brand positioning strategies adopted by the MNCs in India are not influenced by the values and beliefs of the Indian consumer) is rejected whereas the alternate hypothesis ($H1_{\alpha}$: The brand positioning strategies adopted by the MNCs in India are influenced by the values and beliefs of the Indian consumer) is not rejected.

HYPOTHESIS 2A: PRODUCTS TARGETED TOWARDS THE MASS MARKET ARE POSITIONED MORE COMMONLY BY USING THE FUNCTIONAL ELEMENTS OF BRAND POSITIONING.

The study revealed that while positioning brands of fast moving consumer goods in the Indian market, most of the brand managers from multinational companies prefer to use either the functional elements, emotional elements or hedonistic elements of the message content strategy.

Chi Square test has been used to find out which element of the advertising message strategy is commonly used to position a brand of consumer packaged goods by the MNCs operating in India.

As the p value for the item 'preference of functional elements' (0.465) at degree of freedom 1 is more than 0.05, the statement that "Brand Managers prefer to use functional elements while positioning" is not rejected. Therefore the null hypothesis (H2A: Products targeted towards the mass market are positioned more commonly by using the functional elements of brand positioning.) is not rejected.

HYPOTHESIS 2B: PRODUCTS TARGETED TOWARDS THE MASS MARKET ARE POSITIONED MORE COMMONLY BY USING THE CULTURAL ELEMENTS OF BRAND POSITIONING.

Most of the brand managers working for multinational companies dealing in fast moving consumer goods in the Indian market have been found to have a higher preference for the use of either functional elements, emotional elements or hedonistic elements of the message content strategy for positioning FMCG brands and a significantly small percentage of brand managers prefer to use the cultural elements of the message content strategy. In the Chi Square test conducted to test the hypothesis, as the p value for the item 'preference of cultural elements' (0.003) at degree of freedom 1 is lesser than 0.05, the statement that "Brand Managers prefer to use cultural elements while positioning" is rejected (Refer Table 7.18). Thus the null hypothesis (H2B: Products targeted towards the mass market are positioned more commonly by using the cultural elements of brand positioning.) is rejected.

HYPOTHESIS 3: THE CULTURE OF THE COUNTRY FROM WHERE THE BRAND ORIGINATES HAS ITS IMPRINTS ON THE POSITIONING OF THE BRAND

Null Hypothesis 3 (H3$_0$): The culture of the country from where the brand originates does not have its imprints on the positioning of the brand.

Alternate Hypothesis 3 (H3$_a$): The culture of the country from where the brand originates has its imprints on the positioning of the brand.

Chi Square test was conducted to test the null hypothesis which states that "The culture of the country from where the brand originates does not have its imprints on the positioning of the brand".

As the calculated value of chi square for the variables 'Culture of Brand Origin Reflected in the Brand' is 5.00 which less than the table value of chi square (9.488) at degree of freedom 4 and level of significance 0.05, and as the p value for the variables is 0.287 (ie, more than 0.05), the null hypothesis 3 ($H3_{\emptyset}$) is not rejected (See Table 7.21). It implies that the 'Culture of Brand Origin' (COBO) is not significantly represented or reflected by the FMCG brands from the stable of multinational companies in the Indian market.

Thus the null hypothesis ($H3_{\emptyset}$: The culture of the country from where the brand originates has its imprints on the positioning of the brand) is rejected.

HYPOTHESIS 4: ECONOMIC CHARACTERISTICS OF THE TARGETED MARKET SEGMENT HAVE AN IMPACT ON THE BRAND POSITIONING STRATEGIES OF THE PRODUCTS.

Null Hypothesis 4 ($H4_{\emptyset}$): Economic characteristics of the target market segment do not have an impact on the brand positioning strategies of the products.

Alternate Hypothesis 4 ($H4_{a}$): Economic characteristics of the target market segment have an impact on the brand positioning strategies of the products.

Chi Square test was applied to test the null hypothesis which states that "Economic characteristics of the target market segment do not have an impact on the brand positioning strategies of the products". The sub hypotheses were stated as follows:

Null Hypothesis 4a ($H4a_{\emptyset}$): Earning Pattern of the Consumer does not have a significant impact on the brand positioning strategies

Null Hypothesis 4b ($H4b_{\emptyset}$): Disposable Income of the Consumer does not have a significant impact on the brand positioning strategies

Null Hypothesis 4c ($H4c_{\emptyset}$): Saving Habit of the Consumer does not have a significant impact on the brand positioning strategies

As the calculated chi square values for the variables 'Influence of the earning pattern of the consumer on brand positioning' and 'influence of the disposable income of the consumer on brand positioning' at degree of freedom 4 and level of significance 0.05 are 19.667 and 20.000 respectively, which are greater than the table value of chi square (9.488) at degree of freedom 4 and level of significance 0.05 and as the p values for these variables are 0.001 and 0.000, both of which are less than 0.05, the null hypothesis $H4a_{\o}$ and the null hypothesis $H4b_{\o}$ are rejected. However the calculated chi square values for the variable 'influence of the consumer's saving habit' at degree of freedom 4 and level of significance 0.05 is 7.333, which is less than the table value of chi square (9.488) at degree of freedom 4 and level of significance 0.05. Also the p value for the variable 'influence of the consumer's saving habit' is greater than 0.05. Thus the null hypothesis $H4c_{\o}$ is not rejected (See Table 7.24).

It implies that the factors earning pattern of the consumer and the disposable income of the consumer have a significant influence on the brand positioning strategies adopted by MNCs dealing in FMCG in India but the brand positioning strategies of these companies are not significantly influenced by the consumer's saving habit. On the whole it may be concluded that the economic characteristics of the target market have an influence on the brand positioning strategies adopted by the MNCs in positioning FMCG brands in India.

Thus the null hypothesis ($H4\o$: The economic characteristics of the target market segment do not have an impact on the brand positioning strategies of the products) is rejected whereas the alternative hypothesis ($H4_{\alpha}$: Economic characteristics of the target market segment have an impact on the brand positioning strategies of the products) is not rejected.

HYPOTHESIS 5: GLOBAL BRANDS EXPERIENCE HIGHER PURCHASE LIKELIHOOD AS COMPARED TO LOCAL BRANDS.

Null Hypothesis 5 ($H5_{\o}$): Global brands do not experience higher purchase likelihood as compared to local brands.

Alternate Hypothesis ($H5_{\alpha}$): Global brands experience higher purchase likelihood as compared to local brands.

To figure out if the Indian consumers have a higher preference for the purchase of global brands, the respondents (consumers) were asked if they prefer to buy brands that have a global presence and whether they prefer such Indian brands which have become global. To test the null hypothesis which states that "Global brands do not experience higher purchase likelihood as compared to local brands", Chi Square test was applied. Chi Square test was applied to the two hypotheses which were stated as follows:

Null Hypothesis 5a (H5a$_\theta$): Consumers do not prefer to buy brands that have a Global presence.

And

Null Hypothesis 5b (H5b$_\theta$): Consumers do not have a higher preference for Indian brands that have expanded into other countries.

As the calculated value of chi square for the variables 'Preference to buy brands that have a global presence' and 'Preference to buy Indian brands that have expanded into other countries' are 115.216 and 138.832 both of which are greater than the table value of chi square (7.815) at degree of freedom 3 and level of significance 0.05 and as the p values for the variables 'Preference to buy brands that have a global presence' and 'Preference to buy Indian brands that have expanded into other countries' are less than 0.05, the null hypothesis H5a$_\theta$ and H5b$_\alpha$ are rejected (See Table 7.29). It implies that consumers have a significantly high purchase preference for global brands in comparison to their purchase preference for local brands.

Thus the null hypothesis (H5$_\theta$: Global brands do not experience higher purchase likelihood as compared to local brands) is rejected whereas the alternate hypothesis (H5$_\alpha$: Global brands experience higher purchase likelihood as compared to local brands) is not rejected.

IMPACT AND SIGNIFICANCE OF THE 'COUNTRY OF ORIGIN' IN BRAND POSITIONING OF FMCG BRANDS BY MNCs IN INDIA

It has been found from the study that a huge majority of the Indian consumers claim that they prefer to use Indian brands of fast moving consumer goods as compared to brands originating from other countries as they perceive the Indian brands to be higher in reliability and superior in quality and performance.
However, in none of the category of FMCG brands taken up for the study, the consumers' preference of the brand is significantly influenced by the 'Country of Origin' of the brand.

Although a major percentage of the brand managers are of the opinion that highlighting the 'Country of Origin' of an FMCG brand has some degree of positive influence on the image of the brand in the consumers' minds, 'Country of Origin' of the brand does not have a significantly strong bearing on the brand positioning strategies of FMCG brands in the Indian market.

The study also revealed that though the brand managers working for the multinational companies dealing in FMCG brands in India were of the opinion that 'Country of Origin' of a brand does not have any significant influence on the positioning of the brand or on the consumers' perception of the brand, most of these brand managers feel that their brands reflect the culture of the country from where they have originated up to a moderate or significant level.

FACTORS AFFECTING BRAND POSITIONING STRATEGIES OF MNCS DEALING WITH FMCG IN INDIA

(a) **Influence of Product Related Factors on Brand Positioning**

Out of the several product related factors, 'Unique Characteristics of the Product' emerges as the most influential factor in affecting the brand positioning strategy for a brand followed by the 'Product Category'.

(b) **Influence of Competition Related Factors on Brand Positioning**

In competition related factors, the brand preference and loyalty enjoyed by competing brands have the strongest influence on the brand positioning strategies of FMCG brands followed by the number of competitors in the market.

(c) **Influence of Company Related Factors on Brand Positioning**

It has been found that 'Marketing Philosophy of the Company' has a significant influence on the brand positioning strategies for Fast Moving Consumer Goods in the Indian market.

(d) **Influence of Consumer Related Factors on Brand Positioning**

Amongst all the consumer related factors 'Culture and Tradition of the Consumer' was found to have the strongest influence on the brand positioning of FMCG brands offered by multinational companies in the Indian market. The other factor which was found to have a significant influence on the brand positioning strategies designed for FMCG brands in the Indian market was the 'The Value System of the Consumer'.

(e) **Influence of Consumer Behaviour Related Factors on Brand Positioning**

The 'Pattern of Consumption and Consumption Habit of the Consumer' as well as the 'Purchase Habit of the Target Consumer' has been found to have a significant influence on the brand positioning strategies formulated by the multinational companies for their FMCG brands in the Indian market.

Table 15.2 summarises the factors that influence the brand positioning strategies of MNCs offering FMCG brands to the Indian market.

Table 15.2: Factors Influencing Brand Positioning Strategies of MNC offering FMCG Brands in India

Category of Factors	Factors
Product Related Factors	(a) Unique Characteristics of Product (b) Product Category
Company Related Factors	(a) Preference and Loyalty for Competitors (b) Number of Competitors
Competition Related Factors	Marketing Philosophy of the Company
Consumer Related Factors	(a) Culture & Tradition of the Consumer (b) Value System of the Consumer
Consumer Behaviour Related Factors	(a) Pattern of Consumption & Consumption Habit

BRAND POSITIONING STRATEGIES ADOPTED BY SELECTED INDIAN MNCs DEALING WITH FMCG IN INDIA

The study analysed the brand positioning strategies adopted by three of the best performing and most well known Indian multinationals in the FMCG sector, Godrej Consumer Products Ltd., Dabur India Ltd. and Marico Ltd. These three Indian multinationals have a significant presence in the International market and a formidable market share in the domestic market.

(a) Brand Positioning Strategies Adopted by Godrej Consumer Products Ltd.

Godrej Consumer Products Ltd. is the second largest player in India in the toilet soap segment and is a market leader in Hair Colour and Household Insecticide categories. The company is a leader in the liquid detergent category with a market share of more than 75%.

In the domestic market as well as in the International market GCPL sells different brands of products in the three product categories: Home Care, Personal Wash and Hair Care. The name 'Godrej' has strong brand equity. This is what the company tries to leverage through its branding strategy. The brand positioning strategy of the company tries to leverage the image and goodwill that the company has established over the years. Besides reaping the benefit of a strong brand name and powerful brand image, the company also wanted to portray itself as a young and contemporary company. This has been achieved through the endeavour of the holding company to reposition the brand 'Godrej' to reflect its commitment to innovation and better living. The changes brought about as a result of this exercise was a colourful brand insignia- the brand name embellished with vibrant stripes of colours and the introduction of the brand slogan and concept "Brighter Living".

Depending on the type of the product, GCPL was found to use benefit positioning, attribute positioning or application positioning as brand positioning strategies. Functional element of the message strategy was found to be commonly used by the company for positioning its brands. Physical element and Hedonistic element of the message strategy is also used by the company in a few cases. The brand positioning strategies of GCPL are influenced by the cultural factors of the target market which include the culture of the consumer and the consumer's value system. The strategies of the company are also influenced by the purchase habits of the consumers, product characteristics and the brand positioning strategies of competitors. The factor considered most important by the company and primarily taken into account while formulating the positioning of the brands from GCPL is the culture and belief of the consumer.

(b) Brand Positioning Strategies Adopted by Dabur India Ltd.

Dabur India Ltd. is the fourth largest FMCG Company in India with a turnover of over Rs. 5300/- crore. It is an ethnocentrically oriented company that has expanded into the international market through the organic route. The international business of the company is worth Rs. 678 crore and contributes to a fifth of the revenues of Dabur India.

As the strength of Dabur lies in its Ayurvedic legacy, Ayurveda and Nature forms the basis of its brand positioning strategy in the domestic market as well as in the international market. At the beginning of the new millennium Dabur revamped its brand architecture and transformed itself from a herbal product manufacturer to a pure FMCG company differentiated by virtue of its expertise in manufacturing natural and ayurvedic/herbal products. Struck by the realisation that Dabur was perceived as an ageing brand, the company took the initiative to reposition the ageing brand and endow it with the spirit of youth and vibrancy. The old and overbearing Banyan tree in the logo was replaced by a youthful, vibrant looking, animated image of a Banyan tree. The fresh looking leaves of the tree and the broad trunk symbolize energy and stability respectively. Even the font used in the brand name was changed to give a young and contemporary look to it. "Celebrate Life" became the new brand concept and the brand slogan. As a part of this repositioning venture special marketing attention was focused on 'Dabur', 'Vatika', 'Anmol', 'Real' and 'Hajmola' brands.

Dabur offers different brands across four distinct business portfolios: Personal Care, Health Care, Home Care and Foods. The study found that for positioning most of its FMCG brands and OTC brands, Dabur uses either benefit positioning strategy or a combination of attribute positioning and benefit positioning. For a few of its products like Dabur Amla hair oil and Odonil, the company uses competitor positioning and application positioning respectively. Dabur frequently uses celebrity appeal in its advertisements for promoting its brands. In line with its brand concept 'Celebrate Life', Hedonistic element of the message content strategy is frequently employed by the company to convey the positioning of its brands to the consumers. Functional element and Physical element of the message content strategy are also used by Dabur.

The main factors that influence the brand positioning strategies of Dabur are the rural/urban background of the consumer, the value system of the consumer and the marketing philosophy of the company. The factor that is primarily taken into account while designing the brand positioning strategies is the background of the consumer (urban/rural/suburban) followed by the culture and belief of the consumer.

(c) Brand Positioning Strategies Adopted by Marico Ltd.

Marico is an Indian multinational company that operates in more than twenty five countries and has a turnover of Rs. 3,128 Crore (in the year 2011). The company operates in the beauty and wellness space. It has expanded in the international market using both the organic and inorganic routes.

The motto of the company "Be More. Everyday" forms the basic brand positioning credo for the company in all its markets and constitutes the brand concept of the company. In the Indian market Marico offers products in the categories of Hair Care, Skin Care, Home Care and Foods. 'Parachute' is the flagship brand of Marico and is the largest selling brand of hair oil in the country. Benefit positioning is the type of positioning strategy that is mainly used by Marico Ltd. for positioning its brands in the Indian market. The element of the message content strategy commonly employed by Marico for conveying the positioning of its brands is the functional element. Emotional element is also used by the company.

The study found that the brand positioning strategies of Marico are strongly influenced by the characteristics of the target consumer as well as the characteristics of the competing brands. The culture and tradition of the consumer and his value system also influence the btrand positioning strategies of the company in the Indian market. The factors that are primarily taken into account by the brand managers at Marico while formulating the brand positioning strategies are the cultural factors (which include the culture and belief of the consumer and the traditional customs and practices in the target market) and the lifestyle of the target consumer.

SUGGESTION

As the consumers' preference of FMCG brands in the Indian market is strongly influenced by factors like the technology used in the product, the quality of the product, goodwill and popularity of the company, conformance of the brand with the consumer's lifestyle and economy offered by the brand, it would do good to the multinational companies selling FMCG brands in the Indian market to take these factors into account while designing their brand positioning strategies.

The brand managers dealing in FMCG brands, besides focussing on the quality of the brand, may also consider highlighting the global nature of the brand so as to target their brands to the female consumers and effectively position the brands in their minds. FMCG brands targeted at Indian housewives may be positioned on the basis of 'Economy' benefit and lifestyle conformance as well as the duration of presence of the company in the market provided the company is an established one and has been in the market for a long period of time. Brands targeted at the businessmen and working professionals may be positioned by virtue of the size of the company and duration of the company respectively. The Indian origin of the brand may be used as a positioning criterion for FMCG brands targeted at the older generation consumers.

The study indicates a conformance between the brand managers' perception of the impact of emotional and functional elements of the message strategy on brand positioning and the actual impact of these two elements on brand positioning (manifested and noted as the consumers' perception of the brand). However an undue importance seems to be given by the brand managers to the hedonistic message element for positioning brands of Fast Moving Consumer Goods. Mellowing down the intensity of use of the hedonistic element and stepping up the use of the functional and emotional message elements may be considered by a brand manager to strengthen the positioning of a brand of FMCG product in the Indian market.

Despite the fact that culture is increasingly being used as an element of brand positioning, cultural positioning does not always ensure a distinctive competitive advantage to the brand. Brand managers need to make a judicious use of culture as an element of the message content and use it to position a brand in those situations where it is indeed required. For positioning brands of fast moving consumer goods, brand managers may consider using Local Consumer Culture Positioning for brands categorised as Ritualistic Masses and use Global Consumer Culture Positioning for brands categorised as Global Followers.

LIMITATIONS

Though the researches presented in the book treat FMCG as one brand category, it is a well understood fact that the FMCG sector comprises of numerous sub categories of products, each of which may require a different kind of strategy. The brand positioning for each sub category may be influenced by a different set of factors and the suitability of the elements of the message content may also vary with the sub categories within the FMCG sector. As the studies take FMCG sector as one category and have been conducted by taking into account brands from several sub categories of products, the findings presented in the book are generalised findings for all categories of FMCG products. However, further probe into the strategies adopted for brands belonging to different sub categories may reveal certain differences in the brand positioning strategies, use of elements of the message content strategy and the overall brand positioning strategies.

The present set of researches probe into the brand positioning strategies of multinational companies dealing in FMCG brands in the Indian market. Though multinational companies may be classified into different types based on their origin, extent of spread, orientation and mode of functioning, these studies did not endeavour to differentiate between the strategies adopted by different kinds of multinationals. For the sake of practical convenience, even international companies have been considered as MNCs. Similarly, in the course of these studies neither has any attempt been made to distinguish between Indian MNCs and foreign multinationals, nor has the researcher endeavoured to differentiate the strategies adopted by Indian and foreign MNCs.

The author acknowledges the fact that the rural market is not only an emerging market but also an immensely important market for the new generation of marketer. However, the differences in the brand positioning strategies adopted by the multinational companies for the rural markets and those adopted by them for the urban market have not been examined in the study.

The assessment of the factors influencing the consumers' perception of a brand has been done by analysing the responses of consumers from five states of India which may not be representative of the response of the entire population. The findings related to the degree of influence of the various factors on the consumers' image of a brand and those related to the significance of various factors and elements in creating a favourable perception of the brand may not be precisely applicable to the entire population and may not precisely portray the attitude of all Indian consumers towards the factors shaping the perception of FMCG brands, towards communication elements used for positioning and towards FMCG brands.

FUTURE SCOPE OF STUDY

The nuances of brand positioning may be different in different industries. Therefore, like the present study that evaluates the brand positioning strategies adopted for the FMCG brands in the Indian market, there is a need and scope of the study of positioning of brands from various industries in the Indian market like the automobile industry, consumer durables, white goods industry, apparels and textile industry, banking industry, etc.

A comparison of the brand positioning strategies adopted by the multinational companies in the Indian market and those adopted by them in the other markets is beyond the scope of this study. Nevertheless such type of comparison may give an insight into the brand positioning trends of FMCG companies in the international market. One of the limitations of the present study is that it does not make an attempt to compare and differentiate between the strategies adopted by the Indian multinationals and those adopted by the foreign multinationals for positioning their brands in India. Such comparative analysis may be taken up as a topic for future research.

Another dimension which the present study has not touched upon and which may constitute a meaningful topic of research is the study of strategies adopted by Indian and foreign multinational companies for positioning FMCG brands in the Indian rural market. Similarly the difference in the positioning strategies adopted by FMCG companies for the urban market and those adopted by the companies for the rural market may also be taken up as a topic of research.

****

ANNEXURE I

QUESTIONNAIRE FOR CONSUMERS

1. Name: _____

2. Occupation: _____

3. Gender: Male ☐   Female ☐

4. Age: _____

5. Address: _____

   _____

1. While purchasing daily need household items (FMCG), which type of brands do you prefer? (*Rank your preference giving rank '1' for the type of brand that is most preferred, rank '2' for the second most preferred type of brand and so on.*)

(a)	Brands with improved quality	
(b)	Brands that have some unique characteristics	
(c)	Brands originating from India	
(d)	Brands which have their origin in some foreign country	
(e)	Brands sold only in India (local brands)	
(f)	Brands also present in other parts of the world (global brands)	

2. Indicate the extent of impact of the characteristics of the company on your preference for a brand. (Rating Values: *1-Strongly Influence*; *2- Significant Influence*; *3-Moderate Influence*; *4- Weak Influence*; *5- Insignificant or no Influence*)

		1	2	3	4	5
(a)	Size of the company selling the brand.					
(b)	Goodwill and popularity of the company					
(c)	Value and culture of the company selling a brand					
(d)	History & tradition of the company selling a brand					
(e)	The marketing philosophy/ style of the company					

(f)	Geographical coverage of the company					
(g)	The duration of presence of the company in the market					

3. While purchasing consumer non durables, do you have a higher degree of preference for the following category of brands? (*Indicate your answer in the space provided with a (√) mark*)

		Yes	No	Can't Say
(a)	Brands that conform to your value system			
(b)	Brands that reflect your culture and tradition			
(c)	Brands that conform to your faith and belief			
(d)	Brands that conform to or reflect the virtues of your religion			
(e)	Brands that are economical			
(f)	Premium/ Exclusive brands			
(g)	Brands that conform to your lifestyle			

4. Which of the following characteristics should essentially be there in a good brand? (Rating Values: *1-Very Essential*; *2- Somewhat essential*; *3-Somewhat Unessential*; *4- Absolutely Unessential*)

		1	2	3	4
(a)	The brand should conform to your culture and tradition				
(b)	The brand should reflect Indian values				
(c)	The brand should be closely related to the life of the local people				
(d)	The brand should conform to your lifestyle				
(e)	The brand should be friendly to the pocket				
(f)	The brand should be affordable				

5. Which type of advertisement appeal attracts you towards a brand?

(a)	Rational appeal (ads talking about product features, characteristics, usage & technology)		(b)	Emotional Appeal (love, friendship, relationship, belongingness)	

(c)	Cultural appeal (ads highlighting culture and tradition)		(d)	Hedonistic appeal (ads focusing on the pleasant experience from the product)	
(e)	combination of rational & emotional		(f)	combination of rational & cultural	
(g)	combinational of rational & hedonistic		(h)	combination of emotional & cultural	
(i)	combination of emotional & hedonistic		(j)	combination of cultural & hedonistic	
(k)	Any Other				

6. Brands with which type of association do you find easy to remember?

(a)	Celebrity		(b)	Health	
(c)	Festivals and Events		(d)	Culture and Tradition	
(e)	Performance		(f)	Special experience	

7. Brands from which of the countries do you prefer to use?

(a)	India		(b)	USA	
(c)	Germany		(d)	France	
(e)	Japan		(f)	China	

Any other country: _____

8. Brands from which of the countries do you find more reliable?

(a)	India		(b)	USA	
(c)	Germany		(d)	France	
(e)	Japan		(f)	China	

Any other country: _____

9. Brands from which of the countries offer the best quality and performance?

(a)	India		(b)	USA	
(c)	Germany		(d)	France	
(e)	Japan		(f)	China	

Any other country: _____

10. Indicate your agreement with the following statements.

a) Brand with an English name usually signify superior quality.

(a)	Strongly agree		(b)	Somewhat agree	
(c)	Somewhat disagree		(d)	Strongly disagree	

b) Brands with a french name signify elegance.

(a)	Strongly agree		(b)	Somewhat agree	
(c)	Somewhat disagree		(d)	Strongly disagree	

c) Foreign brands offer better quality as compared to Indian brands.

(a)	Strongly agree		(b)	Somewhat agree	
(c)	Somewhat disagree		(d)	Strongly disagree	

d) Brands associated with local culture are close to my heart.

(a)	Strongly agree		(b)	Somewhat agree	
(c)	Somewhat disagree		(d)	Strongly disagree	

e) I can easily associate with brands that reflect my beliefs.

(a)	Strongly agree		(b)	Somewhat agree	
(c)	Somewhat disagree		(d)	Strongly disagree	

f) I prefer to be associated with brands that reflect a global culture.

(a)	Strongly agree		(b)	Somewhat agree	
(c)	Somewhat disagree		(d)	Strongly disagree	

11. Indicate your agreement with the following statements:

a) I prefer to buy brands that have a global presence.

(a)	Strongly agree		(b)	Somewhat agree	
(c)	Somewhat disagree		(d)	Strongly disagree	

b) Local brands offer a better value for money.

(a)	Strongly agree		(b)	Somewhat agree	
(c)	Somewhat disagree		(d)	Strongly disagree	

c) I prefer to buy Indian brands.

(a)	Strongly agree		(b)	Somewhat agree	
(c)	Somewhat disagree		(d)	Strongly disagree	

d) I prefer to buy those Indian brands that have also expanded into other countries vis-à-vis those Indian brands which are only locally available.

(a)	Strongly agree		(b)	Somewhat agree	
(c)	Somewhat disagree		(d)	Strongly disagree	

e) When it comes to quality, performance and safety, I prefer to buy foreign brands.

(a)	Strongly agree		(b)	Somewhat agree	
(c)	Somewhat disagree		(d)	Strongly disagree	

12. Indicate the country of origin of the following brands:

A. TOOTH PASTE

		Indian	Foreign
(a)	CLOSE UP		
(b)	PEPSODENT		
(c)	COLGATE		
(d)	BABOOL		

B. TOILET SOAP

		Indian	Foreign
(a)	LIFEBUOY		
(b)	LUX		
(c)	CINTHOL		
(d)	BREEZE		
(e)	DOVE		
(f)	PEARS		
(g)	NIRMA		

C. SHAMPOO

		Indian	Foreign
(a)	SUNSILK		
(b)	VATIKA		
(c)	CLINIC PLUS		
(d)	HEAD & SHOULDER		
(e)	PANTENE		

D. DETERGENT

		Indian	Foreign
(a)	SURF		
(b)	ARIEL		
(c)	TIDE		
(d)	WHEEL		
(e)	SUNLIGHT		
(f)	NIRMA		
(g)	RIN		

E. TEA

		Indian	Foreign
(a)	LIPTON		
(b)	BROOKE BOND		
(c)	TAJ MAHAL		
(d)	TAZAA		
(e)	AGNI		
(f)	NESTEA		

F. COFFEE

		Indian	Foreign
(a)	NESCAFE		
(b)	BRU		

G. CHOCOLATE/ TOFFEE

		Indian	Foreign
(a)	CADBURY DAIRY MILK		
(b)	CADBURY BORNVILLE		
(c)	CADBURY ECLAIRS		

(d)	BAR ONE		
(e)	FIVE STAR		
(f)	KIT KAT		
(g)	MUNCH		
(h)	ALPENLIEBE		
(i)	POPPINS		
(j)	HAJMOLA		

H. COSMETICS

		Indian	Foreign
(a)	PONDS		
(b)	FEM		
(c)	GARNIER		
(d)	L'OREAL		
(f)	VASELINE		
(g)	BOROLINE		
(h)	BOROPLUS		

I. FOOD AND BEVERAGES

		Indian	Foreign
(a)	MAGGI		
(b)	ACTIVE		
(c)	EVERYDAY		
(d)	TROPICANA		
(e)	REAL JUICE		
(f)	MINUTE MAID		
(g)	FROOTI		
(h)	MAAZA		
(i)	AMUL		

13. Indicate your preference of the brands on a scale of 1 to 5. (*1* stands for *highrst preference* & *5* stands for *lowest preference*)

A. TOOTH PASTE

		1	2	3	4	5
(a)	CLOSE UP					
(b)	PEPSODENT					
(c)	COLGATE					
(d)	BABOOL					

B. TOILET SOAP

		1	2	3	4	5
(a)	LIFEBUOY					
(b)	LUX					
(c)	CINTHOL					
(d)	BREEZE					
(e)	DOVE					
(f)	PEARS					
(g)	NIRMA					

C. SHAMPOO

		1	2	3	4	5
(a)	SUNSILK					
(b)	VATIKA					
(c)	CLINIC PLUS					
(d)	HEAD & SHOULDER					
(e)	PANTENE					

D. DETERGENT

		1	2	3	4	5
(a)	SURF					
(b)	ARIEL					
(c)	TIDE					
(d)	WHEEL					
(e)	SUNLIGHT					
(f)	NIRMA					
(g)	RIN					

E. TEA

		1	2	3	4	5
(a)	LIPTON					
(b)	BROOKE BOND					
(c)	TAJ MAHAL					
(d)	TAZAA					
(e)	AGNI					
(f)	NESTEA					

F. COFFEE

		1	2	3	4	5
(a)	NESCAFE					
(b)	BRU					

G. CHOCOLATE/ TOFFEE

		1	2	3	4	5
(a)	CADBURY DAIRY MILK					
(b)	CADBURY BORNVILLE					

		1	2	3	4	5
(c)	CADBURY ECLAIRS					
(d)	BAR ONE					
(e)	FIVE STAR					
(f)	KIT KAT					
(g)	MUNCH					
(h)	ALPENLIEBE					
(i)	POPPINS					
(j)	HAJMOLA					

H. COSMETICS

		1	2	3	4	5
(a)	PONDS					
(b)	FEM					
(c)	GARNIER					
(d)	L'OREAL					
(f)	VASELINE					
(g)	BOROLINE					
(h)	BOROPLUS					

I. FOOD AND BEVERAGES

		1	2	3	4	5
(a)	MAGGI					
(b)	ACTIVE					
(c)	EVERYDAY					
(d)	TROPICANA					
(e)	REAL JUICE					
(f)	MINUTE MAID					
(g)	FROOTI					
(h)	MAAZA					
(i)	AMUL					

****

ANNEXURE II

QUESTIONNAIRE FOR BRAND MANAGERS

Dear Sir /Madam

This questionnaire has been designed to understand the nuances of brand positioning strategies of MNCs dealing in FMCG products in India. The study undertakes to get an insight into the factors affecting the positioning of FMCG brands and to understand the positioning elements that can be effectively used for positioning FMCG brands by multinational companies in India. The information gathered through the questionnaire would be used for the academic research work **"A CRITICAL EVALUATION OF THE BRAND POSITIONING STRATEGIES OF MNCs DEALING IN FMCG PRODUCTS IN INDIA"**. Your cooperation and support is earnestly solicited for this research work. You are requested to kindly fill in the questionnaire to the best of your knowledge and without leaving out any question/ statement. I assure you that the information provided by you shall be strictly used for academic purpose only and your identity shall be kept secret if you so desire.

1. Name: _____

2. Designation:_____

3. Company: _____

4. Address: _____

    _____

5. Indicate the extent of influence of the product related factors on the brand positioning strategies. (Rating Values: *1-Strongly Influence*; *2- Significant Influence*; *3-Moderate Influence*; *4- Weak Influence*; *5- Insignificant or no Influence*)

		1	2	3	4	5
(a)	Product category					
(b)	Technology of Product					

		1	2	3	4	5
(c)	Unique characteristics of the product					
(d)	'Country of origin' of the Brand					
(e)	Geographical presence of the brand (Local or Global)					

6. Indicate the extent of influence of the competition related factors on the brand positioning strategies. (Rating Values: *1-Strongly Influence*; *2- Significant Influence*; *3-Moderate Influence*; *4- Weak Influence*; *5- Insignificant or no Influence*)

		1	2	3	4	5
(a)	No. of competitors in the market					
(b)	Market share of the competitors					
(c)	Size of the competing firms					
(d)	Brand preference & loyalty that competing brands command					
(e)	Positioning strategies of competitors					

7. Indicate the extent of influence of the company related factors on the brand positioning strategies. (Rating Values: *1-Strongly Influence*; *2- Significant Influence*; *3-Moderate Influence*; *4- Weak Influence*; *5- Insignificant or no Influence*)

		1	2	3	4	5
(a)	Value and culture of the company					
(b)	History and tradition of the company					
(c)	The marketing philosophy of the company					
(d)	Geographical coverage of the company					
(e)	The duration of presence of the company in a given market					

8. Indicate the extent of influence of the consumer related factors on the brand positioning strategies. (Rating Values: *1-Strongly Influence*; *2- Significant Influence*; *3-Moderate Influence*; *4- Weak Influence*; *5- Insignificant or no Influence*)

		1	2	3	4	5
(a)	The value system of the consumer					
(b)	Culture and tradition of the consumer					
(c)	Faith and belief of the consumer					
(d)	Religion of the consumer					
(e)	Geographic location and origin of the consumer					

9. Indicate the extent of influence of the consumer behaviour related factors on the brand positioning strategies. (Rating Values: *1-Strongly Influence*; *2- Significant Influence*; *3- Moderate Influence*; *4- Weak Influence*; *5- Insignificant or no Influence*)

		1	2	3	4	5
(a)	Purchase habits of the target consumer					
(b)	Pattern of consumption & consumption habits of the consumer					
(c)	Media habits of the consumer					

10. Indicate the degree of influence of the following economic and demographic characteristics of the consumers on the brand positioning strategies. (Rating Values: *1-Strongly Influence*; *2- Significant Influence*; *3-Moderate Influence*; *4- Weak Influence*; *5- Insignificant or no Influence*)

		1	2	3	4	5
(a)	Rural/ Urban background of the target consumer					
(b)	Earning patterns of the target consumer					
(c)	Disposable income of the target consumer					
(d)	Saving habits of the target consumer					

11. Which factors do you take into account while designing the brand positioning strategy? Rank in order of importance. *(A ranking of 1 would indicate the highest importance)*

(a)	Rural/ Urban/ Suburban background of the target consumer	
(b)	Occupation of the consumer	
(c)	Education of the consumer	
(d)	Family life cycle	
(e)	Family Size	
(f)	Culture and belief of the consumer	
(g)	Cherished traditional practices	
(h)	Religion of the consumer	
(i)	Gross income of the consumer	
(j)	Disposable income of the consumer	
(k)	Lifestyle of the target consumer	

12. Which type of advertisement appeal guarantees a better response from the consumers?

(a)	Rational appeal		(b)	Emotional Appeal	
(c)	Cultural appeal		(d)	Hedonistic appeal	
(e)	combination of rational & emotional		(f)	combination of rational & cultural	
(g)	combinational of rational & hedonistic		(h)	combination of emotional & cultural	
(i)	combination of emotional & hedonistic		(j)	combination of cultural & hedonistic	
(k)	Any Other				

13. Which type of advertisement appeal ensures a stronger brand recall?

(a)	Rational appeal		(b)	Emotional Appeal	

(c)	Cultural appeal		(d)	Hedonistic appeal	
(e)	combination of rational & emotional		(f)	combination of rational & cultural	
(g)	combinational of rational & hedonistic		(h)	combination of emotional & cultural	
(i)	combination of emotional & hedonistic		(j)	combination of cultural & hedonistic	
(k)	Any Other				

14. Which type of brand association ensures a better brand recall?

(a)	Celebrity		(b)	Health	
(c)	Festivals and Events		(d)	Culture and Tradition	
(e)	Performance		(f)	Special experience	

15. Which of the following elements do you or your company prefer to use while positioning your brands?

(a)	Physical elements (attributes of the product)		(b)	Functional elements (usage of the product)	
(c)	Cultural elements		(d)	Emotional elements	
(e)	Sensory elements (Experience of the consumers)				

16. Upto what extent do your brands reflect the culture of the country from where they originate?

(a)	Very strongly		(b)	Significantly	
(c)	Moderately		(d)	Insignificantly	
(e)	Do not reflect				

17. Upto what extent does highlighting the country of origin of the brand strengthens its position in the minds of the consumer?

(a)	Strongly fortifies		(b)	Somewhat fortifies/strengthens	
(c)	Somewhat weakens		(d)	Has no impact	

18. Do you agree that if your brand reflects and conforms to the culture and belief of the consumers it experiences a higher degree of acceptance amongst the consumers?

(a)	Strongly agree		(b)	Somewhat agree	
(c)	Somewhat disagree		(d)	Strongly disagree	

19. While positioning a brand in different economic segments do you or your company use different positioning criteria and strategies?

(a)	Yes		(b)	No	

20. If your answer to question no. 19 is 'Yes', then indicate your level of agreement with the following:

   a) The positioning strategy is changed with the change in the gross income of the target consumer.

(a)	Strongly agree		(b)	Somewhat agree	
(c)	Somewhat disagree		(d)	Strongly disagree	

   b) The positioning strategy is changed with the change in the purchasing power of the target consumers.

(a)	Strongly agree		(b)	Somewhat agree	
(c)	Somewhat disagree		(d)	Strongly disagree	

   c) The positioning strategy is changed with the change in the disposable income of the target consumer.

(a)	Strongly agree		(b)	Somewhat agree	

(c)	Somewhat disagree		(d)	Strongly disagree	

d) The positioning strategy is changed with the change in the occupation of the target market segment.

(a)	Strongly agree		(b)	Somewhat agree	
(c)	Somewhat disagree		(d)	Strongly disagree	

e) The positioning strategy is changed with the change in the lifestyle of the target market

(a)	Strongly agree		(b)	Somewhat agree	
(c)	Somewhat disagree		(d)	Strongly disagree	

21. While positioning a brand in different geographic segments within the country do you or your company use different positioning criteria and strategies?

(a)	Yes		(b)	No	

22. If your answer to question no. 21 is 'Yes', then indicate your level of agreement with the following:

a) The positioning strategy changes according to the urban/ rural background of the target consumer.

(a)	Strongly agree		(b)	Somewhat agree	
(c)	Somewhat disagree		(d)	Strongly disagree	

b) The positioning strategy changes with the change in the geographical regions or states within the nation.

(a)	Strongly agree		(b)	Somewhat agree	
(c)	Somewhat disagree		(d)	Strongly disagree	

c) The positioning strategy changes with the difference in the climatic conditions of the target segments.

(a)	Strongly agree		(b)	Somewhat agree	
(c)	Somewhat disagree		(d)	Strongly disagree	

23. On the basis of your experience do you feel that brands with a foreign brand name experience a higher brand preference as compared to those with a local sounding name?

(a)	Strongly agree		(b)	Somewhat agree	
(c)	Somewhat disagree		(d)	Strongly disagree	

24. Do you agree that global brands and foreign brands have a higher brand preference as compared to local brands?

(a)	Strongly agree		(b)	Somewhat agree	
(c)	Somewhat disagree		(d)	Strongly disagree	

25. What is your opinion about repositioning a brand? (Rating Values: *1-Always*; *2- Often*; *3- Sometimes*; *4- Seldom*; *5- Never*)

		1	2	3	4	5
(a)	Repositioning rejuvenates the brand					
(b)	Repositioning helps to reinstate a falling brand					
(c)	Repositioning is essential when the brand doesn't perform in the market					
(d)	Changes in consumer preference necessitate repositioning					
(e)	Repositioning a brand has a neutral (ie, neither positive nor negative) impact on the brand preference of the consumer					
(f)	A well established brand should not be					

316

	repositioned					
(g)	Frequent repositioning should be avoided					
(h)	Repositioning dilutes the brand image					
(i)	Repositioning damages the credibility of the brand					

Please express if you have any other opinion or view on brand repositioning.

_____

_____

_____

_____

****

ABOUT THE AUTHOR

Dr. Subho Chattopadhyay
Associate Professor
LBSIMT, Bareilly (India)

Dr. Subho Chattopadhyay is a UGC-Net qualified Management teacher and academician with interest in the areas of Marketing and Brand development. Presently he is working as an Associate Professor at LBSIMT, Bareilly (India). He is teaching in the areas of Marketing and International Business. During his career as a management teacher, he has conducted MDPs and has been a resource person for training programmes conducted for the Ministry of MSME, University teachers and Chartered Accountants and entrepreneurs. He has presented several research papers in national and international conferences. His published work includes research papers in national and international journals, articles in magazines and chapters in books. Some of his research papers have been listed in Econbiz, Proquest and EBSCO database.

He holds a Doctorate in Business Administration and his research interests include the study of brands and brand development, positioning of brands, brand positioning strategies in FMCG and International Marketing.

www.ingramcontent.com/pod-product-compliance
Lightning Source LLC
Chambersburg PA
CBHW080650190526
45169CB00006B/2056